Theoretical Issues in Psychology

An Introduction

Sacha Bem and Huib Looren de Jong

SAGE Publications
London • Thousand Oaks • New Delhi

SAGE Publications Ltd
6 Bonhill Street
London EC2A 4PU

SAGE Publications Inc
2455 Teller Road
Thousand Oaks, California 91320

SAGE Publications India Pvt Ltd
32, M-Block Market
Greater Kailash – I
New Delhi 110 048

British Library Cataloguing in Publication Data

A catalogue record for this book is
available from the British Library

    ISBN 0 8039 7826 X
    ISBN 0 8039 7827 8 (pbk)

Library of Congress catalog record available

Typeset by M Rules
Printed in Great Britain by Biddles Ltd, *www.biddles.co.uk*

Contents

Preface

This book is about theoretical and philosophical issues in psychology. Two questions stand out: what is *science* in general, and the science of the mind or psychology in particular; and what is *mind*, one of the most important objects of psychology?

Twentieth-century philosophy of science has passed through a tumultuous development. It came into being by the light of the Vienna Circle of logical positivist philosophers, scientists and mathematicians who thought it was high time to stop metaphysics and its boundless speculative discussions, and 'to set philosophy upon the sure path of a science' (Ayer, 1959: 9). This new ideal for philosophy brought along a kindred ideal for science. Prescriptions for meaningful statements turned into rules for scientific theories. Empirical observation had to be the solid anchor for the logical justification of theories. And so the first, positivist, phase in the twentieth-century philosophy of science was characterized by the search for a demarcation criterion to distinguish science from mere speculative thought.

Though it is fair to say that the second phase of philosophy of science started in 1962 with Kuhn's seminal *The Structure of Scientific Revolutions* (1970), the ensuing debate about the positivist law and order, and what is and what is not scientific, had already been anticipated by Wittgensteinian analytic philosophers. Not to mention the continental philosophers who, educated mainly in an idealist context, were anti-positivists and anti-empiricists by nature. The bone of contention was the empirical doctrine of given, objective, sense data as the foundation for objective science; this was replaced by the notion of the theory-ladenness of observation. It turned out then, that science had its subjective side; though at the same time the rationality and objectivity of science were at stake. Alongside this philosophical debate, Kuhn's work gave rise to a wealth of studies on the historical and social context of scientific theories, merging with studies from the continental, partly Marxist, side which started from what was seen as the ideological nature of science and technology.

Attention to the subjective, social origins of science divided into studies of broad socioeconomic or cultural influences on the development of theories and scientists, and into work which focused on social and psychological constraints on epistemological issues, such as the construction of facts, theories and scientific culture. In these empirical studies on what scientists really do, we can also discern a turn towards psychological, in particular cognitive issues: research on observation, thinking, problem-solving, creativity, etc. So, alongside sociological interests, psychological interests for science came to the fore.

This cognitive turn in science studies interbred with cognitive psychology in general. The contribution of philosophy of mind to studies of cognition is impressive. Mind, intentionality, representation, consciousness are issues of hot debates and are among the most important theoretical issues in psychology. The so-called 'Cognitive Revolution' started as a rather abstract, grammar-inspired and linguistically modelled study of cognition. This mechanistic, logical view of mind was accompanied by research in Artificial Intelligence. A few decades ago, however, the shortcomings of this abstraction became obvious: neuroscience, evolutionism and pragmatism influenced ideas about the interaction between mental or brain functions and (social) environment, though not one but many different theories and models – mechanistic, biologically plausible, anti-mechanistic – issued from the debates.

We discuss the two theoretical issues in psychology, the one about *science* and psychology, and the one about the nature of *mind*, in four chapters along the lines of the brief story we have just told.

In the first chapter we introduce the concept of science and its tools, such as theories, facts, explanations, and some of its central concepts, such as reasons and causes.

We begin the second chapter with the story of the philosophy of science, of positivism and its decline; much of this is now history. The stage of normative philosophy of science is now so far in the past that it seems (post)modern students find it difficult to understand its ideal of autonomous science and detached truth. The second part of this chapter deals with subjectivist counterattacks, in particular with regard to psychology as a social science. The chapter ends with the debate between realist, relativist and pragmatist conceptions of science.

In Chapter 3 we give attention to various versions of the sociological approach to science, which has a rather strong grip on the 'science of science'. The final section of this chapter turns to psychological studies of science, a domain which is growing today but still in need of a framework.

The last chapter is devoted to the other main theoretical issue in psychology, the question: what is mind? As we already indicated, philosophy of mind has been booming during the last three decades, especially since the so-called 'cognitive revolution' in psychology. We present an overview of the most important issues, leading actors and discussions on the nature of mind, on minds and computers, minds and brains, consciousness and so on. In the last section of this chapter the mainstream 'mechanist' or cognitivist view of mind is contrasted with some alternative ideas emphasizing the embodied nature and the social roots of mind.

This book has, not unusually, its roots in courses in the philosophy of science and philospohical psychology for students majoring in psychology at the Leiden University and the Free University of Amsterdam. We are grateful to our students who have already been acquainted with parts of the content of this book and whose reactions were of influence, and to our colleagues Lex van der Heijden, Jeroen Jansz, Fred Keijzer, Monique Lamers, Hans van Rappard, Maurice Schouten, Sybe Terwee, Marietta Vis, and to Raoul Wirtz for their comments and suggestions. We are also indebted to Marijke Burgel for helping prepare the manuscript.

1

Theory of Science for Psychology

1.1   Introduction

An almost unconditional trust of, and esteem for science seems characteristic of modern societies. Laboratory tests count as a guarantee of the quality of drugs, food and cosmetics; and mathematical certainty is the hallmark of certainty and objectivity. No one seems to question the almost magical ability of scientists to estimate the safety of a new nuclear plant in terms of the probability of an accident, per million years. Apparently, science is seen as the epitome of rationality; most people seem to believe that science and technology have led us on the way to more welfare, health, freedom and prosperity (Toulmin, 1990). In our society common sense yields to scientific knowledge; calling something 'unscientific' is a rebuke.

Strangely enough, philosophers of science have found it impossible to produce an airtight demarcation between science and pseudo-science, or even a clear definition of scientific method. Nowadays, some reject the idea of a difference in principle between science and other social activities, and consider the practice of scientific inquiry the subject matter of sociology (see Chapter 3), to be explained in the same way as one might study primitive tribes or groups like Hell's Angels: acceptance of theories is governed by 'mob psychology' rather than by objective 'scientific' criteria. Some consider methodology pedantic nonsense, at best irrelevant to science, at worst a crippling suppression of common sense and creativity, and advocate methodological anarchism: 'anything goes' (Feyerabend, 1975; see Chapter 2). These social and the anarchistic approaches tend towards relativism; one theory is as good as the next one, and preferences for any scientific approach are due to arbitrary, irrational factors such as power, mob psychology, political pressure, etc.

We will defend the view that scientific practice is *not* arbitrary and that scientific knowledge has a legitimate claim to truth; that it, in a way, corresponds to an external reality, while at the same time we recognize that it is subject to a host of social, pragmatic and sometimes irrational influences, and that scientific truth is not something separate from human concerns.

An impressive feature of science is that it can explain disconnected phenomena as effects of underlying causal structures. A bewildering variety of chemical reactions, for instance, can elegantly and parsimoniously be explained by Mendeleyev's table of elements, which in turn is explained by the composition of chemical elements (atoms, consisting of electrons, neutrons and protons), governing binding and so on. A good example in psychology (although a controversial theory) would be psychoanalysis, which shows how underlying traumas produce neurotic behaviour. Such reductions of everyday phenomena to something more basic have the disquieting consequence that the former are 'really' nothing but atoms and molecules, physiological mechanisms or whatever (see, for the problem of reduction, section 1.6). Explaining, for instance, the physiological mechanisms of consciousness or memory seems tantamount to eliminating the interesting aspects of mental life, and reducing real people like you and me to drab machines.

Another meeting point of science and culture is that science has been associated with a critical attitude, open-mindedness, and Western liberal democracy (e.g. Popper, 1966). Historically, the rise of empirical critical investigation and the rejection of authority have gone together on several occasions. It was characteristic of Protestantism and the associated New Learning movement in England in the middle of the seventeenth century, which combined a politically progressive (if not subversive) demand for freedom of speech and press, with the development of science, mathematics and medicine (see Schafer, 1983).

Others, however, see science as the stronghold of political oppression: it has been identified (especially in psychology and the human sciences) by, among others, Marxists and feminists with repressing human concerns in a methodological strait-jacket, providing the establishment with ideological legitimations and/or the technological means for maintaining the status quo of capitalist exploitation and unthinking technocratic dominance (Marcuse, 1964; Weizenbaum, 1976).

More generally, science has been part of the project of modernity (e.g. Toulmin, 1990) seeking rational criteria for conduct in a wide range of human activities. Thus, it has received its share of postmodernist criticism, which rejects the idea of universal criteria for rationality (Rorty, 1979; Feyerabend, 1975).

This kind of debate on the proper place of science, its limitations and strengths, may be elucidated (if not decided) against the background of a principled account of the nature and limitations of knowledge, and of scientific knowledge in particular. Philosophers have a special branch of their trade that deals with evaluating the claims of knowledge: epistemology.

In this first chapter we will present some central concepts in the philosophy of science. Almost every concept in the field has been the subject of intense debate and though we cannot introduce them without some philosophical discussion, here we will try to present the consensus with respect to fundamental concepts in the theory of science; the next chapter deals with different and sometimes conflicting philosophical views and ideals of science. The latter has more or less a chronological structure, from positivism in the first half of this century to postmodern views. The disputes and positions concerning the important concepts we tackle in the present chapter feed the various accounts of the nature and limitations of scientific knowledge we review in Chapter 2.

In the next section we will introduce two extreme views on the nature of scientific knowledge and the scope of truth: realism and relativism. These epistemological positions bear upon the question of how much objectivity science can claim. This question will keep coming back again in other chapters. In this section we will also list some characteristics of science.

In section 1.3 a number of epistemological concepts such as deductive and inductive arguments; laws, theories and facts; justification and discovery of theories, will be discussed.

Some philosophers contend that the social sciences require a methodology of their own. In section 1.4 we discuss the contrast between explanation and understanding in science.

Purpose is an important concept in explaining behaviour. In section 1.5 we will talk about functional and teleological explanations used, for instance, in biology and psychology.

In section 1.6 we will present a discussion about the problem of reduction. It concerns the questions of materialism and the autonomy of (folk-) psychology, a subject we will return to in Chapter 4.

In giving explanations and accounts of behaviour we use causes as well as reasons. What is the difference between these accounts and what distinguishes behaviour from actions? These problems are the subject of the final section of this chapter.

1.2 Knowledge, everyday knowledge and science

Knowledge is, according to most authors, justified true belief. Of course, one may ask what constitutes justification. In broad outline, two possible grounds for justification have been proposed – one, idealism, focusing on the knower, the individual or social processes leading to knowledge claims; the other, realism, focusing on the known, the object of knowledge.

Realism says that knowledge corresponds to reality; more precisely, that terms of our theories refer to, 'correspond' with, real things in the world. Perhaps the archetype of scientific realism was (logical) *positivism*, which may still determine the (largely implicit) image most working scientists have of what empirical investigation really is. It assumed that reality consists of elementary atomic facts, which are reflected in observation statements, plus the logical connections between them. Such observation statements thus represent elementary states of affairs ('facts') in the world, and they are connected by tautological logical rules, so that the build-up of knowledge makes a kind of mental blueprint of the world, a theory. Language reflects reality in a mirror-like fashion, like a picture, or perhaps more accurately, like a blueprint. The common view of *truth* in realism is *correspondence*: theories are true if they correspond with nature. The unsolved (and unsolvable) problem, however, is that there is no measure for agreement between language and reality – if only because it would have to be put in language, in the form of a theory. Hence, objectivity in the sense of letting the world speak for itself, and objective knowledge as gathering its reflections in the mirror of our theoretical representations, is an illusion.

The alternative, *idealism*, holds that the world as we know it is somehow a creation of the mind. Our knowledge is a subjective product, and does not necessarily correspond to an outside world; it is not even clear what the concept of an outside world exactly means, if it is construed as independent of a knowing subject. Idealism tends to *relativism*; if all knowledge is a subjective construction, there is no rational, objective way to choose between different points of view. If theories are completely in the eye of the beholder, and have no relation with reality, then anything goes. Idealists like Berkeley, Kant and Descartes were forced to introduce God or Universal Human Nature to arrange for some correspondence between representations in individual minds and the represented things in the world. The common view of *truth* in idealism is *coherence*: theories are true if they are consistent with the rest of our knowledge.

So we seem to have two equally unattractive options: the mind makes up the world, perhaps entirely confabulates it; or we must assume that the world as it is in itself, independent of human exploration and theorizing, is accessible to us. The latter option, which assumes that there is some criterion for matching a 'God's eye point of view' (Putnam, 1981) with our own view, is of course paradoxical. As Rorty (1979: 298) puts it, it involves the notion 'that we are successfully representing according to Nature's own conventions of representation', rather than 'that we are successfully representing according to our own'. In other words, there is no criterion for comparing our theories directly with the world, since any such comparison must be, it seems, a theory, so that there is no way of getting beyond, or stepping out of, theory. Thus, realism in the epistemological literal sense is impossible.

Indirect support for *scientific realism* is sometimes sought in the empirical success of empirical investigations, especially in physics (Boyd, 1984). If new findings fit with and extend existing theories, and our world image seems to converge towards a final theory, then these theoretical terms (atoms, quarks, etc.) will probably correspond to something real; hence the name for this position, *convergent realism*. However, patently wrong theories can be quite successful predictors (Laudan, 1991).

We postpone a more elaborate discussion of realism and relativism until Chapter 2, but let us offer you a preview of our own position.

The pragmatic view: functional knowledge

Our position in the realism–idealism dichotomy is that knowledge is inter-active, is the product of actively exploring the world, revealing reality by acting on it. This is in a sense an intermediate position between realism and idealism (Bem, 1989), between subjectivism and objectivism. The idea is that 'the mind and the world jointly make up the mind and the world' (Putnam, 1981: xi). The product of this conjunction is subject-relative but not subjective or relativistic in the sense of arbitrary. We call this a functional view of knowledge. It holds that knowledge is a kind of interaction of subject and object, rather than being either passive picturing or subjective constructing. Knowledge is a methodologically regulated, constrained form of human action (praxis), and therefore is evaluative and value laden. In Rorty's (1979) words, knowing is coping with the world rather than mirroring it. Therefore we should expect that the meaning of theoretical terms derives from their practical use, and that manipulation is a determinant in the structure of knowledge.

To sum up, the notion of functional knowledge designates an interactional view of the nature of knowledge, which avoids the extremes of rationalism and empiricism, of focusing exclusively either on the subjective, or on the objective pole.

Everyday knowledge and scientific knowledge

The difference between everyday knowledge and scientific knowledge is loosely related to questions concerning the nature of scientific methodology and scientific explanation, to the tension between methodological reduction and phenomenological experience, and to the relation between explanation and understanding. These questions we will set out later in this chapter.

The philosopher Wilfred Sellars (1963) made the classic distinction between the manifest and the scientific image. 'Image' refers to the concept of man in the world, the framework in terms of which man views himself. The manifest image is the world of objects and persons of sophisticated common sense, including traditional philosophical systems which are reflections on and refinements of primitive self-consciousness. The scientific image is the world of particles and forces posited by advanced science. Thus, the difference is 'not that between an unscientific conception of man-in-the-world and a sci-entific one, but between that conception which limits itself to what correlational techniques can tell us about perceptible and introspectible events, and that which postulates imperceptible objects and events for the purpose of explaining correlations between perceptibles' (Sellars, 1963: 19).

So, on the one hand there is the image of refined categories of common sense, on the other hand the image in terms of postulated underlying reality; and these often seem in conflict, each claiming to be the true and complete account of man in the world. The scientific image aims at replacing the mani-fest one; it holds that water, for instance, is really H_2O; that only the scientific table as described in physical terms is real, the common-sense table is an illlusion; that a person and her thoughts and feelings are really neurophysiological processes.

Three ways of confronting both images suggest themselves: (1) we may assume that they are identical – this is obviously wrong, since strictly speaking, molecules are not wet or coloured; (2) the manifest image is real, and the scientific image is only an abstract or condensed way of describing it; (3) the scientific image is real, and the manifest image is only an appearance. Sellars assumes that the scientific image is in principle adequate/and true.

Sellars wants to unite two images in 'stereoscopic' vision; we should realize that science is not finished, but might progress and recreate in its own terms the concepts of the manifest image. A fine example of this approach is Dennett's (1991) theory of consciousness, which tries to incorporate consciousness in a state-of-the-art cognitive-neurophysiological theory (see Chapter 4, p. 136 ff.). However, Sellars has also a more utopian view of integrating science with the goals of a community, appropriating the world as conceived by science into a rational and meaningful way of life.

To sum up, the relation of science and common sense is often conceived as a border dispute, with science in the role of the invader. The view taken in this book is that the relation between science and common sense is a continuum, in the sense that scientific methods are a restricted and regimented outgrowth of human praxis. In our view science can be best understood against the background of practice. A large part of Chapter 2 will be devoted to a discussion of a pragmatic view in the philosophy of science, as contrasted with the theory-centred view.

Some characteristics of science

Historically, science is no doubt continuous with the knowledge and concerns of daily life. In Western society practical problems, such as optimizing fertility in agriculture, measuring land, traditional healthcare, etc., have more or less smoothly merged into chemistry, geometry, biochemistry. There is apparently no sharp division between pre-scientific and scientific knowledge. Science is organized common sense.

The methodically definite form of science as we know it began at the end of the Middle Ages. Later, in seventeenth-century England and the Netherlands, the demand for practical knowledge in artillery, fortress building, irrigation, and canalization boosted the study of mathematics and physics. What distinguishes this new scientific method from previous commonsense solutions is its systematic nature, and its endeavour to provide explanations for the phenomena observed. In a nutshell, science is systematic in the sense that it tries to formulate laws that apply everywhere, not just in traditionally established habits, and is explanatory in the sense that it tries to answer 'why' questions, providing an answer to the question of why the phenomena are as observed. Such explanations are both systematic and controllable by factual evidence. As Nagel (1961: 4) puts it: '[I]t is the organisation and classification of knowledge on the basis of explanatory principles that is the distinctive goal of the sciences.'

The following list of characteristics may be used to get the gist of scientific method (Nagel, 1961; Sanders et al., 1976).

1. *Systematicity*. Theories must be applicable across the board, the theoretical edifice must be coherent and if possible hierarchical; the domain of application is specified at the outset, and no *ad hoc* exceptions are allowed.
2. *Well-defined methods* (Kuhn, 1962). Methods also specify what count as legitimate subject matter, facts and explananda. Psychologists, for instance, will be reluctant to investigate poltergeists as phenomena in their own right; chemists disown the philosopher's stone: they fall outside the framework, do not count as observation.
3. *Reduction*, both in the sense of ignoring certain aspects of reality (which are supposedly accidental) at the descriptive level, and in the sense of reducing phenomena to underlying principles at the explanatory level. As a simple example of the latter, water, steam and ice are explained as the same chemical substance under different conditions. A more complex example: all matter may ultimately be explained by the final laws of a (future) complete physical theory in terms of elementary particles or fields.
4. *Objectivity*, in the sense of being controllable, reliable and intersubjectively observable. For instance, so-called slow schizophrenia, which could only be observed in Soviet dissidents by Soviet psychiatrists trained by Professor Snezjnevskij in KGB clinics, and nowhere and by nobody else (Joravski, 1989), is not a scientific concept.
5. *Clarity*. Scientific statements are phrased unambiguously, in principle addressed to the public domain.
6. *Never closed*. Scientific knowledge is open, is at all times revisable and never definitive.

So the dictum that science is organized common sense is reasonable, but a lot remains to be said about the specifics of the mode of organization.

Notions of *classification* and taxonomy play an important role in reflections on scientific method. 'Cutting nature at the joints' is essential for organization of knowledge in the systematic way. The suggestion that some term is 'merely' descriptive, and therefore unimportant and arbitrary, is certainly wrong. In biology the choice of taxonomy (mammals, reptiles, fish, insects) is a *sine qua non* for a viable science; the classification of whales as mammals, rather than fish, is no trivial or linguistic matter, but an essential feature of the systematic nature of science.

Classical accounts emphasize explanation as the hallmark of science (e.g. Nagel, 1961), describing the underlying mechanisms that account for or cause surface phenomena. The explanatory aspect of science can be seen in its extensive use of unobservables, underlying explanatory entities (like atoms, or the Freudian unconscious) that try to explain the observed phenomena. This may sometimes have the unpleasant consequence of parting with the layman's view, as discussed above.

Furthermore, systematicity implies that phenomena are isolated into small and unambiguously observable units, with the aim of subsequently integrating them in a larger system of facts. Science attempts to provide a logically unified body of knowledge, ideally in the form of a closed, axiomatic, deductive system (see p. 9 ff.) in which propositions can be derived from theories describing empirical facts. A nice example would be Mendeleyev's system.

In its *testability* science also goes beyond commonsense knowledge; common sense employs broad and relatively fuzzy concepts, whereas science refines these into precise notions. The greater determinacy of scientific concepts contrasts with the loose generalizations elsewhere, and allows more rigorous testing. It makes knowledge claims more vulnerable, but also provides more opportunities for neatly fitting them into a larger clearly articulated coherent theory. Thus, previously unconnected facts can be related and systematized. Common sense is relatively dependent upon unchanging conditions and a number of unarticulated background assumptions, whereas science is explicit as to its assumptions. Scientific knowledge is systematic and coherent in the way that everyday knowledge is not, and unlike common sense, it is explicit about the range of application of its concepts. Science avoids the inconsistencies common sense is not concerned about and tries to build a homogeneous network of concepts.

In our view, then, science is to be considered from a pragmatic perspective. Its methods are to be evaluated with respect to its central aim, producing knowledge about the world, and finding generalizations ('laws') that apply to the world (Chalmers, 1990). Thus we can circumvent, at least for practical purposes, the unsettling problems of relativism. Briefly, the view that pragmatism is relativist and irrationalist, and cannot distinguish between accidental success and genuine scientific rationality, only follows from the hidden assumption that a philosophical account of how knowledge is anchored in some form of contact with the world is the only defence against absurdity and fraud. We think that there is no need for a single, fixed ahistorical canon of scientific method. Knowledge about the world comes in many varieties, and should be evaluated pragmatically, in the light of practice.

1.3   Arguments, laws, theories, models and facts

The objective of knowledge is to understand (parts of) the world in order to get on in it. Science is a special branch of knowledge; it is usually not content with the immediate environment, and probes deeper than common, everyday knowledge; and most important, science is a controlled enterprise. Scientists want to comprehend *why* things happen, what are the mechanisms or processes *behind* the phenomena. To form their opinions, to convince others, to provide evidence and to predict events they use different means – assumptions, observations, arguments, explanations, predictions, descriptions, theories, models. In this and the following sections we will discuss some of these basic scientific concepts.

Arguments

Arguments are sets of statements (the premisses) connected in such a way that a conclusion follows from them. In some arguments, the conclusion is definitively supported. An example is:

Men are bigger than mice
Mice are bigger than ants
∴ Men are bigger than ants

Because the premisses 'contain', so to say, the conclusion, or the conclusion can be 'extracted' or deduced from the premisses, these conclusive arguments or inferences are also called *deductive*. If you accept the premisses of a deductive argument then you also must buy the conclusion; otherwise you produce a contradiction. The soundness of conclusive arguments is a consequence of the meaning of the relations (in the example, 'are bigger than') and the arrangement of the terms (the names which stand for the subjects). This pattern can be abstracted from inferences about specific states of affairs, and can be formalized as follows:

$$x \, R_t \, y$$
$$y \, R_t \, z$$
$$\therefore x \, R_t \, z$$

where R_t stands for a transitive relation, such as 'bigger than', 'smaller than', 'older than'. So, we have here a valid inference-pattern which can be interpreted by any transitive relation between two different entities. This is what logicians do (among other things): they abstract from or generalize about specific arguments and study under what conditions arguments are valid, in what respect they are similar or different, etc. Unlike other scientists and people in their everyday discourse, a formal logician is not interested in the subject matter or content of arguments, only in the formal structure.

Among conclusive arguments *syllogisms* are well known. Here is an example:

All politicians are liars
All members of parliament are politicians
∴ All members of parliament are liars

In this example it is easy to see that a conclusive argument that is perfectly valid can be doubtful or even false, because the first of the premisses is. The truth has something to do with the content of the inference; the soundness with the pattern or form. So, the conclusion of a deductive inference is true on two conditions: (1) the argument must be valid or sound; and (2) the premisses must be true. In other words, if an argument is deductively valid, it is impossible for the premisses to be true while the conclusion is false.

This promise of absolute certainty constitutes the appeal of the deductive method. Ideally, one could start with a few unquestionable truths or axioms and then deduce other statements or theorems from them. The geometry devised by Euclid, the Greek geometer who lived in the third century BC, was such an *axiomatic system*. Very much impressed by the elegance of this system the French philosopher René Descartes (1596–1650) thought it possible to deduce all scientific statements from some axioms, which were put into us as innate ideas by God. Many other scientists in the sixteenth and seventeenth centuries also thought that nature was mathematically structured, that the world was a machine, or clockwork, working according to precise mathematical laws, that the human mind was designed in accordance with that system and could comprehend it, and that knowledge reflected that system. In our century the behaviourist Clark Hull (1884–1952) had a similar ideal in mind for psychology. Psychology, he thought, is a natural science and since nature is a mathematical and mechanical system the mental is nothing but physical and behavioural, and psychology can be formalized into one single deductive system. In the end behaviour is the complex result of basic physical entities like electrons and protons. Since psychology is a chapter of the whole scientific system, theories and predictions about behaviour can be deduced from clearly stated principles (Leahey, 1992).

However, Hull's system didn't work out. Apparently, we cannot put our knowledge so rigorously and absolutely into a comprehensive, unified and fixed system. Scientific theories happen to be fallible and changeable. As we said before, science is never closed.

Inductive arguments

We cannot rely on deductive arguments exclusively; in science as well as in everyday discourse we mostly apply non-conclusive arguments. While the premisses of a conclusive argument logically already 'contain' the conclusion, which therefore must be accepted, the conclusion of a non-conclusive argument is only, more or less, supported by the premisses. If you do accept the premisses, but still doubt the conclusion you could be reproached for being stubborn or an arch-sceptic but you cannot be reproached for contradicting yourself. Among the non-conclusive arguments are *inductive* arguments which are generalizations from statements of lesser scope: what is true of a number of members of a class is likely to be true of all members. Here is an example:

> I know five psychologists and, boy, are they arrogant!
> Therefore, I think that all psychologists are arrogant.

If someone said this he had perhaps not been very fortunate in his meetings with psychologists, and was rather hasty in drawing this general conclusion from the poor sample, because there are thousands of psychologists. Suppose, however, that the sample of arrogant psychologists is not five but 100, or 1,000: wouldn't we be moving from less to more evidential support? Thus, inductive support for the conclusion comes in degrees; it depends on the amount of evidence in relation to the extent of the conclusion, and it varies with different types of subject matter. It is reasonable therefore that people who are confronted with inductive conclusions should want to know the weight of the evidence. In order to accept, for instance, the assertion that frequent use of marijuana or hashish every day will impair your memory, one wants to know how the study which constitutes the evidence has been done, how many subjects have been examined (the sample), what data have been gathered, etc. A subclass of inductive arguments are *statistical* arguments in which the degree of probability is given in numbers or percentages; often you will find non-numerical terms such as 'many', 'nearly all', or 'never' in the conclusion.

The 'problem' of induction

In an inductively strong argument, then, if the premises are true, it is only probable that the conclusion is true. Some logicians think it better to speak of a successful induction not as a valid but as a strong argument; they reserve the notion of validity for deductive arguments. No matter how strong the inductive reasoning, it will always be an inconclusive argument: the conclusion will always go beyond the evidence. For this reason philosophers of science have had a love–hate relationship with induction. On the one hand, it is acknowledged that inductive arguments provide new empirical knowledge, that is, knowledge that is not already contained in the premises as with deduction. Science is to a great extent empirical and inductive; it generalizes from observed instances and it predicts by inferring what will happen from what has happened. This, one could say, has contributed to scientific successes. But on the other hand, it does not provide the ardently desired certainty, one cannot anticipate future cases or predict with certainty; and one has seldom witnessed all the cases in the past. There is always room for *scepticism*, as the empiricist David Hume wrote:

> *That the sun will not rise tomorrow* is no less intelligible a proposition, and implies no more contradiction than the affirmation, *that it will rise*. (Hume, 1963: section iv, 25–6)

On reflection you would perhaps point to the general presupposition upon which expectations of natural events are based: that the course of nature is uniform and continuous. This means that, other things being equal, if nothing interferes, nature will operate in the same way. But, replies Hume, that again gives you an inductive inference: up till now nature behaved . . . etcetera. And then you realize that you are merely begging the question; you are going in circles.

Hume's conclusion of his discussion of induction is sceptical and negative: inductive arguments cannot be justified by (logical) reasoning; there is no rational foundation for them. There is no cogent line of reasoning that leads from premises to conclusion, no absolute certainty in the manner of deduction. We arrive at inductive conclusions by a non-rational process: by habit. The process of inference is not logical thinking but a psychological step. We are used to the fact that the sun rises every morning, and the prediction that it will rise tomorrow is not the conclusion of a rational – read: logical – argument but a psychologically understandable expectation. For Hume 'rational' is deductive certainty and, except in mathematics, most scientific reasoning is 'merely' inductive.

This lack of certainty or, more precisely, the suspicion that scientific inference is not justifiable, and consequently that science is unfounded, has been called *the problem of induction*. Some scientists think the problem can be ignored, saying that only if you think that science has to search for absolute certainty, only if you think that truth has to be absolute, do you have a problem because you ask too much; it is enough that science scores its successes without strong logical justification. This is the pragmatic response. Others also deny that there is a problem, saying that not only science but also life would be impossible if the zillion everyday expectations stood in need of strong foundation, such as: if I collide with that tree my car gets smashed up. Some philosophers of science, however, are not satisfied with the idea that the factual success of science and scientific reasoning lacks justification, and hence is simply fortuitous. Many have been trying to find a logic of inductive justification.

Inference to the best explanation

Inconclusive reasonings are often used in explanations. Coming home you find the fridge open. Since your partner, the only other inhabitant, has lately developed the bad habit of showing some negligence in this matter, you conclude that he, again, has left open the door of the refrigerator. Of all the possible other explanations this is the best; but is the conclusion more logically legitimate than others? What you did was arrive at a hypothesis. The question is, how do we do that, and on what basis?

This kind of probably reliable explanation, inference to the best explanation as it is called today, the pragmatist C.S. Peirce once christened *abduction*. It is a kind of reasoning in which an explanatory hypothesis is derived from a set of facts and has the following structure:

S is the case
If R then S is normally to be expected
∴ It is highly probable that R was the case

Peirce was very much interested in the testing of these hypotheses and he tried to construct a logic of it. How do we arrive at hypotheses? And what criteria can we legitimately use for testing them? This logic of testing and of finding rules and criteria for hypotheses is also called the *logic of discovery*.

Context of justification and context of discovery

Some philosophers, however, denied that there can be a logic of discovery because discoveries are too different and complex to be captured in logical and methodological rules. There is no algorithm for discovery, or a recipe that inevitably and mechanically leads to new facts and generalizations. And they contended that the acquisition of scientific facts or theories is not the business of philosophy but of psychology. All kinds of extrascientific factors induce discoveries, such as Archimedes sitting in his bath and discovering the way to calculate the volume of solid objects; and Newton guessing the law of gravitation by observing an apple falling from a tree. These philosophers consider it the task of the philosophy and methodology of science to guard the rationality of science and to analyse whether the scientific products, the finished theories can be justified, abstracting from the messy ways in which scientists arrive at their conjectures: What is the argumentative basis? What are the empirical data? How strong are the logical connections between the statements? What are the norms for good theories? Romantic flashes of insight and other personal histories are non-rational or irrational and irrelevant to the task of justification.

This led to the distinction between the *context of justification* and the *context of discovery*, introduced by traditional empiricist philosophers to demarcate the domain of scientific rationality. Others, in direct opposition, demonstrate the importance of the historical, social and psychological contexts of scientific discoveries (see Chapters 2 and 3). Apart from the question of whether there is a discovery algorithm, they argue that

> to ignore discovery, innovation, and problem solving in general is to ignore most of the scientists' activities and concerns, in many cases not only the most interesting phases of scientific research but also (more importantly) phases highly relevant to epistemology, e.g., to the theory of rationality and the understanding of conceptual change and progress in science. (Nickles, 1980: 2)

In fact, sociologists and psychologists took over segments of the epistemological domain that philosophers traditionally claimed for themselves – guarding rationality and setting the rules for scientific method. This takeover is part of what has been called *naturalistic epistemology*. In this project, initiated by the philosopher W.V.O. Quine, epistemology is seen as a part of natural science because it 'simply falls into place as a chapter of psychology' (Quine, 1969: 82). It can be contested whether psychology is entirely a natural science, but if one takes 'naturalistic' in a broader sense, meaning 'continuous with science', one might appreciate our suggestion that the sociology of science, psychology of science and/or psychology of cognition are legitimate chapters in the programme of naturalizing epistemology. We consider this project as an inquiry into the processes by which scientists tend to arrive at their scientific beliefs. In Chapters 3 and 4 we will pursue this line of thinking.

Facts and theories

It is sometimes said that the job of science is to discover facts. This has to be qualified, however. The empiricist Francis Bacon (1561–1626) thought that collecting facts like a bee gathers honey is the right method of doing science: doing research is systematically collecting observations and compiling lists of data and if the scientist does that carefully the scientific laws will be discovered automatically. However, it is highly implausible that science has ever been done in such a way, because it is not an automatic process at all. One always departs from preconceived ideas when gathering data. You cannot do science without some power of imagination, without some idea what to look for. For Bacon, however, imagination and fantasy constitute dangers for science, which should eschew prejudices ('idols'), and he put all his money on 'pure' empirical facts.

The tension between facts (meaning here, direct observations) and theory (meaning here, going beyond direct observations) has always haunted philosophers of science. It is, of course, a major concern of science to understand what happens and what will happen. To this end scientists have to generalize about relations between different facts. We saw earlier that empiricists reached the view that inductive reasoning was highly problematic; this is why Hume became sceptical about science. Logical positivists, who built their idea of science upon strict empiricism, had to accept probability and a certain amount of uncertainty, but clung to observations as the stronghold of science. At least observations can be intersubjectively agreed upon, they thought, and they required exact statements about observations as the foundation of theories.

However, to comprehend underlying structures, to formulate what have been called 'laws' of nature, scientists have to venture beyond the mere inspection, enumeration and description of what can be observed. This very often makes them decide to conjecture *unobservable entities* and relations, such as protons, gravitation, energy, attitudes, motives, personality traits, or the cognitive map.

You can imagine that the empiricists' focus on observable facts made them suspicious about theoretical imagination. Strict empiricists do not want to have anything to do with unobservables. However, criticism of strict empiricism has become so loud since the 1950s and 1960s that almost nobody thinks any more that science can be exciting, or can be done at all, without conjectures about unobservables. Moreover, the notion of theory-neutral data to be 'read off' from the world has been severely attacked and has given way to the notion of the 'theory-ladenness' of observations: observation is always partly determined by one's theoretical assumptions (see Chapter 2). 'Facts' are not directly given events in the world but are the statements about those events one holds to be true. A fact is a conviction or a belief that something is the case and is never independent of other notions one happens to believe.

Hence, the one-time demand that every scientific statement should be reducible to (an) observation statement(s), has been replaced by the notion that theories can be underdetermined by data. Cognitive science, for instance, would be impossible if we had to stick to direct observations.

This is not to say that empirical tests can be dismissed. On the contrary, to use your imagination in order to construct bold theories is one thing; to stay open-minded and to revise and even refute your theory in the light of evidence to the contrary is another. This is a far cry from mere speculation, superstitious explanation and prejudice. Unscientific explanations, like these, tend to be final and dogmatic, invoking revelation or authority, without giving reasons and seeking evidence. Science, on the contrary, should be open to tests and arguments and sensitive to evidence, including empirical evidence. For this reason, the logician Irving Copi wrote: 'The vocabulary of "hypothesis", "theory", and "law" is unfortunate, since it obscures the important fact that *all* of the general propositions of science are regarded as hypotheses, never as dogmas' (1961: 423).

As we said before, scientific knowledge is at all times revisable and never definitive. Though scientists may have good reasons and may have good evidence for thinking that their theories are true, they can never be certain in an absolute sense.

Theories

Informally speaking, a theory is a set of statements that organizes, predicts and explains observations; it tells you how phenomena relate to each other, and what you can expect under still unknown conditions. De Groot (1969: 40) gives the following more formal definition:

> [A theory is] a system of logically interrelated, specifically non-contradictory, statements, ideas, and concepts relating to an area of reality, formulated in such a way that testable hypotheses can be derived from them.

A theory, to some extent, fixes the vocabulary in which observations are phrased. A feature of natural sciences is that its vocabulary consists of a limited set of unambiguously defined terms; mathematical symbols are the most telling example, but also in physics the description of what is observed is limited to what can be expressed in terms of force, mass, velocity, etc.

From a theory predictions can be derived, and predicting is tantamount to explaining. When your theory predicts the position of the planets, that is, when a prediction can be derived in an unambiguous way from the theory, you can be said to have a model that explains (a relevant part of) the movement of the planets.

What 'deriving' predictions exactly means is tricky. As discussed elsewhere, the original idea (with the logical positivists) was that theories have a formal structure, like an abstract calculus, and deriving predictions is considered an exercise in formal logic. In physics, mathematical theories do indeed permit such quantitative predictions. In the history of psychology, however, Hull's attempt to build a formal deductive system for the prediction of behaviour was a failure. In most cases we have to rely on informal but still reasonably uncontroversial ways of deriving predictions from a theory. Usually, additional assumptions are therefore required, and some kind of translation of theoretical terms in empirical phenomena is needed.

Laws

A law can be defined as an empirical generalization. Ideally, it has the form: for all x at any time and place, if x is P, then it is Q – for example, frustration leads to aggression: all individuals, if frustrated (P), will exhibit aggression (Q). Of course, all kinds of exceptions and conditions will usually have to be specified.

Laws then are generalizations, but not all generalizations are laws. A nasty problem in the theory of science is, how to distinguish between real laws and accidental generalizations. There is a genuine difference between the law that (all) copper (always) expands when heated, and the fact that all coins in my pocket are silver. The former is a law of nature, the latter is an accidental generalization. The difference is usually expressed in terms of necessity or of counterfactuals.

A law must necessarily hold, even in circumstances which do not now obtain – which is known as *counterfactual*. If we took a piece of copper to the moon and heated it, it would expand, but if I put a copper coin in my pocket, it would not turn into silver. The former generalization is counterfactual-supporting, and thus a real law; the latter is not.

Put slightly differently, we may require that theories exceed the known evidence for them, that is, tell us more than we already knew. A genuine theory is also a commitment about what might happen, under conditions as yet unobserved.

The philosopher of science, Popper made refutability (the possibility that future situations will prove a theory wrong) of predictions the hallmark of real science, as we will see in the next chapter.

Also, being part of a network of theories and concepts, and being as strictly as possible (logically) connected to other laws, is a highly desirable property for laws in science. The system of classical mechanics is a case in point. Hooking up to good theories in other domains enhances the credibility of a theory. In psychology, a good working relation with functional neurophysiology is an asset for a model in cognitive or clinical psychology.

A distinction can be made between empirical and theoretical laws (De Groot, 1969: 76–7; Nagel, 1961). Laws in which *observables* occur are *empirical* generalizations, laws with *unobservables* can be defined as *theoretical* laws. In genetics, Mendelian laws which capture regularities in the inheritance of certain traits (e.g. hair colour, eye colour) are empirical; in contrast, whenever genes or chromosomes are mentioned in a law, this assumes a theoretical character.

As you can imagine, reverting to abstract and/or unobservable parameters goes hand in glove with larger and more theoretical networks. This suggests that there is virtue in constructing theoretical laws. First, it enhances the scope and the anchoring of a theory; empirical laws are in danger of just enumerating familiar and trite facts. Second, theories ideally bring together qualitatively different phenomena in a single framework. Empirical laws capture commonalties at a phenomenal level, but theoretical laws suggest a deeper insight into underlying mechanisms and, consequently, the possibility of bringing together disparate observations under the same conceptual umbrella. Unification, the subsumption of many domains of empirical observation under a single conceptual framework, is an important goal of scientific inquiry. A classic example is Newtonian mechanics, which applies to falling apples as well as to the movement of the planets, and more recently to launching missiles, accelerating motorcycles and whatnot.

The difference between empirical and theoretical laws is not absolute, but gradual: observations in empirical laws are *theory laden* (the theory to some extent determines what counts as a phenomenon), and unobservables in theoretical laws must also be verified by observation – only indirectly (see the paragraph on operationalization, p. 18). Nevertheless, it is useful to be clear about the difference. A nasty example in psychology where it is ignored is Freud's psychoanalysis, where theoretical constructs were confused with clinical observations. The result was a closed and sectarian school of thought, where presumed 'observations' were only understandable and verifiable to true believers, and which as a consequence lost touch with the mainstream of science.

Models

A model is a kind of mini-theory: it provides a more or less visualizable representation of the theory, as in some kind of analogy. A classic example is the model of the atom as a collection of coloured balls (electrons) circling around a core composed of differently coloured balls (protons and neutrons).

The term 'model' is also used for a more or less abstract picture of a part of reality in a field of inquiry where no fully fledged theory is (yet) available. Psychology is rich in models: in any textbook of cognitive psychology you will find pictures of boxes and arrows that purport to model things like the working of memory (say, different kinds of storage from which information is retrieved), or attention (which may be modelled as a searchlight focusing on selected objects or a glue integrating features to objects). Sometimes, the model takes a mathematical form. Such models are for example used in economics to express relations between economic parameters (say, between average wage and unemployment) and can be used even if the underlying causes of such relationships are still unknown, that is, when a real theory is not available. In psychology, computer programs that simulate cognitive processes, like learning or problem-solving, can be regarded as models in the above sense. Whether such simulations qualify as a genuine *theory* of the domain they model is a moot point (De Groot, 1969: 335–42).

Causality

A notorious problem in philosophy is the notion of causality. We will ignore the metaphysical niceties, and focus on the notion of causal laws. If we take a law to be a generalization connecting several events, then there is, intuitively, a difference between mere contiguity of two events and a causal relation: in Boyle's law, pressure and temperature are related, but you cannot say that one is caused by the other.

Philosophers have spent considerable effort in investigating the metaphysical foundations for the notion of cause (see, e.g., Bochenski, 1973; Sosa and Tooley, 1993): do causes really exist as a part of the furniture of the world? The answer to that question is still debated. We only want to remark here that, in practice, what counts as a cause depends on the context and the *explanatory interests* of the investigator. You may say that religious extremism was the cause of Rabin's death, or sloppy security, and for a pathologist it would be the biomechanics of bullets and human tissue – it depends on what your explanatory interests are. Nagel (1961: 74) lists four conditions for causal laws. First, there must be an invariable relation between cause and effect, the cause must be both a necessary and a sufficient condition for the effect. Second, cause and effect must be in the same spatial domain, or there must be an intermediate chain of causes connecting them across space. Third, the cause must precede the effect and be temporally close to it. And fourth, the relation must be asymmetrical: sunlight causes shadows, but not vice versa. Thus many laws of nature are not causal: it is a law that water is H_2O, but this is not a causal relation; Boyle's law is not causal; and so on.

Empirical cycle

The notion of an empirical cycle (De Groot, 1969) nicely captures the interplay of data and theory, deduction and induction, in the practice of science. It consists of the following stages: observation, induction, deduction, testing and evaluation (De Groot, 1969: 27 ff.).

Observation is the stage where empirical material is collected and ordered. As a first approximation, it is systematic perception (recall that organized – or systematic –common sense was our 'quick and dirty' definition of science). Tentative or implicit hypothesis formation also occurs in this stage – if only because no perception is possible without (perhaps implicit) concepts and presuppositions, without some point of view. What is selected and observed reflects implicit hypotheses and theories; these are made explicit in the next stage.

Induction (including abduction) then is the phrasing of an explicit hypothesis. 'Explicit' means that the hypothesis yields specific, verifiable predictions that can be empirically tested. *Deduction* refers to the derivation of predictions from hypotheses. The logical positivists demanded that all theories have a strictly logical or mathematical form, so that in their view deduction was an exercise in formal logic or mathematics. Such strictly formal theories however are very rare in psychology, if they exist at all, and as mentioned before, attempts by, for instance, Hull to force such an abstract calculus on psychology were unsuccessful –some would say, just silly. However, even in a less formalistic conception of hypothesis, the requirement that empirical consequences of a theory must be specified (and subsequently tested) remains. One of the ways to derive testable predictions from theoretical concepts is *operationalisation*. This means that a concept is defined in terms of measurement operations. A good example is intelligence, defined as the score on an intelligence test. The choice of quantifiable behavioural indicators for psychological constructs is an important aspect of psychological experimentation.

The aim of the *deduction* stage is to formulate predictions, in such an explicit, precise and unambiguous way that they can be tested against empirical data.

The *testing* stage is about the confrontation of these predictions with empirical data. It must be emphasized that a hypothesis is a generalizing statement: it refers to a class of events, not to single facts (it is, possibly, a law that stress is conducive to premature ageing; it is not a law that John has grey hair). This implies that predictions must contain references to new situations, which are not already observed. For example, the law that frustration leads to aggression should be tested by comparing the prediction with the behaviour of a new population.

Finally, in the *evaluation* stage the results of the test are used as feedback for the more general theory from which the hypotheses are derived. Depending on the situation, one of two competing theories might have to be rejected in favour of the other, but more frequently, no such choice is available, and the theory will be expanded, qualified or amended; for instance, frustration leads to aggression only in certain circumstances, or in certain populations. There are no hard and fast rules for the interpretation of the results; the decision what to change in one's theory will to some extent remain subjective, influenced by prejudices and opportunism. For example, the investigator may blame contradictory results on artefacts, or nuisance variables or whatever, or may invent *ad hoc* hypotheses to save his or her favourite theory. Alternatively, unexpected results may lead to new discoveries completely beyond the hypothesis tested (so-called serendipity). This stage then is at least partially to be situated in the context of discovery.

In any case, the new theory will again spawn new hypotheses, to be tested on new data, leading to new tests and interpretations: the empirical cycle starts all over again. Bad ideas will fade away when no empirical evidence for them is found. The empirical cycle is thus a never-ending circular process, where subjective decisions will always in principle be formulated in (at least partially) objectively testable form. Thus, the *context of discovery* and the *context of justification* are both in play. Induction is as indispensable as deduction.

1.4 Explanation and understanding

Explanation: the classical view

The job of science is to explain phenomena and events in the world. In the first half of this century, philosophers opted for a philosophy of science as a normative branch of philosophy, stating criteria for clearly demarcating science from non-science, laying down strict conditions for theories, etc. (Chapter 2). For an explanation to be really scientific it had to satisfy certain logical norms. The orthodox theory of scientific explanation accepted two models of explanation: the deductive and the probabilistic model.

If I have to explain why my dog salivates when eating his food, I have to search for a theory that explains this event. This theory is formulated as a law of nature, let us say: 'Whenever a mammal gets food in its mouth it salivates.' The phenomenon or the event to be explained is shown to have occurred in accordance with a general regularity of the nature of mammals. It is said to be a consequence of this general law of nature and some initial or specific conditions pertaining to the situation in question: for example here we have a dog which is a mammal and gets food in its mouth. This model of scientific explanation is called the *covering-law model* because the event to be explained, the *explanandum*, is subsumed under or covered by a law of nature; the explanation is also called a *deductive-nomological* explanation (the Greek word *nomos* means law). The law of nature, or the theory, and the specific conditions which together explain the event or phenomenon are called the *explanans*.

It could be that we still are not satisfied by the explaining theory. Perhaps we want to hear more about salivation. Why do mammals salivate? Of course, we could extend the theory, i.e. add more general laws. However, this doesn't affect the logical structure of the covering-law model of scientific explanation. Normally, it is presented as follows:

$$\frac{\begin{array}{l} L_1 \ldots, L_n \\[4pt] C_1 \ldots, C_m \end{array}}{E}$$

$\}$ together the explanans

the explanandum

The explanans consists of two premises: one about one or a set of general laws (L); and the other about a set of specific conditions (C) relevant to the event (E) to be explained. The explanation is a deductive argument of which the explanandum is a logical consequence of the explanans. But the relation between explanans and explanandum in reality is not clear and has been an object of lively debate. The conditions referred to in one of the premises may be called the cause of the event and the explanation is sometimes called a causal explanation. But there are cases for which explanation the conditions cannot straightforwardly be called the cause of the event. Among these cases are *dispositions*. Is the molecular structure of glass the cause of its brittleness, if we take, as usual, a cause to precede its effect, but the glass has not been broken yet? The disposition, its brittleness, is a tendency: only after the glass has fallen to the ground does it break.

Prediction and probability

Besides explanation, prediction – saying what will happen or how somebody will behave – is an important objective of science. To strengthen the predictive power of a theory and then to test it, is the royal road to strong *empirical support* for the theory. The standard most important criterion of a good theory is its *empirical content*, the amount of predictive information (Hyland, 1981).

Philosophers took it as a corollary of the covering-law argument that the same model for explanation could be used for prediction. There is a symmetry between deductive-nomological explanation and prediction. If we know the laws of nature and control the conditions of an experiment, for instance, we can predict with certainty the outcome. This may be true in the ideal case. However, universal laws are rare; and even in physical science we have to accept statistical probabilities. Some 'laws' of science are to our best knowledge no more than statistical. And predictions too are not always certain;

sometimes only statistical predictions can be produced, when, for instance, one does not know, or cannot be sure of all the variables, as is mostly the case in psychology. Here is an example of a probabilistic generalization: the probability that persons with different sexual partners who do not have safe sex will become sero-positive is x percent.

Besides the deductive model which requires a universal law, philosophers of science had to accept a probabilistic model. The explanans of a probabilistic explanation contains a statistical 'law'. But, of course, the connection between a probabilistic explanans and the event to be explained or predicted is weaker than in a deductive-nomological explanation or prediction. It is possible that the explanans is a good one for most cases and that it nevertheless fails to explain or predict the event at hand. Thus, there is no airtight logical deductive relation between explanans and explanandum in these cases. Some orthodox philosophers who could not accept the resultant ambiguity, attempted to assimilate statistical explanation as closely as possible to deductive explanation, and considered this latter model as the ideal against which all forms of explanation are to be measured.

Certainty or reliability?

Behind this strict requirement for explanation lies an interpretation of science as the pursuit of certainty, the endeavour to establish scientific truth once and for all. It should provide us with a science that is universal in that it is ahistoric; a science that is not infected with local and temporary interests. This idea has inspired confidence in the deductive model because an explanation or a prediction according to this model will work without flaw only if the explaining general theory and observations, that is, the premises, are true.

However, the problem is, we never can be absolutely sure about that. History teaches us that human knowledge is fallible. The history of science is full of what we now see as lapses. So, we should have to prepare ourselves for failures. But on the other hand, we would like, and even are obliged, to trust our scientific efforts and results for pragmatic reasons. Should we say then that every time or every community has its own truths? This would be too much relativism. After all, that we could be wrong about features of the world does not preclude the possibility that we could be right and that we should trust our theories when they fit the best (practical) evidence we can get. Moreover, if we could not trust in principle our knowledge we would not survive. So, it seems best to balance a realistic picture of science against some relativism; that is, to take a realistic stance towards science, but nevertheless to be modest and open-minded about our theories and models.

Another problem, mentioned before, is the non-neutrality of observations. We arrange new observations in theories we already cherish. We apply categories and classifications we are already familiar with. We embed new concepts in networks of already existing concepts, and seldom concoct them out of the blue. Facts, observations, explanations, laws never just speak for themselves. If such is the case in natural science, all the more, so it seems, in social science.

Explanation in the social sciences

What we seek to explain in social science and psychology is (*inter alia*) people's behaviour, or *actions*. For a deductive argument to work logically the explanandum must be defined independently of the explanans, the cause of the event. To explain the fact that, say, this lump of sugar has dissolved in your coffee by saying: 'because sugar is soluble', does not help very much. In this way we sometimes produce explanatory fictions, or pseudo-explanations. The famous example is Molière's mock-explanation of the working of opium. 'Why does opium put people to sleep?' is the question put before the candidate doctor in Molière's play *Le Malade imaginaire* (1673). And the man answers, to the enthusiastic cheers of the examiners: 'Because it has "Vis dormitiva"' – a power that puts you to sleep. It sounds professional, but it explains nothing; exactly what the French playwright had in mind, because he loathed the pedantry of doctors.

A related demand is that the meanings of the terms in the argument have to be unambiguous. These requirements seem to present a major problem when we have to define and explain someone's action. In describing an action we are already taking account of the attitudes, motives and intentions by which we would like to explain the act. Other than a mere movement, the description of an action is not in the least unequivocal. Consider the following descriptions: 'He raised his arm', 'He greeted someone', 'He called a halt', 'He saluted the "Führer"'. The same movement of the arm could be described in various ways and the descriptions are not independent of the very intentions or motives we would use in the explanation of the act. What is observed can be interpreted and described differently.

The terms used in the social sciences are mostly derived from everyday discourse and carry their indeterminate interpretative and sometimes vague meanings into science. Take for instance attitude, role, belief, unconscious. It is hardly possible to restrict the connotations without loss of meaning or without changing them beyond recognition. Moreover, for many concepts, like 'ideology' or 'libido', definite descriptions are incomplete; they require the whole context of the theory. And this goes for natural scientific concepts as well, although perhaps to a lesser extent.

Hermeneutic understanding: an alternative to classical explanation

Describing an action or ascribing behaviour is not reporting a bare fact that forces itself upon us in a simple observation. In social sciences explanations often consist of more than subsumption under general laws. For a relevant description of human behaviour we need to grasp the meaning, to understand the context, and sometimes even the culture. To capture the idea, the anthropologist Clifford Geertz (1973) borrows a notion of the philosopher Gilbert Ryle (1971), *thick description*. To understand the meaning of human behaviour one has to go beyond a passive camera-like registration of movements; one has to give a thick description, a 'sorting out the structure of signification . . . and determining their social ground and import' (Geertz, 1973: 9).

Whether, for example, the contraction of an eyelid is an involuntary twitch, a conspiratorial signal, or a parody cannot be 'read off' the movement, which is identical in each case. Behaviour or human actions are part of a 'culture which consists of socially established structures of meaning' (ibid: 12).

The need for understanding and interpretation is the reason why some philosophers of science contend that the social sciences need a completely different methodology from the natural sciences. As early as the second half of the nineteenth century, when sociology and psychology were still in their infancy, a *Methodenstreit* (dispute about methods) took place. German philosophers such as Dilthey, Rickert and Windelband distinguished on the one hand *Naturwissenschaften* (natural sciences) and on the other *Geisteswissenschaften* (literally the sciences of the spirit, the humanities), including history, the history of art, and philology. Historical science was seen as very important in these sciences because it supplies one with the sensitivity to understand the wealth and variety of human life. While the natural sciences try to find universal laws of nature and generalizations – their *nomothetical* (*nomos* is law) characteristic – the human sciences and history try to understand or to interpret unique events – their *idiographical* (*idios* is particular, personal) characteristic. These different and irreducible orders of phenomena, namely the natural and the mental, require radically different methods. While in natural sciences we are concerned with explanation (*Erklären*), with subsuming a multitude of equal and disconnected objective facts under general laws, with replicable experiments and observations, and with causal connections, in human sciences we have to understand (*Verstehen*) actions, meanings and intentions. Understanding is about lived experience, about creating one's culture and self, about unique and unrepeatable individuals, cultures and historical epochs, not about general laws of nature.

What many philosophers hoped for was that understanding actions and other human or mental aspects would develop into a methodology typical of the human sciences, *hermeneutics*. Originally conceived as a method in theology, philology and jurisprudence in order to make sense and to be able to reconstruct the meaning of classical and authoritative texts, hermeneutics was extended to all cultural products that were supposed to reflect any meaning, intention and feeling. Historical periods, texts, artefacts were all interpreted as reflecting some kind of spirit – the spirit of the Middle Ages, the meaning of *Hamlet*, the intentions of Julius Caesar.

Wilhelm Dilthey (1833–1911) and others dreamt of making hermeneutics into a strong and central methodology of the human sciences. It was their intention to protect these studies against the obtrusive natural sciences and to guarantee their autonomy. The central idea is that human creations such as literary products, arts, buildings, laws, social institutions and behaviour cannot be objectified as things disconnected from human subjects; instead they are laden with values and must be understood in the context of their time and cultural setting. While the mathematical-natural way of explaining requires an analysis into meaningless elements, the historical understanding necessitates the part being held up against the whole, and vice versa – *the*

hermeneutic circle – meaning that we can never understand a particular product without considering its cultural background. Hermeneutics aims at
reconstructing the meanings and experiences objectified in cultural products.

It is hopeless to explain the French Revolution in terms of laws and causes
and disconnected events; rather one has to feel its spirit, reconstruct its
unique meaning. Enumerating a lot of objective observations, and trying to
state a causal law about them, simply misses the meaning of it all; the meaning has to be understood, 'read off' the context, lived through, so to say.

It seems that such a methodological divide is still with us, when it is argued
that subjectivity and meaning can never be explained by scientific methods.
Psychology still seems to be haunted by an antithesis between scientific
respectability and human interest, between scientific explanations and understanding lived experience (e.g. Bruner, 1990; Varela et al., 1991).

In psychology, understanding is not generally considered a viable method,
since one of the criteria for a scientific method is that it can be stated in the
form of explicit instructions, in principle understandable and learnable by all.
Psychotherapy, in psychoanalytic and Rogerian settings, has something in
common with the hermeneutic enterprise (see Terwee, 1990): the therapist is
concerned with reconstructing meaning, with exploring the way a unique
individual (the patient) makes sense of the world, rather than with observing
objective facts (like behavioural movements *per se*). She has to bring in her
own feelings and prejudices to get the dialogue going. Unfortunately, therapy
is a highly subjective and intractable affair, with dozens of deeply divided
schools and approaches. That points to a problem with hermeneutics considered as a scientific method: lack of objectivity.

The hermeneutic considers interpretation not as a kind of detached objective observation, but more as a dialogue where the interpreter brings his own
'horizon', his cultural baggage, his opinions, subjective norms and prejudices
and confronts them with the cultural spirit of his text. Such a cultural background is indispensable, but is never competely made conscious.
Interpretation is in fact only possible when it starts from such 'prejudices'
(more about this in Chapter 2) and never completely detaches itself from
them. When these predjudices are revised in confrontation with the meanings
of the text, there is no external objective criterion for correct understanding,
there is only different (revised and refined) understanding. The hermeneutic
dialogue is a circle, from which there is no escape to objectivity.

In modern times the ideal of a *methodological* hermeneutics has been
transformed, at least in the German tradition, by philosophers such as
Martin Heidegger and Hans-Georg Gadamer, into a *philosophical* hermeneutics. The claim is that humans have a fundamental hermeneutic relation not
only with their cultural products, but with the world in general. This relation
with the world is mediated by our knowledge, formed by language and therefore saturated with the subjectivity of tradition and communication. Humans
are historical and social beings and so is their most important product,
knowledge. *Verstehen* is, therefore, the fundamental epistemological characteristic of human beings and turns hermeneutics into the foundation of

philosophy. In our days, in the hands of Jürgen Habermas, Richard Rorty and others, hermeneutics has become a critical philosophy questioning the role of science and technology and the course philosophy itself has taken in the Western world.

In this section, the classical nomological view of explanation (subsumption under causal laws), and the hermeneutic view (understanding unique and individual intentions and meanings) were explained. We suggest that hermeneutics is closest to real-life concerns, and serves as the matrix for more specific investigations (since 'science is organized common sense'). Understanding and explanation can be considered as lying on a continuum from real life to more rigidly regimented forms of inquiry. Nomological explanation is, roughly, the standard in the natural sciences. Some kind of hermeneutic understanding seems crucial for social sciences. In the next section, a third methodological approach, functional and teleological explanation, is discussed, which seems adequate for biology and the 'lower strata' of psychology.

1.5   Functional and teleological explanations

What is function and teleology?

Function ascription is a crucial, but somewhat problematic element of biological explanation. On the one hand it seems natural and illuminating to describe or explain the presence of properties or organs as serving some goal or function; we have lungs to breathe, a heart to pump blood, etc. However, such explanations face criticism of triviality, vacuousness and vitalism. The assumption that a property must be there for some reason may lead to pseudo-explanations; for example the cork-oak's *raison d'être* is to enable us to cork our wine bottles. In Voltaire's novel *Candide* (1759), Maître Pangloss specializes in explaining that things are what they are because we live in the very best of all possible worlds – which is of course the most vacuous explanation you can imagine. Ascribing functions in biological and psychological contexts often involves the evolutionary notions of adaptation and fitness. Explanations that argue from these notions run the risk of 'panglossian' reasoning (Gould and Lewontin, 1979): the heart is there because it should be there, otherwise it wouldn't be there, *quod erat demonstrandum*.

Functional explanations may also lead to what is called *adaptationism*, the unhappy idea 'that natural selection is an optimizing process' and 'that there is a direct evolutionary explanation for *every* striking feature of an organism' (Clark, 1989: 76 ff.). The result is that you may focus on the wrong feature, a by-product, overlooking the very feature that needs explaining.

In an attempt to provide a sound workable notion of function, the functional explanation of some trait or organ (e.g. the function of the heart is to pump blood) can be construed as holding that such a trait exists 'in order to'.

Functional explanation is teleological, explains by invoking some goal or function (Wright, 1973, 1976).

The concern about functional and teleological explanation in the philosophy of science in the late 1950s was whether it was not a form of crypto-vitalism, appealing to immaterial causes or backward causation. More precisely, the question was whether functional explanation could be fitted into the received view, the D-N (deductive-nomological) model; by replacing *goal-directed* explanation by an equivalent *causal* explanation. Such attempts have not been successful (see Salmon, 1990). If, for example, John makes loud noises, in order to scare off a possible burglar, you cannot say that the 'possible burglar' is the cause of John's making loud noises.

The attempt to reduce teleological and functional behaviour to pre-existing *representations of a goal* (scaring off a burglar) in the organism (e.g. Boden, 1972) shifts the problem from function to the equally problematic notion of representation (Bigelow and Pargetter, 1987; more about the concept of mental representation in Chapter 4). Also, the mentalist assumption that some kind of intention, design or representation underlies functional or teleological behaviour ignores the fact that natural teleology includes organisms too simple to have mental states (Bedau, 1990); can a spider be said to have a blueprint of its web, or a beaver of its dam, and to work towards it? And does such talk really explain anything; is there a real difference between such expressions and attributing a representation of comfortable temperature to a thermostat, or a desire to a river to reach the sea?

At present the consensus seems to be that functional explanation is *sui generis* and has a legitimate place alongside causal explanation (Cummins, 1983; Rosenberg, 1985; Mayr, 1992).

Evolution and survival

Functional laws predict that in a system with a certain goal a form of behaviour will occur because it brings about the goal. The 'because' in such statements might be explicated in terms of *natural selection*, which would shift the problem from the notion of function to the notion of *adaptation*. However, function ascription can be detached from evolutionary considerations; as Boorse (1984) suggests, Wright's (1973) focus on causal history is just one among a number of possible perspectives on goals, and is not part of the meaning of the concept of function. The functions a physiologist ascribes to an organism under study would not change if some evolutionary missing link were found where the same organ had a different role. Influenced by classical epistemological analysis, Wright primarily answers the philosophical question: 'Why is a trait there?', rather than the scientific question: 'How does the system containing that trait work as a whole?' The latter question refers to the contribution a part makes to the whole system, independent of evolutionary concerns (Boorse, 1984).

So, functional explanation should be distinguished from issues of survival. First, identifying system properties is a study in its own right, independent of, and preceding, evolutionary explanation. Second, function ascription is not to be reduced to explanations in terms of actual survival (Sober, 1985). The concept of function should be detached from evolution, in the sense that survival value is not required to underwrite functional analysis, which is a good thing, considering the danger of the 'panglossian' and *post hoc* character of evolutionary explanations.

Function and environment

The 'backward-looking' tendency, which makes function too much dependent upon more or less contingent, evolutionary events in the past, can be amended by emphasizing a forward-looking, dispositional and environment-relative nature of functions: '[A] structure has a certain function when it has a propensity for selection in virtue of that character of structures having the relevant effects' (Bigelow and Pargetter, 1987: 194). In this 'propensity' account, function ascription refers to a relevant effect on appropriate occasions, so that something can count as a function even before it has actually contributed to survival. Functions are furthermore relative to their surroundings; they would constitute a survival-enhancing property in a specific environment.

To sum up: (1) function may be considered a respectable explanatory concept in its own right; genuine functions can in principle be distinguished from accidental ones; (2) it is not conceptually dependent on, nor does it have to be reduced to, considerations of evolutionary fitness; (3) function is clearly tied to teleology, to serving a goal; (4) function refers intrinsically to certain environmental conditions; (5) functions are not fixed properties, but depend on explanatory purposes (some say: are in the eye of the beholder), which cross-classify with causal laws and anatomical structures, and answer different questions.

Functionalism

Some proposals exist on how to use the concept of function as an explanation of behaviour. Functional explanation has been widely discussed with regard to the nature and the role of mental states. For this reason functionalism is also considered as part of a solution to the mind–body problem. This is in fact the subject matter of Chapter 4, but to give an impression of functional explanations in psychology we cannot avoid this problem altogether here.

Since the decline of behaviourism, it is widely accepted that observed behaviour is not enough in accounting for human behaviour. Fear is not fully understood when only somebody's external terrified behaviour – the anxious cry, wide-open eyes, etc. – and the circumstantial happenings are established, registered and related. To account for human behaviour, cognitivists claim that we need to go behind the scenes; we need to know the nature and role of what scientists, since the cognitivist turn in psychology, think is responsible for human behaviour: mental states, like thinking that Al Pacino is one of the best actors, or hoping that your plane will land safely.

But what are mental states? If we want to avoid Cartesian dualism – and most scientific psychologists nowadays reject the idea that mental phenomena are ontologically completely unlike other things in the world – we have to come up with a story about mental states that is continuous with neurological, biological and other natural sciences. We have to explain how material beings can have mental states; how matter can become mindful. There are downright materialists who assert that mind is nothing but brain; that being angry is nothing but specific neuronal firings. This is called the *mind–brain identity theory*. The main problem of the identity theory is its *type-materialism*. In this strong conception of materialism a type of mental state (e.g. being angry) is held to be identical with a certain type of brain state (say, the firing of the specific neurons x, y, and z). Thus every token of that mental state of being angry, everyone's anger, is exactly that brain state. But this identification of mental states is too specific. It pins down my Tuesday anger and my Sunday anger in exactly the same way to such-and-such neural events; and it identifies my and your anger in exactly the same neural way. Moreover, the theory precludes other species with a different neurological make-up from being in the same mental states.

To avoid this 'species chauvinism' cognitive philosophers proposed functionalism. What is important, cognitively speaking, is not the question of what pain *is* neurologically, but what it *does* to the organism. The focus of attention is not the elements or the *structure* of a mental state, but its *function*; the functional role it plays, that is, its relations to the 'input' (perception) and 'output' (behaviour) and other mental states. So, the functionalists came to distinguish the concrete *neurophysiological level of brain states* and the more abstract *cognitive level of mental states*. And they came to believe that the neurophysiological level bears no cognitive importance. They liked to compare the two levels with the hardware on the one hand, and the software or the computer program on the other. Just as a computer program can be realized or implemented by different hardware configurations, so can a mental 'program' be realized by different organisms or systems with different physiological or physical make-up, be it humans, dogs, computers, aliens from another galaxy, or the stones of Stonehenge. Instead of the 'chauvinism' of the identity theorists, functionalists opted for 'liberalism' (Block, 1978): they ascribed mental states to many things. In this theory, you and a robot could share mental functions, without sharing underlying physical structure. Functionalists regarded cognition in general as computational information processing (for more on the computational theory of mind, see Chapter 4, p. 107 ff.).

Functionalism is based on the less strong kind of materialism, *token-materialism*. A whole type of mental states is not being identified with a certain type of brain state, as in type-materialism, but each token of a mental state is *a* physical state, whatever. So, it is materialism without reduction of every mental state to a particular neural state. But what is more, it is a materialism not of things (structure) but of functions, of roles. Therefore, in the cognitive view, mental states are material systems in which mental states play causal roles, hence are causally related to input, to output and to other mental states. Paul's hope that his girlfriend will come tonight is causally related to, say, his belief that she will not have to work on the night shift, and to his buying her favourite drink. So, Paul's behaviour, being in the super-market and buying Sambuca, can be explained in terms of its causal connections with mental states and sensory stimulation. What Paul's beliefs and hopes are made of, the question of their material realization (or 'imple-mentation'), is irrelevant, according to these cognitivists.

The early functionalists (e.g. Putnam, 1961; Fodor, 1968) regarded the study of cognition as a mechanistic study of the computational network of mental states, the study of an abstract machine (or 'virtual machine'); they characterized mental states in logico-mathematical terms. Recently, some functionalists criticized this *machine functionalism* and came up with another idea of psychological explanation. They contend that the machine function-alists have stripped the concept of function of its teleology and that genuine function has to be 'put back into functionalism' (Sober, 1985), meaning that cognition has to be explained in a biologically plausible sense, and that the notion of mechanistic causality has to be replaced by the notion of biological purpose. This new *teleological functionalism* does not want to split organisms into independent levels (the neurophysiological and the cognitive). Cognition cannot be abstracted rigorously from its biological and neurological realiza-tion. The biological and neurological constrain the psychological, and the teleological notion of function is part of it. The machine functionalists are guilty of too much liberalism.

If, however, functions are not fixed properties, but depend on explanatory purposes and cannot be identified with mental states, might that be a problem for (teleological) functionalism? Especially when we label striking higher-order cognitive tasks which are suggested by folk-psychological expressions, such as attention, planning or feeling as functions, we run the risk of what we earlier called adaptationism. These 'functions' may easily be constituted in the eye of the beholder. On the other hand, the structure/function distinction is a problem mainly when your materialism consists of a predilection for concrete things or structure. The question is, can there be a world without functions, without the workings of things? Do we not, in fact, encounter the structural/functional hierarchical relation on every level of analysis?

Analysing and decomposing functions

Wilkes (1978) and Cummins (1980, 1983) have elaborated the notion of func-tion into a real explanation of complex systems, which deviates from the classical causal view of explanation. They propose that mental processes can be explained by analysing them as functions, and Cummins contrasts this type of explanation with the causal model which others (e.g. Fodor, 1991) think fits the bill. The question to be answered by functional analysis is about instantiation rather than causation: in virtue of what can a system have such and such properties or capacities? Functional explanation according to Cummins *decomposes* functional capacities (or dispositions) into a number of simpler functions, *subfunctions*, which together instantiate the analysed function. In principle, functions can be instantiated in different structures, and no relation between form and function is assumed. Since multiple instantiations are possible of one property in different physical structures, instantiation is not compatible with the classical reductionist strategy. Functions can be *hierarchically decomposed*. For a given function, a structure can be specified which can in turn be considered as a function, to be specified by further analysis into subfunctions. This results in a sort of Chinese boxes procedure: a progressive decomposition into simpler and more elementary functions until a basic level of mechanism, brain structures or perhaps individual neurons, is reached.

Wilkes proposes this model as a solution for the mind–body problem: the functions of the nervous system can be analysed in terms of (sub)functions and subserving structures, and she suggests that this is the strategy for neuropsychology (Wilkes, 1980). One might think of the functional explanation of a mental capacity as a decomposition into systems described at the level of functional neuroscience, which may then in turn be decomposed into increasingly anatomically localized and mechanistically explainable structures. In Wilkes' model such typical mental concepts as intentions and representations only figure at the very top of the functional hierarchy. The general picture is that mind is a hierarchy of functions situated between an intentional representational level at the top, and a mechanistic causal level at the bottom. The level of mechanisms which can be explained causally, and where functional explanation becomes trivial, is the lower boundary of functional analysis.

So, function according to these authors is a separate type of explanation, and a distinct level of analysis (or a hierarchy of levels), situated above the level of physical mechanisms.

Function, environment and teleology

The biological conception of function implies an appeal to environmental constraints. This element is missing, or at least not prominent, in Cummins' (1983) non-teleological functional analysis (Bechtel, 1986). It can be argued that the role of the environment is crucial, not only in biological, but also in psychological explanation. Harman (1988: 11) writes:

> Psychological explanation is a kind of functional explanation in the way that some biological explanation is. . . . *Wide* functional explanations . . . typically appeal to an actual or possible environmental situation of the creature whose activity is being explained. . . . *Narrow* functional explanation appeals only to internal states of the individual, and says nothing about how the creature functions in an actual or possible environment. (italics added)

Wide functional analysis thus entails that in psychological explanation there is (usually implicit) reference to the environment, and that it involves teleological considerations about the relation between the organism and its

environment. Harman (1988: 20) thinks that 'only a wide psychological functionalism can motivate appropriate distinctions between aspects of a system,
irrelevant side effects and misfunctions'.

So, functional analysis should be amended to include more emphasis on
the role of the environment. Bechtel (1985) called attention to the similarity
between a relational construal of mind and the concept of function. The relation of a system to its environment is the crux of biological functions; hence
ascribing function to (part of) a system implies its environment. Teleological
functional analysis should according to Bechtel (1986) distinguish three levels: the components, the system, and the environment; whereas Cummins
considers only the first two levels. Applied to psychology, this notion of teleological functional analysis means that one should look beyond the mental
apparatus as such (narrowly construed), to the way it deals with its environment: *wide functionalism*.

Conclusion

Functional analysis, in the fashion of Cummins and others, holds that the
way a system is organized explains some of its activities. These systemic properties can be seen in the components. Furthermore, following Bechtel and
others, the environment is seen as an additional constraint on these system
properties, involving a higher level of analysis; reference to the environment
explains what these properties are really doing, why they are adaptive or not.
It seems that functional explanation concentrating on organism–environment
relations is the basic pattern in biology and to some extent in biologically ori-
ented psychology.

Functional explanation is a form of explanation that exists alongside
nomological (causal) and hermeneutic methods. It can be seen as a separate
level of analysis, tailored to biological and psychological phenomena. In general psychology, many processes are described functionally, in terms of what
they do, like working memory, stages of processing, independently of the
underlying causal physical mechanisms (Cummins, 1983, 1989). Such a stratified approach (several levels of explanation) may bring some clarification to
the confusion of methods in psychology.

1.6   Reduction, supervenience and strata

Reduction

Reduction has a bad reputation in some of the many mansions of psychology.
It is often associated with a 'nothing-but perspective' – man is nothing but a
machine, nothing but a digital computer, a neural network. Especially in the
'soft' parts of psychology such views are immensely resented; it seems that
typically human, warm concerns are replaced by cold mechanisms.

We feel that sometimes reduction is legitimate, as when it eliminates errors
and illusions; for instance, thunder is 'nothing but' an electric discharge, it is
not the wrath of the thunder god riding the sky. Furthermore, some

reductions, especially in psychology, are even positively interesting; knowing the mechanisms of memory, for instance, makes comprehensible why you cannot retain more than seven digits in memory. Finally, knowing the trick does not necessarily eliminate or debase the phenomenon; knowing that life is a matter of duplicating RNA does not make it less interesting than it was under the old explanation in terms of a *vis vitalis* (life force) or *generatio spontanea* (spontaneous generation); rather, it increases our sense of wonder (Dennett, 1991). At the very least, proposals for reduction in the human sciences can serve to sharpen our sense of what exactly is left out in reduction, and in exactly what way human beings are more than science explains.

In a sense, the business of science is reduction; in the philosophy of science, the narrow definition of reduction is traditionally *theory reduction*. On the one hand, some scientists raise(d) the defence that all sciences can ultimately be reduced to one basic science (some future idealized physics), and can be unified in one theoretical structure, so that laws about complex events (say, human behaviour, politics, economics) can be deduced from general theories plus knowledge about initial conditions under which these laws operate.

On the other hand, it can be objected that the variety of knowledge interests, interesting questions, phenomena and styles of explanation is too diverse for a single framework. The most interesting cases of reduction or elimination in psychology are no doubt those where inter-level relations are found, for example neuropsychological explanations for psychological deficits.

The structure of the world

Reduction is sometimes put forward as a claim about the logical structure of the world. An intuitively plausible view of reduction is that it involves a chain of 'whys' and 'becauses'. To borrow Weinberg's (1992) example: Why is chalk white? – because it reflects the whole spectrum, and does not absorb a particular wavelength; this, in turn, is so because light comes in photons, and chalk does not absorb photons; because a photon has a definite energy and the atomic structure of chalk does not have an electron that could absorb a particular photon of any wavelength.

This implies a view on reduction as going through a series of more and more fundamental principles, until the final theory dealing with elementary particles is reached. The idea is that the arrows of reduction all point the same way and converge on a final theory that does not require reduction to other principles. As you may guess, the final theory does not yet exist, though physicists (e.g. Hawking, 1988; Weinberg, 1992) are confident that it may be found one day.

This view of reduction is in fact a claim about the logical way the world is made, and assumes that physics deals with the fundamental laws of nature. The converging arrows of reduction point towards the most basic constituents of the world. Reality consists of elementary constituents, and can be understood as an aggregate of these. The idea goes back at least to Newton, who thought that reality at the most basic level consists of particles in motion (forces), and the ultimate aim of Newtonian physics was to know the position and velocity of all particles. That is really all there is to know. It amounts to a complete knowledge of the universe and allows perfect prediction of everything in it.

This complexity assumption is also the background of the positivist model of science. It is associated with the notion of 'explanation', which in turn, as mentioned in section 1.4, is traditionally understood as deducing a statement describing a state of affairs from a general law. Reduction then amounts to the displacement of a theory or a research programme if it provides a competing and adequate explanation for its phenomena, thereby proving the first programme dispensable. An example might be the sociobiological explanation of altruistic behaviour, which reduces altruism to the influence of selfish genes, and thus aims at displacing moral and psychological explanations.

Logical positivism and theory reduction

A more rigorous, logical conception of theory reduction is a part of the positivist view of theory building in science. In the modern phase of positivism, at the beginning of this century, theories were conceived as axiomatic, logical and unified logical structures. Logical positivism's ideal is *unification* of all sciences in a single theory, under a single methodology, according to the deductive-nomological (D-N) model of explanation, set out earlier in this chapter (section 1.4).

The logical positivists' view of the reduction of a science to basic science is an outgrowth of their view of explanation. It is assumed more or less implicitly that complex entities are composed of elementary more basic entities. Organisms, for instance, are complexes of cells, which are complexes of macro-molecules which are complexes of chemical elements. A lower-level science can explain the phenomena or laws of a higher more complex level: for instance neurosciences might explain behaviour; biochemistry explains genetics. 'Explanation' is working one's way back to the basic elements; and because physics provides the ultimate, most fundamental 'explanations' this view is called *physicalism*.

The model conceives of reduction as a relation between theories in the sense that a more complex theory can logically be derived from a more basic one. Logical positivists envisage reduction as a logical deduction of higher-level laws from lower-level laws plus boundary conditions specifying the qualifications under which the latter operate.

Reducing a theory to another one involves *bridge laws*, establishing equivalences between the two theories, connecting concepts across levels. The standard example of bridge laws is the identification of heat with average kinetic energy in statistical thermodynamics. Thus the equivalence of the sets of laws is more or less a matter of translation.

This equivalence is in itself not yet a complete reduction. In addition to bridge laws, it must be possible to *derive* higher-level laws from lower levels. Assuming, as logical positivism does, that explanation is deducing a statement (the explanandum) from general laws plus statements describing initial conditions, then reduction is a special instance of explanation. It consists in deducing higher-level laws from lower-level laws plus boundary conditions.

The interesting question then becomes: is the higher-level theory dispensable if the same empirical predictions can be derived from the lower-level theory? If we agree that explaining is deriving a statement from a general law, and we can get that from, say, physics, then higher levels like physiology and psychology are bound for oblivion. An obvious problem is whether or not something (or in fact quite a lot) is lost in the process.

Why the D-N view on reduction is untenable

For a number of reasons, the D-N view is untenable. We have already mentioned some problems (see p. 20 ff.). In this discussion on reduction we will point out some other reasons.

First, theory reduction has never been very successful: the reduced theory is almost always corrected, or even entirely eliminated. Bridge laws are about as frequently seen in actual science as the Loch Ness monster. Furthermore, deduction is not the same as explanation. Explanation is asymmetrical, but deduction is not. Take the position of the sun: it can be deduced from the position of a sundial, and vice versa. However, the position of the sun explains the shadow on the sundial, but the sun surely isn't explained by the sundial.

Second, there is what could be called the non-transitivity of explanation (Putnam, 1980). From the fact that the behaviour of a system can be deduced from its description as a system of elementary particles it does not follow that it can be explained from that description. The relevant features may be buried in a mass of irrelevant detail when we go, for instance, from elementary particles to macroscopic objects; explanation is not transitive. In Putnam's example, the fact that a square peg does not fit into a round hole is explained by the rigidity of the material, and the rigidity of the material is explained by its microstructure; however, an interesting explanation of the rigidity of macro-objects is not an explanation of someting which is explained by this rigidity.

The organization of elements determines the higher-level features. Thus the latter are accidental from the point of view of physics. Hence, although the system has a physical basis, it cannot be explained by it. The fact that elements are organized in a particular way suggests a kind of autonomy of higher-level features, like psychology and sociology. The idea of deduction of higher from lower level is a mistake because it ignores the structure of the higher level.

To sum up then, it is by no means clear that the theory reduction model reflects real scientific practice, and we should be wary of philosophers using it to promote or debate metaphysical or a-priori claims about the structure of the world.

Nothing-but: reduction and elimination of everyday concepts

In the chain of 'whys' leading down from everyday phenomena to elementary particle physics, the organization of higher-level phenomena is lost. If that fact is overlooked, it is easy to interpret reduction as 'nothing-buttery': the idea that most of the everyday phenomena we know can be explained away by science. Altruism is 'nothing but' the blind drive of the selfish gene, sociobiologists tell us. Thinking is 'nothing but' symbol manipulation; consciousness is 'nothing but' the working of a neural network. Thus it is suggested that any reduction leads to elimination; in psychology this would mean the displacement of so-called 'folk'-psychological explanation by presumably neurophysiological language, so that we turn out to be causally determined machines, rather than intentional and rational beings.

More precisely, the idea here is that reduction equals *elimination*, that is, entails a correction or displacement of the reduced theory. To use a well-worn example: 'Water is really H_2O' means that only H_2O exists, and the everyday use of the word 'water' refers to an illusion. However, it can also be argued that the possibility of reduction does not affect the legitimacy of everyday reducible concepts, and even that the discovery of a physical correlate legitimizes the everyday concepts. If pain has a distinct neurophysiological correlate, such mental events are real.

The archetype of this problem is Eddington's two tables (Schwartz, 1991); the scientific one of elementary physics, and the everyday one. The apparently solid table is an illusion, from the viewpoint of physics; the real table is, as physics tells us, a void full of electric charges. The scientific table is according to Eddington the only real one, and there is no obvious way to connect the two. It is also arguable that the scientific story underwrites the commonsense story about the table. The solidity of the everyday table can be explained, to some extent perhaps corrected, by the theory of molecular bonds. In this view, we are talking about the same table.

Thus reduction can be conservative with respect to common sense; in psychology, mental concepts can be preserved to some extent (and perhaps to some extent corrected) in a future psycho-neuroscience. We will come back to this in Chapter 4.

Supervenience

Behind the ideal of reduction is the metaphysical conception of physicalism, the claim that basically everything is physical and, ultimately, only physics can describe and explain the nature of the world. It is especially in view of mental phenomena that physicalism and reduction raise doubts. Reductionism mostly boils down to the *identity* theory of matter (brain) and mind, and many philosophers of mind would not accept that one-to-one identity of mental concepts and, say, neural concepts could be found; that, for example, to be in love is *nothing-but* and can be translated without loss of meaning into the activities of specific neurons. They assume that psychology somehow should be independent of the physical sciences. But then they face the other horn of the dilemma, *dualism* of mind and matter, running the risk of leaving mind as a non-natural and rather mysterious entity. This option is out of fashion among philosophers of mind and psychologists. The theory of functionalism, set out a moment ago, seems to be meant to reconcile materialistic monism with an autonomous psychology. It allows a less radical kind of materialism than the reductionism of the identity theory. Functionalism chooses a level of describing mental phenomena as functional states of physical entities, but not necessarily of brains.

The concept of supervenience (literally 'follows') has been proposed in order to understand the close relationship between different domains, say, the mental and the physical. The notion should represent a causal bond that makes room for a kind of non-reductive materialism.

The philosopher Donald Davidson is one of the first who made mention of this supervenience relation in the context of the mind–body problem:

> [M]ental characteristics are in some sense dependent, or supervenient, on physical characteristics. Such supervenience might be taken to mean that there cannot be two events alike in all physical respects but differing in some mental respect, or that an object cannot alter in some mental respect without altering in some physical respect. (Davidson, 1980b: 214)

Supervenience does not entail reducibility because mental phenomena cannot be explained in purely physical concepts, according to Davidson.

The mental–physical is, apparently, not the only supervenience relation. We might say that the liquidity of water depends on and is determined by its molecular structure; that the functions of a table supervene on its physical composition on the one hand and on its spatial construction on the other. So, it seems to be a matter of a hierarchy of domains such that one domain d_1 supervenes on another d_2, if there can be no change in domain d_1 without change in d_2; in other words, if properties of domain d_1 depend on and are determined by d_2 properties. What the supervenience relation rules out is that the relation is reversible: the relation does not hold in the d_2/d_1 direction, it would be implausible that the physical supervenes on the mental; and it rules out that the properties of d_1 are nothing-but the properties of d_2. But this last idea is controversial according to one's reading of 'depend' and 'determine' (Heil, 1992).

Strata

If we follow the non-reductive line we have a conception of the world as being stratified, that is, built in layers or strata forming a non-reductive hierarchy. But other pictures of the world are conceivable, such as physicalism, according to which everything is physical and, in the end, can be explained in pure physical terms. Another view is a world of domains which are completely distinct from each other; phenomena or events in the one domain occur alongside events in the other, as in psychophysical parallelism according to which events in both domains, the physical and the mental, occur independently of each other.

We cannot hope for conclusive evidence in questions about the ontology, the fundamental construction of the world. We meet here a metaphysical stand-off. Nevertheless we opt, with many philosophers nowadays, for a stratified world, at least in our epistemological approach, that is, in our descriptions and explanations. We think there is overwhelming theoretical and practical evidence for believing that every level – chemical, anatomical, physiological, neurophysiological, biological, mental, social – has its own theoretical concepts and theories with their own explanatory power, though the one level does constrain the other. This is termed by Clark (1989) the multiplicity of explanation. Your brain is a necessary condition for your being in love, but does neurological knowledge provide us with a sufficient condition for understanding your being in love? We think that in order to understand this mental and emotional phenomenon we need other levels of explanation.

1.7   Reasons and causes

As we said earlier, human behaviour, in general, can be taken as the subject matter of the social sciences. Some psychologists classify psychology among the social sciences for this reason. Many claim, however, that psychology studies determinants of behaviour, some of which are, but others are not, social. These psychologists prefer to designate psychology as a behavioural science. If we give credit to this idea of determinants we will have to confront the classic problem of 'reasons for' and 'causes of' behaviour. Are these expressions equivalent, or not? We have already referred to the concept of action as a terse and adequate description of human behaviour. In the context of the earlier discussion we suggested that along explanations of human behaviour there is much room for understanding human actions. In this section about reasons and causes we hope to clarify the connected distinctions. By doing this we will have the opportunity to make a case for the conceptions of different epistemological strata and the multiplicity of explanation.

What do we want to hear when asking the question why John slammed the door? Probably not that John put more than average energy into his act, giving the door more speed (which resulted in a heavy collision of the door with the doorpost, a loud noise and the lamp rocking back and forth). We normally are not interested in a report of the chain of causes and effects leading up to the slamming. Neither do we expect to hear a report about microprocesses in John's body causing his movements. The why-question asks for reasons – 'He felt offended', for instance. Even when we think in a materialistic frame of mind that the state of being offended can be traced in John's brain, even then we normally will not be interested in an answer in neurological terms. So, normally, in our day-to-day why-questions about people's actions we expect to hear about their reasons.

But are reasons different from causes? Are actions nothing but movements, and if so, should not science trace the causes that set bodies in motion, by identifying, let us say, motives, attitudes, traits; or even further by showing up these psychological entities as neuro-activities? Are not reasons and actions in fact clumsy or facile expressions of ordinary language? Some radical materialists, who deny such expressions' scientific status, think that reasons are part of *folk psychology*, the commonsense psychology we use every day, which consists of bad theories, a totally obsolete and inadequate account of our internal activities. 'The folk psychology of the Greeks is essentially the folk psychology we use today, and we are negligibly better at explaining human behavior in its terms than was Sophocles' (Churchland, 1989: 8).

When doing science, according to Paul Churchland, we do better to eliminate these concepts just as we got rid of 'phlogiston', the fire principle that in the seventeenth century was thought to depart when a body burned. Scientific psychology has to be a physical, a neuroscientific, enterprise.

A less radical materialist proposition, defended once by Donald Davidson (1968), is to consider reasons as causes. Actions are caused or produced by a set of beliefs plus desires (or 'pro-attitudes'). So, we have a causal relation between two types of material event; mental events which are inner and distinct both in time and in place from outside behavioural, that is, bodily events.

We have already in a preliminary way dealt with some materialist positions concerning the mind–body problem and we will return to this problem, but for the moment we assume that actions are not the same as movements, that reasons cannot be equated with the causes of these movements and that therefore everyday psychology rightly acknowledges the differences.

Consider an illustration, given before, of the fact that one and the same movement can express different actions – by raising one's hand one can greet, urge someone to stop, or simply mimic. Sometimes one acts by not even stirring a finger, when protesting by not shaking hands, for instance, or when offering resistance by not speaking up. Some actions are so comprehensive that it is unclear what movement could be responsible: for instance the act of committing fraud.

We think that actions have another ontological status; that they exist in a different way than as the movements or non-movements by which they are expressed. Actions and movements do not belong to the same category. Actions are more like descriptions and interpretations of these events and movements. They convey meanings, have symbolic import and take their identity and meaning from the context. That is why they have to be 'understood'. The same can be said of reasons. Reasons, framed in intentions, desires, emotions and beliefs, are heavily laden with meanings and interpretations communicated between people. We ask about someone's reasons when we want to assess her conduct. Actions and reasons share the same level of explanation, and the relation between them is normative, not causal. Reasons are appreciated as arguments and are not 'like forces whose intensity can be measured in advance and whose effects can therefore be accurately predicted' (Moya, 1990: 168).

So it does not help to trace reasons in the micro-activities of the actor's brain. And it remains to be seen if throwing away ordinary psychological language will provide a better psychology. Isn't this what at least part of psychology is all about – understanding people's behaviour?

Some philosophers of science maintain that because of this 'change' of cognitive interest – from 'explaining' why the actions *qua* events in space and time had to come about, to 'understanding' actions from reasons and intentions – social sciences are in essence hermeneutic sciences. To 'understand' persons as agents is not to confront them as objects in the same sense as in a non-organic nature, but to meet them 'as "subject-objects" who in relation to us preserve their status of being virtual co-subjects of interaction and communication . . . This virtualization of the dialogical relationship to other persons seems to me to be the very condition of the possibility of hermeneutic sciences' (Apel, 1982: 33).

Is there, then, nothing left to be 'explained' about people's behaviour? Of course there is! There is more to understanding people than is revealed in communication only. If John acts over-sensitively there could be reasons, but also somatic causes. We should expect mixed explanations in such cases. We do not need an a-priori ontological commitment, materialistic monism or psychophysical dualism, and nevertheless acknowledge that we cannot *act* without our brain and body; that our neurophysiological and bodily make-up are among the necessary conditions for thoughts and behaviour. We have to admit that psychology is a science with more than one or two levels of explanation. It consists of different types of question and accordingly different types of answer. There is not necessarily a competition among the answers; they do not have the same explanatory power (Noble, 1990).

Does this mean that the epistemological strata or levels of explanation constitute different domains of psychology and that these levels and domains are autonomous? There is no clear-cut answer to this. In many psychological phenomena, especially the cognitive ones such as perception, learning skills, memory and emotions, the conceptual interdependence of different levels is, we think, pretty obvious and as scientists we should, therefore, make use of different levels and models. To simplify, we could say that many psychological phenomena have a process side and a content side – the 'how' (our physical make-up) and the 'what' (we as persons) of psychological behaviour.

Suggested reading

About explanation in a classical presentation:
    Hempel (1966)
The classic book about the logic of scientific explanation is:
    Nagel (1961)
Classic on methodology in psychology:
    De Groot (1969)
Recent developments in explanation:
    Salmon (1990)
A short, informative introduction to theory construction and theory testing in psychology:
    Hyland (1981)

Some introductory books to the philosophy of (social) science:
Brown (1977)
Greenwood (1991b)
Hughes (1990)
Lessnoff (1974)
Ryan (1970)
Trigg (1985)

A good book about modern hermeneutics:
Bleicher (1980)
A reader with modern texts about hermeneutics:
Hollinger (1985)

About reduction and supervenience (rather technical):
Heil (1992)
Kim (1993)

A recent introduction to actions and reasons along our own lines:
Moya (1990)
A more materialistic handling of this subject matter:
Dretske (1988)
For a classical action theory, also in connection with the explanation – understanding issue:
Von Wright (1963, 1971)
A reader on 'social action':
Seebass and Tuomela (1985)

A reader on the explanation of human behaviour from a social science perspective:
Secord (1982)

2

Philosophy of Science for Psychology

2.1   Introduction: scientific methods and rationality

In the previous chapter, some characteristics and basic concepts of science were sketched out. We now turn to a more principled reflection on the scientific enterprise: philosophy of science. The philosophy of science has for a long time been characterized by the quest for a so-called *demarcation criterion* to distinguish science from pseudo-science, and to be used as a yardstick against which to measure progress. A demarcation criterion is an account of a universal, ahistoric and general method for rationality that can be applied in an algorithmic fashion, leaving nothing to subjective factors like individual taste or judgement, or to social and historical factors. The (logical) positivist movement in the philosophy of science was motivated by the conviction that only a universal, general and ahistoric account of the methods of science can distinguish science from pseudo-science.

Furthermore, a clear account of scientific *method* is required to account for scientific *progress*: what makes chemistry better science than alchemy, Einstein's theory better than Newton's, cognitive psychology better than behaviourism.

The political and ethical import of this idea will be appreciated when one realizes that the famous group of (logical) positivist philosophers, the Wiener Kreis (Vienna Circle), operated in the intellectual and moral corruption of post-First-World-War Vienna. One of its members, Moritz Schlick, was actually murdered by a Nazi. Popper's rejection of totalitarian political thought (Hegel, Marx) is of a piece with his attempt to demarcate science from pseudo-science (Freud).

Recently, the quest for a demarcation criterion has come under fire. Toulmin (1990) explains the restriction of rationality and the obsession with mathematical certainty in the seventeenth century (Descartes and Newton) as a reaction to the failure of Montaigne's open, sceptical and tolerant view in the face of religious conflicts. He interprets the Wiener Kreis as part of this modernist 'quest for certainty', which acknowledges only one type of rationality, and discards the possibility of open dialogue between different points of view within a historical context.

Feyerabend, who was the most vociferous antagonist of methodological standards, seemed motivated by a loathing of pompous, pontificating philosophers, who claim the authority to tell other people what to do, who see themselves as guardians of a supposedly universal rationality, and who stifle spontaneity and common sense.

The foundationalist attempt to find an Archimedean point outside history and society in the pure and undoubtable certainties of universal standards of rational conduct, on which a secure science can be built, is now definitely out of fashion, at least among philosophers. It is nevertheless instructive to follow the undoing of the demarcation criterion – paradoxically, its demise was driven by the attempt of its partisans to work it out in a thoroughgoing and coherent way. Internal criticism from within the neo-positivist community has probably contributed more to its collapse than the outside and somewhat faddish rejections of its point of view. Again, it is important to realize the importance of demarcation; in the traditional view, universal method is the only stronghold against barbarism, the hallmark of rationality, a bulwark against metaphysics and ideological muddles.

In the next sections we will discuss the positivist philosophy of science, and how it came under attack in the 1960s and 1970s. This attack on this so-called standard view of science came from two sides. First, empiricism was challenged from within the Anglo-American tradition itself; and the traditional aversions to empiricism on the other side of the English Channel intensified and broadened. The main actors were Sellars, Quine, Wittgenstein, Hanson (section 2.3); Popper (section 2.4); Kuhn, Lakatos and Feyerabend (section 2.5). In sections 2.6 and 2.8 we will give an overview of some alternatives to positivism. One line of alternatives is relativistic in its orientation (section 2.6). In section 2.7 we will discuss some problems of relativism, as well as realism. The other line of alternatives to positivism has a penchant for a moderate, that is, pragmatically reconstructed realism (section 2.8).

2.2 Logical positivism and demarcation

Logical positivism was the dominant philosophy of science from the 1920s to the 1960s. With the ascent to power of the Nazis, many members of the Wiener Kreis (Carnap, Feigl, Neurath) emigrated from Vienna and Prague to the United States, where the Vienna Circle became a major force in American philosophy. Although probably no one would use the label logical positivist these days, the consensus among practising scientists about the nature of empirical research, data, theories, confirmation and so on still reflects the basic ideas of positivism. The previous chapter illustrates this.

The provenance of logical positivism was reflection on the role of *observation* in science, which had become problematic at the beginning of the century. The classical idea of physics relied on observation as the only legitimate method, and thought that careful experimentation would in the end lay bare the naked facts. This view had never been a very accurate picture of history; Galileo, the celebrated founder of classical mechanics, introduced new concepts that were not directly related to empirical facts, and probably even 'cleaned up' his measurements to fit his theory better. As an ideal, the model was called in doubt by the rise of the theory of relativity and quantum mechanics, in which theoretical considerations rather than experimental results played a leading role. These could not (initially) be verified by direct observation, nor could they be directly compared with the Newtonian theory on empirical grounds. Concepts like space, time and causality, which had seemed evident for all the world to see, also became problematic. This poses a problem: if carefully collecting objective empirical facts is not the (whole) business of science, then what is?

The members of the Wiener Kreis were hard-nosed scientists, mathematicians and logicians. Their philosophy aspired to be as precise and exact as science. In their analysis of the legitimacy of scientific knowledge, they demanded that statements should be empirically verifiable. The meaning of a statement is the way it can be verified; and if and to the extent that a sentence does not specify how it could be proven true or false, it is just nonsense, meaningless. Pure observation statements ('The liquid in the test-tube is coloured red.') and operational definitions ('Intelligence is what an intelligence test measures.') are models of meaningful utterances. Metaphysics, poetry, Heideggerian philosophy, and theology are meaningless – one does not, strictly speaking, know what they are saying.

However, the logical positivists understood that scientific textbooks and papers contain many theoretical terms that are not directly observable, such as 'electron', or 'personality'. It is of course unacceptable to abandon these as 'meaningless'. Their solution to this problem is aptly summarized in the label 'logical positivism': science consists of statements describing positive objective facts, plus logical relations between these statements. These should be knit together in a closed logical system, built from elementary axioms, in such a way that the statements of a theory (a collection of statements describing states of affairs) can be logically derived from the axioms. Axioms are connected with observation statements through so-called correspondence rules. Thus, theoretical terms without direct empirical content are through a deductive network linked to empirical observations. Those statements that cannot in any way be logically connected with observations should be purged from the theory.

Such a system supports a deductive-nomological methodology. Hypotheses (predictions, explanations: see Chapter 1) can be deductively derived from the theory. A statement, for instance, that a particular piece of copper will expand when put on the stove can be derived from the general law that all copper expands when heated. Thus, explanation is subsumption of statements describing events under a general law. Reduction is establishing relations between theories – Mendelian genetics, for instance, can be reduced to molecular genetics: the gene can be identified with the chromosome, and the 'rational reconstruction' (axiomatized theory) of both laws allows derivation of Mendel's laws from biochemical laws. Thus, science is ideally a single unified system, in which the same methods can be applied across the board, and higher-level sciences (biology, psychology, sociology) are just special cases of, and reducible to, basic sciences (physics). Psychology, history, etc, were supposed to use the same physical language, and to be formalized in the same nomological framework as physics. To the extent that they do not fit, they are simply not real sciences.

Whereas the positivist view has yielded interesting and illuminating analyses of the structure of theories and explanations in physics, it has been far less successful in clarifying the nature of research in psychology and the social sciences, which indicates that unification is probably not such a good idea.

This idea of unification also indicates that science is cumulative: research is incorporating ever more facts into an integrated deductive network, comprehending ever more complex higher-level laws.

The logical positivists argued that what really matters in scientific knowledge and rationality is justification, and that this can be expressed in deductive-nomological theories; all other considerations, such as Einstein's, and Galileo's theoretical preferences, and other contingent circumstances at the moment of discovery, can be considered as belonging to the context of discovery, and may be left to psychologists. This distinction between the two contexts, justification and discovery (see also Chapter 1), opened up the possibility of rational reconstruction of scientific practice. It is obvious that not all (good) scientists (not even physicists) spend their time juggling axioms and logical formulae. Nevertheless, philosophers hold up logic as an ideal of scientific rationality

The main, and the most hotly disputed, presuppositions of the positivist philosophy of science, or the 'standard view' of science as it was also called, can be summed up as follows:

- The basic elements of scientific knowledge are sense data and the observation statements reflecting them; the senses give us direct access to the facts of the world.
- Theoretical terms and expressions are only to be admitted in theories if they can be deduced from carefully controlled observations; there is a sharp distinction between theory and observations.
- Science has a deductive-nomological structure (see Chapter 1); the different sciences use the same method and can, therefore, be unified. Unification in practice means the annexation of other sciences by physics.
- In the assessment of scientific products, like hypotheses and theories, it is only the 'context of justification' that counts, that is, strictly logical, methodological and sound epistemological criteria. This evaluation has nothing to do with the 'context of discovery', the historical, social or psychological process and circumstances by which these products are discovered and created.

- Science is cumulative; scientific progress is reflected in technical achievements that benefit society.
- The task of philosophy of science is to explain how and why science is succesful, and to discover, protect and promote the permanent criteria and standards for sound scientific method.

2.3   Problems with the standard view of science

In this section we will set out epistemological arguments put forward by Anglo-American philosophers to challenge positivist empiricism. These arguments affected the basics of the image of science created, from 1930 till 1960, by positivist or logical-positivist (sometimes called 'neo-positivist') philosophers of science. The resulting revolution in the philosophy of science was of importance to psychology because it made it possible for cognitive psychology to replace behaviourism as the leading theory (see Chapter 4).

Sellars on the 'Myth of the Given'

The 'Myth of the Given' is perhaps the central pillar of Western epistemology, which held up from the seventeenth century until the demise of logical positivism in the 1960s. The myth has been the target of devastating attacks on the foundations of psychology and traditional epistemology by Richard Rorty, Daniel Dennett, Paul Churchland and Paul Feyerabend.

In Wilfrid Sellars' (1963) diagnosis the myth holds that (at least some of) our mental states are 'given', that is, we can be directly aware of them. Unlike external perception of the external world, direct awareness of our mind cannot be wrong, and does not need cognitive elaboration. The internal eye is infallible and incorrigible: someone can be absolutely sure that he remembers standing on the Eiffel Tower – his recollection may be wrong and he may never have been in Paris, but his feeling of remembrance, the mental state, is indisputable. Further, this direct access is also privileged and incorrigible: no one else can tell whether a person indeed has a specific mental state. Finally, direct access implies that mental states are self-evident, self-transparent, self-disclosing and provide their own cognitive legitimation.

With only slight exaggeration, it can be said that the Myth of the Given – that (some) mental states are directly known, essentially private, self-presenting, self-justifying and incorrigible – was generally accepted by philosophers for centuries. Somewhat surprisingly, it has never been quite clear what these given, self-evident mental states and processes were. Rationalists like Descartes thought they involved innate ideas, abstract non-empirical knowledge, like mathematical evidence and the certainty of the *cogito* (I am thinking). Empiricists on the other hand had in mind sensory states, like pain, colour or sensations.

Richard Rorty, endorsing Sellars' criticism, summarizes the Cartesian view as follows: 'the notion of a single inner space in which bodily and perceptual sensations . . ., mathematical truths, moral rules, the idea of God, moods of depression, and all the rest of what we now call "mental" were objects of quasi-observation' (Rorty, 1979: 50). These mental objects are directly present to consciousness ('given') as the states they are, since mind knows itself best. These mental objects provide absolute certainty, and thus can serve as the foundation of knowledge. As this phrasing suggests, psychological and epistemological issues are lumped together by the myth.

Looking first at psychology, *introspection*, the observation of the events in one's own mental realm, was the method of investigation during most of psychology's history. Unfortunately, different schools saw different scenes in the mental theatre, and as a method of psychology introspection has long been defunct. There are serious doubts that reports by experimental subjects on the way they have found the solution to problems are reliable, let alone that they have direct and infallible access to the workings of their own mind. This indicates that there is something wrong with the Myth of the Given.

One introspective psychologist, E.B. Titchener (1867–1927) coined the notion of 'stimulus error' for experimental subjects who described the object they saw, rather than the internal processes they were supposed to observe. It will be clear that such a methodology assumes the existence of an internal mental world that can be observed in a more direct and certain way than the external world. In fact, the external world is in this view only accessible as indirect reconstruction from the directly perceived (given) sensory data in the mind.

This brings us to the second area where the myth has reigned supreme until recently, *epistemology*. Traditional epistemology was built upon the idea of directly given sensory (or, sense) data (e.g. Russell, 1988), also known as knowledge by acquaintance, from which knowledge of the external world must be inferred. The mind is a repository of representations, somehow mirroring the world. This suggests that beliefs are 'given' to us by experience. The foundation of knowledge is in this view the given, what is before the inner eye. In the rationalist tradition, exemplified by Descartes, mathematical insight, the experience of evidence, is the foundation of true knowledge. For the empiricists, like Locke, sensations, the primary qualities of the senses, are true evidence.

While Ryle (1949) made a devastating attack on the psychological offshoot of the myth, ridiculing the view of mind as an inner theatre observed by an inner eye, Sellars axed its epistemological branch. Sellars (1963) contrasts the 'Myth of the Given' with a story invented by himself, the 'Myth of Jones'.

Let us assume that our ancestors were practising behaviourists, and that one of them, a certain Jones, hit upon the idea that all behaviour is directed by language – through verbal instructions, sometimes through inaudible inner speech. Jones now develops the habit of explaining the behaviour of his fellow men as a result of internal statements, that is, he predicts their behaviour as guided by their 'thoughts'. This strategy works, even if these people would not admit to finding such internal statements in their minds. Next, Jones goes a step further: he finds that the strategy can be applied to himself. He starts to think of his own behaviour in terms of his thoughts. The first-person use ('I think') is predictively even more accurate than the third person ('he thinks'): Jones is obviously an authority on his own thoughts. Jones' method becomes common usage, till this very day.

Thus, mythological Jones has invented both third-person and first-person mental language. The moral of the story about Jones, as Sellars would like us to interpret it, is that reports of the presumed 'given' are not directly perceived, but are basically 'theory laden': like any empirical claim about the external world, they are of a theoretical nature, and hence fallible, and empirically falsifiable. The story suggests that thinking is a kind of language, and that although first-person mental discourse may be to some degree more reliable than third-person discourse, it is not fundamentally private or infallible.

The radically new epistemological consequence then of the 'Myth of Jones' is that knowledge becomes irredeemably linguistic – suspended as it were in discourse, and that it loses its moorings to an intrinsic indubitable given. Attempts to ground knowledge in secure facts in mental space has become impossible. Knowing something is defending it in the face of one's linguistic peers, rather than having mental data, or, as Rorty puts it: 'think of knowledge as a matter of being disposed to utter true sentences about something, rather than in terms of the metaphor of acquaintance' (Rorty, 1982: 331). Vindication of knowledge claims must come from prediction and control, not from some sort of intrinsic mental evidence.

In the philosophy of mind, Sellars' 'Myth of Jones' lives on in Paul Churchland's ideas on the elimination of folk psychology and the reduction of the so-called *qualia* (qualitative subjective experiences, like seeing red, or tasting wine) to neural processes (see Chapter 4, p. 137). Like Sellars, Churchland argues that mental processes, such as understanding music or tasting wine, are theory laden, depend on our conceptual apparatus, and are not pure mental data.

Quine on two dogmas of empiricism

Willard Van Orman Quine made an important contribution to the dismantling of *foundationalism*, the idea that philosophy of science has to offer permanent standards for the justification of scientific theories, an ultimate foundation of knowledge, in order to answer the questions – What is good science and what are good theories?

In his widely influential article 'Two dogmas of empiricism' (1961) he attacked two presuppositions of empiricism. One is the belief in some fundamental dichotomy between true statements which are *analytic*, that is, explaining the meaning of their terms (A circle is round); and truths which are *synthetic*, that is, informing about the world (This book has four chapters). The other assumption is the belief that each meaningful statement is in itself a report of immediate experience of the world.

It was Kant who distinguished between synthetic and analytic truths. Whereas analytic statements are merely about language and do not augment our knowledge about the world, synthetic statements do augment our knowledge, do tell us something about the world. Such statements are contingent because the answer to the question of whether they are true or not depends on the state of affairs in the world. Kant called this dependency on experience of the world a posteriori; we have to check empirically whether, for instance, this book has four chapters.

Incidentally, Kant thought that there was also a third category of statements, synthetic statements a priori, which he thought necessarily true, but independent of experience, because they tell us something about a super-empirical reality. The concept of causality, for instance, is not seen in but imposed upon experience.

This latter kind of statement, however, is usually dismissed by the empiricist philosophers. They accept only the first two kinds of statement, synthetic a-posteriori statements about matters of fact, and analytic statements. Following Hume, they believe not only that these two classes, the analytic and the synthetic statements, exhaust the domain of meaningful language, but also that there is a sharp distinction between them.

Now, Quine attacked the dogma of this dichotomy by showing that the distinctive criteria of analytic statements are not clear at all. There are no objections to formal logical statements like 'No unmarried man is married'. The terms can be exchanged without loss of meaning. But what to think of 'No bachelor is married'? Here we have to resort to the concept of meaning. 'Bachelor' and 'unmarried man' have the same *reference*, but do they share the same *meaning*? We have to distinguish what a term refers to and what it means. 'The successor to Kennedy' and 'The 36th president of the US' cannot always be substituted for each other; they refer to the same person, but their meaning is not the same.

So, what is or is not the 'meaning' of a term is not at all absolutely clear, or given. Neither is 'synonym', nor '(true by) definition', because who defined 'bachelor', and when? asks Quine. The meaning or definition of a term is not pre-existing and pre-given, but is grounded in usage and dependent on contexts, according to Quine.

Upon second thoughts then, there is no sharp dichotomy between the synthetic statements, grounded in fact, and these so-called analytic statements, which are supposed to be true by definition, come what may. There are no statements totally based on sense-experience. Nor are there pure analytic and a-priori statements without experiential content at all. The distinction between statements about the world and statements only about language is illusory.

The attack on the other dogma of empiricism follows naturally from this – the belief that it is possible to test a statement in isolation from other statements or context. The positivists thought that every meaningful statement is held to be translatable into a statement about immediate experience; that is, translatable into language about given sense-data; that a single statement maps on to a single state of affairs in the world; and that its meaning can be empirically confirmed.

According to Quine, however, it is misleading to speak of the empirical content of an individual statement. It is a mistake to think that it is possible to compare *single* statements with the world. We confront the world with *whole theories*, of which statements are components. Our statements about the external world 'face the tribunal of sense experience not individually but only as a corporate body' (Quine, 1961: 41). A similar thesis had already been defended by the French philosopher Pierre Duhem in 1906; for this reason it is called the Duhem–Quine thesis. Any statement can be *held* true, 'if we make drastic enough adjustments elsewhere in the system'. And even a 'recalcitrant experience', an observation clashing with the theory, can be accommodated by 'any of various reëvaluations in various alternative quarters of the total system' (Quine, 1961: 44). So there is no neutral, or independent, foundation of given immediate experiences upon which we could build our scientific statements.

We could sum up this thesis – sometimes called *epistemological holism* – in two points: (1) no knowledge is a priori and immune to empirical refutation; and no knowledge is completely theory-independent; (2) in cases of conflict between theory and observations we cannot summon certain statements in isolation; the whole system of beliefs, or large parts thereof, must stand to trial.

What we learn from this is that observations do not have direct access to the world but are interpreted against the background of a whole theory. There is no sharp distinction between observations and theory, because observations reveal their meaning only against the background of the theory. The totality of our knowledge 'is a man-made fabric which impinges on experience only along the edges' (Quine, 1961: 42). Quine considered this epistemological holism (not to be confused with a kind of New Age holism) a form of pragmatism:

> Each man is given a scientific heritage plus a continuing barrage of sensory stimulation; and the considerations which guide him in warping his scientific heritage to fit his continuing sensory promptings are, where rational, pragmatic. (ibid.: 46)

It is this non-given, non-neutral and theory-laden character of observations that became a recurrent theme in the new philosophy of science.

Wittgenstein on language and meaning

Many of Ludwig Wittgenstein's ideas have direct importance for the philosophy of mind (see Chapter 4) and language, and by consequence for the philosophy of science, in which theories of perception, language and knowledge acquisition are pivotal. The first phase of his philosophical work was, along logical positivist lines, about the ties between language and world. He thought that elementary states of affairs in the world are, somehow, *pictured* in language. The 'logical form', or the structure of states of affairs in the world, is mirrored in the logical structure, the logico-syntactic calculus, of language. Elements of propositions, and the logical relations between them, resemble the elements and their relations in states of affairs in the way that the structure of a musical score, or a map, resembles the structure of the piece of music, or the landscape, respectively. In the early 1920s he had put down this so-called *picture theory* of the proposition in his famous *Tractatus Logico-philosophicus* (1961) which had an enormous impact upon the logical positivist movement.

Later, in the mid-1930s he began to criticize the positivist theory of language, including his own. He opens his *Philosophical Investigations* (1953) with an attack on the idea that the meaning of a word is what it stands for; and that we explain the meaning of a word by ostentive definition, explaining, for instance, 'red' by pointing to red objects. The assumption of this *reference theory of meaning* is that there is a timeless and context-free link between language and reality, propositions and facts. He criticized the assumption that propositions, or statements, are to be considered on their own; that they are independent of each other; and that their truth-value and meaning can be tested in isolation. On the contrary, they belong to whole systems of propositions (cf. Quine's holism).

When he wrestled with these ideas he became interested in the analogy of games. Language is like chess and words are like the chess pieces. A chess piece has significance only in the context of the game and its moves. Likewise, a word gets its meaning in the context of the *language game* in which it is used. Both games should be played in conformity with rules. Rules are not found but are the result of the ongoing creativity of language users.

A language game is an activity and the meaning of an element of the game is displayed in the activity. The 'term "Language-game" is meant to bring into prominence the fact that the *speaking* of language is part of an activity, or of a form of life' (Wittgenstein, 1953: para. 23).

This idea constitutes Wittgenstein's theory of meaning: *meaning is use.* Whether the shopkeeper understands my slip marked 'Five red apples' will be made clear by her subsequent actions. Words and sentences get their meaning in a context. Sentences are used as tools to assert, to command, to question, etc. To understand a meaning requires mastery of the practice, the *form of life*. The meanings of words are rooted in a public language; for this reason Wittgenstein dismissed the existence of a private language. The meanings are part of language games which dictate how we see things. The games themselves cannot be true or false; they rest on no foundation of facts, but rather are constitutive of facts. Facts are convictions, the way we see things; they form part of whole language games.

The consequences of this theory for the conception of knowledge and science are dramatic, because it invites us to replace the quest for timeless foundations by the idea of the social character of knowledge; to see science as a social institution, as practices, which may be different in different times and places. It is hardly surprising that some philosophers developed a relativistic viewpoint out of this.

Hanson on the theory-ladenness of observation

Imagine Johannes Kepler on a hill watching the dawn. With him is Tycho Brahe. Kepler regarded the sun as fixed: it was the earth that moved. But Tycho followed Ptolemy and Aristotle in this much at least: the earth was fixed and all other celestial bodies moved around it. *Do Kepler and Tycho see the same thing in the east at dawn?* (Hanson, 1958: 5)

This is the question with which Norwood Russel Hanson begins his *Patterns of Discovery*, his study of observation, theories and what he calls 'the conceptual foundations' of science. Answering that the two astronomers see the same thing just because their eyes are similarly affected would be a fundamental mistake. According to Hanson, there is a difference between a *physical state* and a *visual experience*. To say, as the empiricist would do, that they *see* the same thing because they get the same sensations or sense-data, and that after this experience they *interpret* what they see in different ways, would be a mistake as well. 'One does not first soak up an optical pattern and then clamp an interpretation on it' (ibid.: 9). On the contrary, the 'what' of the seen object is in the visual experience from the outset. There is more to seeing than meets the eye. That Tycho and Kepler *see different things*, though perhaps their eyes receive the same sensations, depends on their knowledge and theories. Seeing is *theory laden*. To observe a watch is to *know* the concept of a watch. The observation is shaped by that prior knowledge and takes with it a background of knowledge; it appears in a context of background information. I could answer questions about what I see and I could tell, for instance, that the little hand indicates the hours and the big hand the minutes, that the figures stand for hours, etc. The eye and knowing fit together. Without this knowledge, nothing seen would make sense.

Because observation is theory laden, science is 'not just a systematic exposure to the world; it is also a way of thinking about the world, a way of forming conceptions' (ibid.: 30). With a wealth of historical illustrations from the work of physicists, such as Kepler, Galileo, Newton, Descartes, Helmholtz and Maxwell, and influenced by the Gestalt psychologists and by Wittgenstein, Hanson criticized the hypothetico-deductive philosophy of science. This system does not tell us how laws are decided on in the first place. When paying attention to what scientists *do*, you have to acknowledge that they do not start from laws, nor from hypotheses: they start from data. However, data appear intelligible only within theories. Theories 'constitute a "conceptual Gestalt". A theory is not pieced together from observed phenomena; it is rather what makes it possible to observe phenomena as being of a certain sort, and as related to other phenomena. Theories put phenomena into systems.' (ibid.: 90).

2.4   Demarcation – Popper

As mentioned, the original impulse of positivism was to distinguish between science and pseudo-science. The main tenets of positivist philosophy were: (1) the verifiability theory of meaning; (2) the notion of confirmations of theories; (3) a strict distinction between fact and theory; and (4) the view of theories as logical edifices, from which predictions can be logically deduced. In the previous section, we discussed some of the deeper reasons why the positivist view of science, language and reality behind these assumptions is untenable. Next, we will consider how later thinkers tried to prevent the disaster that seemed to follow from this failure: the fact that it seems impossible to delineate a criterion for distinguishing good science from pseudo-science.

Karl Popper tried to salvage the ideal of a demarcation criterion while abandoning the criteria of verifiability and confirmation. Recall that the Wiener Kreis thought that only statements that specify how they can be verified are meaningful – it is clear how to find out whether 'Water boils at 100° C' is correct. Unverifiable statements are literally non-sense; it is not clear what the factual content of 'God is love' is, and thus it makes no sense – it cannot even be called false. Essential for the positivist project was the design of a new unambiguous language in which facts can be stated in a purely observational fashion. Ordinary language is too messy, imprecise and ambiguous to denote observations. The positivists conceived the world as a collection of facts (states of affairs), and hence the scientific language as a collection of *Protokollsätze*, basic statements expressing a state of affairs (meter readings, colour of a chemical solution, etc.). *Verification*, then, is comparing statements derived from a theory with observation statements. Thus, verifiability was proposed by the Wiener Kreis as the demarcation criterion, distinguishing legitimate knowledge claims from nonsense, metaphysics and other claptrap.

Verification and confirmation

However, the positivist programme soon ran into considerable trouble. The idea of comparing language with a pre-linguistic world in itself proved incoherent, and the strict theory–observation dichotomy had to be abandoned. Furthermore, verification of general statements (laws, theories) is strictly speaking impossible. A simple hypothesis like: 'All swans are white' may have been corroborated a zillion times by observing white swans, but the logical possibility remains that the zillion-first swan will turn out to be turquoise: this is the notorious problem of induction (see Chapter 1). General laws are about an, in principle, infinite domain, and can never be conclusively verified.

Rudolf Carnap (1891–1970), a member of the Wiener Kreis, introduced the concept of confirmation. It was intended as a more practical and less rigid alternative to verification. Rather than demanding that the truth of a statement can be assessed, Carnap suggested that some degree of confirmation must be possible for a statement to be meaningful. Confirmation is a matter of probability, varying from 0 ('unconfirmed') to 1 ('verified'), and depends *prima facie* on the number of observations that support a statement; usually, scientific knowledge claims will be less than perfectly verified and remain hypothetical. Since general laws can be more or less confirmed, even when not completely verified, that problem was supposed to be solved. Carnap formulated a logic of induction, providing the rules for generalizing from observations to general statements, in more or less the same way that in formal logic the algorithms for deduction are specified. Such a procedure could provide a measure of the degree of confirmation of a theory. However, the logical apparatus never worked. Popper's work suggests some reasons why not.

Popper (1974, 1979) radically rejected the ideas of verification, confirmation and induction as foundations of the legitimacy of scientific knowledge claims. He replaced the notion of confirmation (verification) by *falsification*. While abandoning the 'rock bottom' of knowledge in observation statements, he remained within the tradition in the philosophy of science that tries to create a foolproof demarcation criterion distinguishing science from metaphysics. Keywords of his philosophy are: falsification, criticism, anti-dogmatism.

Popper on confirmation and falsification

Popper argued that, strictly speaking, only falsification is possible, not verification. A lot of accumulated evidence is no guarantee for the truth of a hypothesis: as soon as the first turquoise swan has been spotted, the much-confirmed statement that all swans are white is falsified and must be rejected. Popper shows this by making a simple logical point. He argues that induction cannot be made certain in the way deduction is. Confirmation cannot be measured, since one never knows how many disconfirming instances may be around. However, what is logically certain is falsification: if a theory predicts an effect, and it doesn't turn out, then the theory should be rejected. This idea of falsification becomes the linchpin of Popper's system: don't try to confirm your theories, try to refute them.

The logical form is the *modus tollens*: If *T*, then *P*; not *P*; therefore, not *T*; or in common language, whenever from a theory *T* a prediction *P* can be deduced that turns out to be false in experiment or observation, the theory is rejected. Science should not try to prove theories, but to disprove them. A good theory specifies in advance what observations would make it untrue.

A theory is only interesting to the extent that it (*ex hypothesi*) rules out certain phenomena, and it is more interesting the more it rules out – that is, the more improbable it is. In fact, confirmed and probable hypotheses are the least interesting. It is easy to formulate probable (often confirmed) generalizations, but such a strategy would favour uninformative truisms. The prediction that the temperature will be above zero in August in Amsterdam is highly probable, but hardly informative. Scientific progress can be made only by advancing bold, improbable conjectures, and then ruthlessly trying to falsify them. This should involve as many new predictions, pose new problems, and suggest new experiments and observations as possible; it should not only generalize over already known facts. Popper defines the empirical content of theories as the number of possible falsifications: the more general and precise it is, the more phenomena it forbids. Among competing theories, we should accept the one with the largest empirical content, which has so far survived all tests.

Inventing hypotheses is completely unconstrained, in Popper's view: unlike the Wiener Kreis, he does not think that theory building needs to be regimented by empirical support or logic. The bolder the hypothesis, the better, provided that it is subsequently rigorously tested and mercilessly rejected if found wanting. Hence, bold conjectures and refutations are the staple trade of science. Unlike the logical positivists, Popper sees no conclusively established facts. Knowledge is provisional, always revisable, 'piles driven into a swamp', and there are no absolutely secure foundations.

Theories that have stood the test are only corroborated, never verified or confirmed: they may be proven wrong any time. Although it seems hard to imagine that long-established theories in physics could be proven wrong, that was more or less what happened with the replacement of Newtonian physics by quantum theory. And this indicates that in principle no theory can be immune to refutation. One could consider the process of conjectures and refutations, and provisional corroboration of theories as something like natural selection: unfit theories perish, and the best, most adapted theories survive – for the time being. In this sense there is real progress and growth of knowledge. However, Popper abandons the conception of cumulative growth founded on observation. There is no hoard of objective facts, as the logical positivists thought, but all knowledge is theory laden, and the nature of accepted data may be entirely reinterpreted when theories are refuted. Newton's physics was experimentally corroborated many times, but had to be completely revised after Einstein.

Popper on demarcation and dogmatism

The aim of logical positivism was to provide a secure foundation for science in empirical facts. Popper abandons the quest for certainty, but sticks to the ideal of demarcating science from metaphysics. Having rejected induction, verification and confirmation as yardstick, he defends falsifiability as the hallmark of rationality. Rather than looking for secure foundations on which to build a theory, he accepts the uncertainty and provisional nature of theories, and considers a critical attitude to any knowledge claim as the demarcation between science and pseudo-science. Irrationality should be exorcized by the scientist being ruthlessly critical of any claim to knowledge rather than accumulating bits and pieces of confirmed facts. Popper is a radical anti-dogmatist: discussions should be absolutely free, any hypothesis is in principle legitimate, as long as it is rationally refutable. Refutability (falsifiability) then is the mark of rationality.

Popper sees an absolute difference between critical and dogmatic thinking. Theories that are advertised as certain and immune to criticism are pseudo-science. Examples are Marx and Freud and other builders of closed dogmatic philosophical systems, which can explain anything under the sun, and its negation, for that matter. Such systems cannot be criticized, let alone refuted; they require some dogmatic belief from their followers and are thereby the opposite of scientific rationality. Their aim is not to increase knowledge, but to prove that the believers are right. Especially pernicious is such dogmatism in political philosophy: Popper's targets are systems like Hegel's and Marx's, which he calls 'historicism' (Popper, 1961, 1966), and which pretend to know and understand the Immutable Laws of history, and therefore tend to totalitarianism. A critical, anti-dogmatic attitude is as indispensable for democracy as it is for science.

Problems with falsification

Popper considers repairing a falsified theory by way of *ad hoc* hypotheses dogmatism: the principle of criticism demands that whenever facts turn up that do not fit its prediction, the whole theory is ruthlessly rejected, and a new set of conjectures is drafted, or a competing theory is selected for further testing. Unfortunately, this is not the way researchers work: it was quickly noted that working scientists often consider their favourite hypothesis too good a story to be spoiled by the facts. When a prediction fails, they come up with *ad hoc* hypotheses (faulty apparatus, artefacts, etc.) to explain the deviant results, rather than rejecting the theory. Furthermore, there are not always competitors to choose from. Whereas the philosopher Popper considers dogmatism a sin against the Holy Ghost of science, and a critical attitude as the hallmark of rationality, in reality scientists can be stubborn and dogmatic in upholding a hypothesis against the evidence – and often with success. Sticking to one's prejudices and looking for reasons why reality fails to behave as it should can be a fruitful strategy that brings new discoveries. Since a philosophy of science that prescribes a method inconsistent with real, successful scientific practice must be wrong somewhere, we must conclude that falsification in the strict sense can be no demarcation criterion.

In the 1960s the full consequences of Hanson's and Quine's notion of theory-ladenness began to sink in, namely, that in a sense theories produce their own facts. This implies that theories cannot be matched against theory-independent facts, as required by a strict application of the verification or falsification criterion. Hence facts cannot be used to choose between better and less adequate theories. The full relativistic implications of this view have been elaborated by Kuhn and Feyerabend. Incidentally, Quine (1992) himself is no all-out relativist: he maintained that there is a continuum from almost pure theory (logic and mathematics) to reasonably theory-independent observation. Popper also recognizes that observation statements are never certain, and depend on a (revisable) consensus among researchers on what count as basic facts in their field.

2.5 Demarcation abandoned – Kuhn, Lakatos, Feyerabend

In criticizing empiricism and positivism, post-positivist Anglo-American philosophers effectively moved the centre of gravity from the observed object to the knowing subject. The knowing subject is not the passive observer the empiricists thought he or she was. On the contrary, the things we see and come to know are incorporated in a theory, or even more, they are part of a worldview or of a long-established life-world with roots in history and culture. And this worldview we inherit, build and share intersubjectively. The new philosophers of science, the 'second generation' (Callebaut, 1993), became more interested in the ways by which scientists reached their theories and hypotheses than in the logical structure of theories. They began to highlight context and history, the *context of discovery*, whereas the positivists favoured the *context of justification*, the assessment of the scientific products, and focused on (rationally reconstructed) theories. This introduced an element of subjectivity and interest-relativity that the logical positivists had tried to eliminate, and thus opened the door to relativism.

Kuhn on paradigms and scientific revolutions

Thomas Kuhn introduced the notion of *paradigm*, which has become a label for the dogmatic, self-perpetuating and collectivist aspects of science. A paradigm is (among a lot of other things: see Masterman, 1970) a framework that determines which data are legitimate, what methods may be used, what vocabulary is to be used in stating the results, and what kinds of interpretation are allowed. Furthermore, a paradigm also comprehends the social organization of research, including the perceptual training, the socializing of apprentices in the laboratory and the scientific community at large. Students and junior researchers are trained to adopt the frame of reference, the vocabulary and the methods and techniques of the existing community. In complete contrast with Popper's ideal of open and critical discussion, research communities can be as authoritarian and dogmatic as the Catholic Church or the Mafia. If a junior researcher cannot reproduce the canonical results of the paradigm, he will be out of a job, rather than having falsified the paradigm.

In contrast with the theory-centred view of the logical positivists, Kuhn considers a theory as part of a whole structure of methods, frameworks, concepts, professional habits and obligations, and laboratory practices. This structure determines the general approach to research, it defines what counts as legitimate observations, and without it no research problems would exist. Thus, a paradigm comprises, first, a school, a community of researchers; secondly, all the methods, mathematical techniques, laboratory equipment, etc.; and thirdly, the conceptual frame of reference. It includes practical skills as well as theoretical knowledge; recognizing 'exemplars', paradigm cases, requires training in special ways of looking and in the use of concepts and apparatus. (In section 2.8, the role of skills and practices in research will be discussed, in contrast with the traditional purely theory-centred view.)

Paradigms are *incommensurable*, that is, no rational comparison is possible between competing paradigms. This has the very serious consequence that there is no way to measure progress and rationality in the history of science; or better, that philosophers have been unable to find a hard and fast criterion for rationality. Another important relativist implication is that a paradigm cannot (rationally) be rejected in the way Popper advocated. Facts exist only in the context of a paradigm, therefore selection between and rejection of theories by assessment of their empirical adequacy, according to unambiguous criteria for empirical progress, is impossible.

Kuhn starts his book with a plea for a role for *history,* and he aims to provide a general sketch for the development of science. He emphasizes that the cumulative-progress idea the positivists propagated is not realistic, and that their rational reconstruction does not describe the way science really works. He suggests that the distinction between context of justification and context of discovery does not provide a demarcation criterion; nor are fact and theory separable in the way the positivists thought. So the positivist way of keeping history out of rational science has failed.

The general pattern of historical development Kuhn proposes is as follows. It starts with pre-paradigmatic science, followed by *normal science* after the establishment of a paradigm; then the emergence of anomalous results causes a crisis, triggering a *revolution* after which a new paradigm is established; after a period of normal science the next crisis starts, and so on.

Kuhn's probably most shocking and controversial claim is that paradigm shifts really have the character of revolutions. Rather than through reasonable debate according to rational procedures, paradigms are abandoned as a result of some irrational kind of mob psychology. After a paradigm has run into anomalies (results that it cannot easily explain, or explain away), tensions start to accumulate, which lead, suddenly and inexplicably, into a wholesale rejection of the old paradigm, and the establishment of a new one. Note that there is no conclusive or rational reason for revolution, or for the point where anomalies must lead to crisis: it involves a radical change in viewpoint, where existing results are reinterpreted beyond recognition. Within a paradigm one may decide that anomalies should be put aside for later generations and can be ignored for the time being.

Such dogmatism would be anathema to Popper, who demands outright rejection of a refuted theory. Kuhn however doubts whether falsifying instances in the strict Popperian sense exist at all. Anomalies are not even facts of science, since facts appear only within a paradigm. Therefore, the data cannot be used as a neutral base for judging the merits of the old paradigm and its competitor. Kuhn compares paradigm shifts to Gestalt switches: you cannot simultaneously see both interpretations of an ambiguous figure (like the famous duck-rabbit), but you have to choose one of them more or less voluntarily, and neither view is inherently better or more correct than the other.

Analogously, 'facts' are products of a specific paradigm, and they cannot be used as an observational basis to decide which paradigm is empirically better or more progressive: paradigms are incommensurable. The first effect of a crisis is usually loosening of the rules, so that new phenomena are now recognized as legitimate observations. Paradigm shifts are a matter of persuasion and depend on essentially circular reasoning (the promise to explain the facts better, but these facts are of its own making). Embarking on a new paradigm is a kind of conversion that can, strictly speaking, only be done on *faith*. Note also that a paradigm cannot be abandoned without a new one being chosen: research would simply stop without one.

Revolutions contrast sharply with periods of *normal science*. Here, the framework cannot be criticized. Doing research is essentially puzzle solving, filling in the gaps in a generally accepted framework by applying the generally accepted methods and interpretations. In normal science, work consists of redetermining the previously known; measuring with more precision what was already accepted, establishing more facts that were anticipated by the paradigm, and articulating the theory by finding quantitative laws, seeking new areas of application, etc. Briefly, research is working out the paradigm under the assumption that there is a well-defined solution to the remaining uncertainties which can be found by the usual methods. Only when the puzzles do not come out may a vague desire for new rules, for retooling the approach, raise its head. Therefore, revolutions are necessary for really new discoveries. Feyerabend has capitalized on this intuition with his idea of counterinduction.

It is important to realize that a paradigm is more than a theory. It requires a set of commitments, not only to concepts and theories, but also to instruments and methods, and to metaphysical or foundational assumptions (like materialism, or corpuscularism). Thus, social and pragmatic factors are part and parcel of scientific research. Kuhn emphasizes that the shared commitments in a paradigm are more fundamental than explicit methodical rules and concepts. Learning to be a researcher involves developing the skills and know-how to handle the exemplars (the canonical examples of a paradigm) to interpret results, more than knowing explicit theories. A paradigm may be more specific than explicit methodological rules. The latter may be shared by a number of research communities, who nevertheless have different work styles, other problems and exemplars of typical results and approaches. Research is not a matter of explicit knowledge of abstract rules, and is never learned that way by the junior researcher; it is a matter of doing successful work.

Kuhn compares a paradigm to a worldview; a change of concepts and procedures can transform objects into something else: the data themselves change. Obviously, here the notion of theory-ladenness is taken to its limits. A historical example of such a deep and radical vision is the refusal of Galileo's opponents to verify his claims by looking through his telescope: they simply did not accept it as providing legitimate data about the stars (Feyerabend, 1975: Ch. 10). In their opinion, following Aristotle, the laws governing celestial bodies were essentially different from those on earth. Galileo's innovation was not the telescope (it had been used before for navigation) but the new way of looking and creating data. So there was indeed no compelling rational argument why they should accept his data.

In section 2.7 we will return to the problem of incommensurability, and the relativist conclusions that seem to follow from it.

Lakatos on rational reconstruction

Imre Lakatos (1970) has attempted to combine Kuhn's analysis of paradigms with the possibility of a rational reconstruction of scientific progress, effectively keeping relativism at bay. While acknowledging the dominant role of dogmatism and puzzle solving within scientific research, he tries to stave off relativism by allowing for progress and rationality in terms of competition between *research programmes*. Lakatos defined a research programme as a complex of theories which succeed each other in time. It consists of a set of hard-core hypotheses which are essential and not open to criticism, and a protective belt of auxiliary hypotheses that can be modified to explain deviant results. The hard core defines the negative heuristic: refutation is not allowed here, as long as the programme anticipates novel facts. The test for superiority of one programme over another is whether the empirical content increases. A programme that has to invent an ever increasing set of *ad hoc* hypotheses to counter anomalies in order to protect its hard core counts as degenerating. But when such hypotheses work, open new areas, and trigger new research it is considered progressive. For example, in the history of astronomy, a mathematical theory (a rather cranky one, in modern eyes) led Kepler to postulate yet unknown planets, while retaining the core of the theory. These were *ad hoc* hypotheses (Losee, 1980: 46–50) but the subsequent discovery of Uranus proved them right, so that the empirical content increased.

Scientific progress results from competition between research programmes. Each programme tries to uphold its own hard core by protecting it in a Kuhnian dogmatic way against anomalies through auxiliary hypothesis. However, in contrast with Kuhn, Lakatos thinks that progressive and degenerating research programmes can be discerned. If a programme shows no empirical progress, anticipates no new facts, but only subsists by patching up its core with ever new excuses, it is degenerative. If, however, the programme has heuristic power, its empirical content tends to increase, and new facts are discovered, it will win the competition. In the astronomy example, if the unknown planet is indeed discovered, the programme progresses; if on the other hand the programme has to make all kinds of guesses, none of which is confirmed, it degenerates.

Thus, although Kuhn is right that *within* a research programme dogmatism reigns, nevertheless some form of Popperian fallibilism and falsification can be salvaged: there is a rational choice, according to some kind of demarcation criterion, by way of a-posteriori selection *between* programmes. Progress and rationality can be attained by picking the programme that happened to be on the right track and proved to be more capable of empirical growth than the competition.

So, although there is no criterion for instant rationality, a-posteriori *rational reconstruction* of scientific progress is possible; there may be good reasons to reject a research programme, and paradigm shifts are not entirely a matter of mob psychology. The winning programme is objectively better if it has the same empirical content as its competitor, and a bit more. Unfortunately, there is no hard and fast measure of empirical content, and we do not always have a choice between two programmes.

Feyerabend on science in a free society

Paul Feyerabend (1978) has, in debate with Lakatos, radicalized Kuhn's relativism. His position has become known as *methodological anarchism*; it holds that 'anything goes' in methodology, that there is and should be no demarcation criterion. He argues that the methodological law-and-order approach, implied in the quest for demarcation, is disastrous to scientific progress, and that framing hypotheses which go against established theories is the way science proceeds. Established theories have carried the day usually by coincidence, rhetoric, superior persuasive or political powers of their defenders, and the like. As Kuhn argued, they then produce their own evidence, entrench themselves using the support, grants and prestige that comes from their privileged position. Big science is successful because it controls the resources to churn out ever more results that confirm it. The competition lacks the laboratories and the manpower to produce its own evidence, and hence has no data to show. So it is only natural that new hypotheses should clash with accepted wisdom, and seem ill-supported by the evidence. However, lack of confirmation is in this view no disadvantage. Rather, being counterintuitive is highly desirable, since that is the way to unsettle the established ideologies, and realize real progress. Not surprisingly, Feyerabend became a kind of cult figure in Californian counterculture in the late 1970s.

So, 'anything goes' means that no hypothesis should be rejected as falsified or unconfirmed; on the contrary, notoriously unscientific-like ideas, such as voodoo, magic, or alternative healing, should be given a try. Moreover, they should not be rejected in the face of conflicting evidence; a maximum of empirical immunity should be granted to wild ideas. Application of a universal method that suppresses ideas with insufficient empirical and methodological backing would be disastrous for progress. Scientific progress, rather than being the epitome of rationality, needs a firm dose of irrationality.

It will come as no surprise that Feyerabend does not recognize the distinction between context of discovery and context of justification. The acceptance of new scientific ideas is as much due to social and accidental factors (discovery) as to rational methods (justification). Methodological rules hamper progress; 'counterinduction', choosing the unjustified and unconfirmed, is the road to new discoveries.

Furthermore, he argues that science is not essentially different from ideology and mythology. Only the establishment has a vested interest in selling science as superior to common sense and as the epitome of rationality, and in fostering an uncritical belief in its superiority. Feyerabend defended a separation between state and science, in the same way that church and science have been separated. Children in school should not be indoctrinated with the dominant scientific ideology, and free citizens in a free society should not be patronized by philosophical know-alls.

It should be emphasized that the main thrust of Feyerabend's methodological anarchism is his disdain for pompous philosophers who try to lay down the law for scientists, and try to prescribe to society at large what is rational and scientifically respectable. His style has been deliberately provocative: he cultivated his image as a kind of anti-philosopher and certainly lived up to his own maxim: 'Always contradict'. By his own admission, he did not have a new philosophical doctrine of knowledge (Feyerabend, 1980: 284), but wanted to blow up the established ideology from the inside (ibid.: 285). As a philosopher of science, he probably has made no lasting contribution. Having read (and sometimes enjoyed) his diatribes, one realizes that he fails to answer the rather crucial question: why is it that established science has delivered such impressive results, and alchemy, voodoo and witchcraft have not? What distinguishes the former from the latter?

Moral

To sum up, the vicissitudes of the demarcation criterion have been something like the following.

The Wiener Kreis designated verifiability as the criterion for meaningfulness. Popper realized that verification in the strict sense required is impossible, and proposed falsifiability. Quine undercut the dogma of the distinction between empirical and logical statements and demonstrated that scientific statements are connected with whole theories. Wittgenstein maintained that the meaning of a term or a statement is not once and for all given, but forms part of a 'language game', a 'form of life'. Hanson introduced the notion of 'theory-ladenness': there is no 'immaculate' perception, observations are not independent of theoretical presuppositions, and hence cannot be used to reject or confirm the theory. Likewise, Sellars unmasked the 'Myth of the Given'. Kuhn introduced the celebrated term 'paradigm', one of its implications being that scientific collectives make their own data, which are 'incommensurable' with data from other collectives or periods: paradigms determine what is seen, and no rational comparison in terms of empirical adequacy or progress is possible. Hence no demarcation criterion can be specified, and all-out relativism seems to follow. Feyerabend exploits the notions of theory-ladenness and paradigm in the service of methodological anarchism: any attempt to impose standards is arrogant and paternalistic: so, 'anything goes'. Lakatos tries to rescue rationality in backward fashion, combining dogmatism within a 'research programme' with the possibility of progress through identification of progressive and degenerating programmes.

One could interpret the development from logical positivism to Kuhn and Feyerabend as the demise of a demarcation criterion for scientific rationality, the undoing of the quest for iron-clad methods and standards, and consequently as the victory of all-out relativism.

However, one could also consider it as the introduction of more human and contextual elements in the philosophy of science. Science is now seen as a human activity. Already in Popper, framing hypotheses is an essentially free, creative and unconstrained human activity. Kuhn emphasizes the social nature of science, and the contextual nature of knowledge claims: only on the basis of shared practices within a community is research possible. The later Wittgenstein and hermeneutics reached a similar conclusion: knowledge starts from a pragmatic and social matrix; it depends on prejudices and prereflexive practices. So the development in the philosophy of science seems to converge somehow with strands from continental philosophy. In the next section, philosophies of science which emphasize this social and pragmatic, if you will, hermeneutic matrix of inquiry will be introduced.

2.6   Alternatives to positivism 1 – hermeneutics, constructionism, rhetoric

Hermeneutics in science

We saw in Chapter 1 that in the continental philosophical tradition hermeneutics was already a much respected approach to the social sciences. It was introduced in the English-language philosophy of science by, among others, Thomas Kuhn and Charles Taylor in the 1970s. Criticism of positivism and serious doubts about the idea that the methods of natural science should be held up to the social sciences as the ideal standard merged with the view 'that there is an unavoidable "hermeneutical" component in sciences of man' (Taylor, 1971: 3). Let us rehearse some hermeneutic ideas.

An important element in hermeneutics is the sensitivity to *history*. A major thesis of the influential German philosopher, Martin Heidegger (1889–1976), was that the quest for a timeless foundation of knowledge, for absolute truth and certainty, ignores our own radical, insurmountable historicity and finiteness. In his major work *Wahrheit und Methode* (*Truth and Method*) (1960) the German philosopher Hans Georg Gadamer elaborates this theme and explains the essence of understanding and interpretation in the human sciences by analysing how we should understand a work of art. We understand a work of art not by objectifying it, ourselves being detached and disinterested spectators. On the contrary, in understanding it we are involved in and participate in the work of art, starting from our own situation and prejudices. Or consider attending a tragedy: the spectators are not disinterested; they as well as the players participate in the play. This happening is never finished and never the same; the work of art is never an object in itself: it is the essence of a play and a work of art that they should be perceived by spectators who become involved in interpreting and understanding them. And every time staging and interpretation will be different because the interpreter brings her own history with her and the work of art is passed on through tradition.

In this way interpretation brings with it a sensitivity to history or, what is more, a form of historical existence. To understand the meaning of a work of art, or a text in general, we should become conscious of our own situatedness. We should resist the naive temptation of objectivism, the belief that there is a stable pre-given object or world to be known as a secure truth on its own. Between subject and object there is that historical, hermeneutic interaction. Therefore, in understanding a text we cannot possibly remain neutral or 'objective' observers; on the contrary we should search for our own prejudices. To understand a text from the past, for instance, is to understand it from our own situation, though our situation is also a product of history. To understand something is to re-enact it in our own situation; to interrogate it as it were, in order to get an answer to a question of our own. In this dialectic, dialogue-like, process of questions and answers we do learn things about the world, as well as about ourselves. What a text means does not necessarily coincide with the intentions of the initial author (if any). Human knowledge and experience, in general, is a constant conversation with tradition applied to the questions of our times. As it is the means of communication, language is the most important medium of the hermeneutic experience of the world: the world presents itself in language and communication.

This has to be a very short and fragmented rendering of a typical continental philosophical, broad, sweeping and erudite work, sometimes almost obscure to the reader who is not familiar with continental philosophy. It should give the flavour of hermeneutics which Heidegger and Gadamer turned from a method for the sciences of man and for the interpretation of texts, into a universal or ontological hermeneutics concerned with the fundamental mode of human existence, our being in the world. What does concern us here is that some ideas of hermeneutics tie in with the post-positivistic philosophy of science, such as the Myth of the Given, epistemological holism (the Quine–Duhem thesis), the theory-ladenness of observations, and the importance of history.

Interpretation and meaning   What then is this hermeneutical component of scientific theorizing? Let us follow Charles Taylor (1971) for a tentative answer. The objects of the sciences of man, such as a text, a situation, an action, a reason, a purpose, have meanings; and these meanings are to be interpreted or understood by subjects. Meaning has an essential place in the characterization of human behaviour. Something has a meaning only in a 'field', that is, in relation to the meaning of other things. There is no such thing as a single, unrelated meaningful element. A term like 'shame' refers to a certain kind of situation leading to a certain mode of response, like hiding oneself. But this 'hiding' which is not the same as hiding from an armed pursuer cannot be understood without reference to the feeling experienced. So, we are back where we started: 'We have to be within the circle' (Taylor, 1971: 13). We meet here the *hermeneutic circle*: 'the readings of partial expressions depend on those of others, and ultimately of the whole' (ibid.: 6). We can only make sense of a certain behaviour if we understand it as part of an entire practice. The readings, however, will never be clear-cut and the same, and will not relieve us of the uncertainty of interpretations and subjectivity. This epistemological predicament, Taylor writes, would be intolerable for the positivists, who demanded clarity, certainty and formalization as a way to avoid the circle of interpretation and subjectivity. Behaviourism failed at exactly this point; you cannot define, says Taylor, the response without the stimulus, and vice versa: interpretation gets in between, making any 'objective' definition of situation and reaction to it impossible.

A certain behaviour, say, writing a name on a piece of paper and putting it in a box, makes sense only as part of a whole, namely voting, which is a social practice. Social practices like voting, promising, negotiating, blushing, etc. carry with them certain vocabularies and rules which 'constitute' these practices, not necessarily obtaining in all societies. Here, hermeneutics meets Wittgenstein's notion of 'form of life'. Social practices, rules and vocabularies make up the necessary context of the meanings of particular behaviours. So, understanding human behaviour requires more than knowledge and description of spatiotemporal superficialities, more than 'brute data', as

Taylor calls them, 'whose validity cannot be questioned by offering another interpretation'; understanding human behaviour requires hermeneutical science, a study of the intersubjective and common meanings embedded in social reality.

Natural versus social (human) sciences   But is there, then, a difference between the methodology of the natural and of the social or human sciences? Is there something special about the subject matter of the latter which tells us not to adopt for it the method of the former sciences? Positivist-empiricist philosophers favour the belief that the exact natural sciences set the methodological standard and adhered to a methodological monism. Some hermeneutic philosophers do not believe, for their own reasons, that we should distinguish between natural and human (social) scientific methods. Let us attend to the arguments of the American philosopher Richard Rorty who is very sympathetic to hermeneutics. Rorty takes sides with the *universal hermeneutics* of Gadamer. This is an attitude, a general intellectual position, not a universal method. After the demise of positivism and empiricism there is no place for an objective, ahistorical foundation of any knowledge. There is no ahistoric structure of rationality. 'We have not *got* a language which will serve as a permanent neutral matrix formulating all good explanatory hypotheses, and we have not the foggiest notion how to get one' (Rorty, 1979: 348–9). For this reason Rorty thinks that 'there is no requirement that people should be more difficult to understand than things' (ibid.: 347); that is, there is no essential difference between human and natural sciences; both are hermeneutical, in the sense of interpretation, involving understanding. Neither are we justified in accepting the traditional distinction between *explanation* in the natural and *understanding* in the social sciences. In the formulation of Taylor, who doesn't agree with Rorty, 'The two turn out to be methodologically at one, not for the positivist reason that there is no rational place for hermeneutics; but for the radically opposed reason that all sciences are equally hermeneutic' (Taylor, 1980: 26).

Taylor, however, rejects this claim of universal hermeneutics. The kind of understanding involved in the two kinds of science is different. This is so, because in the natural sciences the task is 'to give an account of the world as it is independently of the meanings it might have for human subjects' (ibid.: 31). But this 'requirement of absoluteness', the requirement to avoid subject-related terms, is inapplicable to human sciences. Here we have to understand the world as it makes sense to the humans themselves. We have to grasp the significance of things for them, which can only be articulated in subject-related terms. In human sciences the experience of subjects plays an indispensable role. Here is one of his eloquent examples:

> When I know that a situation is humiliating, I know more than that the subject is averse to it; I know that his aversion has a different quality than to a situation which is physically painful, or one which is embarrassing, or one which awakens guilt in him, or unbearable pity, or which induces despair. There is here a set of alternative terms for feeling or reaction: 'guilt', 'shame', 'despair', 'embarrassment', 'pity',

which are correlative to and are only understood in terms of the type of situation: wrongdoing, the humiliating, the hopeless, the embarrassing, the pitiable. (Taylor, 1980: 35)

For almost the same reasons Herbert Dreyfus (1980) rejects Rorty's (1980) conclusion that there is no important difference between the natural and the social sciences. We never can escape the hermeneutic circle, because our beliefs, communication, actions, develop against a shared cultural *background* of social practices, of know-how and skills, which cannot be made entirely explicit because it is presupposed. It is the necessary context that makes communication and understanding possible in the first place. But, whereas in natural science the scientists can take this background for granted, making normal science possible, the social sciences must take account of it, thereby constantly disagreeing about interpretations. It is the basic job of the social sciences to explore the background of practices and their meaning, 'the unique feature of human behaviour, the human self-interpretation in our everyday know-how' (Dreyfus, 1980: 17). Natural science 'succeeds by decontextualizing, while the human sciences have to deal with the human context' (ibid: 20).

As mentioned, Rorty denies that we can give a natural scientific account of the world as it is independently of the meanings it might have for human subjects. He repudiates the notion of a 'requirement of absoluteness', because he claims that the notion of 'mind-independent reality' is incoherent. In section 2.7 we will pursue this *realism* vs. *relativism* issue. Rorty sees no distinction between natural and human sciences in this respect: the universal hermeneutics following the demise of positivism is the recognition that inquiry proceeds without a universal canon of rationality.

Mary Hesse (1980) claimed that it has increasingly become apparent that the empiricist standard of scientific rationality has fallen apart; that the logic of the natural sciences cannot serve as a model for the social sciences; and that the traditional contrast between the natural and social sciences should be reconsidered. What counts as facts depends on the theory. Hence, the circularity emphasized by hermeneutics is also apparent in the natural sciences. The language of natural science is 'formalizable only at the cost of the historical dynamics of scientific development and of the imaginative constructions in terms of which nature is interpreted by science' (Hesse: 1980: 173).

Thus Hesse recognizes that human and social factors are intrinsic to all science. She charts the demise of classical positivist philosophy of science and shows much sympathy for the hermeneutic view of the role of interpretation and the hermeneutic circle between data and theory. Because almost every point made about the human sciences has been made about the natural sciences, the resemblances between this post-empiricist/positivist account of natural science and the hermeneutic approach to the human sciences appear very close (see also Bernstein, 1983).

Social constructionism

An important element of classical positivism and empiricism was its theory of truth, the *correspondence theory*, according to which a description is true if it corresponds to the object or event in the world which it describes. This notion of correspondence is the major bone of contention for social constructionists like Kenneth Gergen and John Shotter. What is that correspondence relation supposed to be? It is an illusion to think that we can establish secure and determinate relationships between words and world referents, that knowledge mirrors nature, and that scientific theory serves to reflect or map reality in any direct or decontextualized manner. 'How can theoretical categories map or reflect the world if each definition linking category and observation itself requires a definition?' (Gergen, 1985b: 4). In this kind of criticism they follow the lines of post-positivist argumentation we have already encountered. What makes them rather special is the radical and relativistic conclusions they draw from it. Because the positivist claim that science can and must strive for full objectivity, in terms of mental mirroring of the world, has proved untenable, the social constructionists infer that scientific knowledge is only the product of *social construction* and convention. 'Social constructionism,' writes Gergen, after Rorty (1979), 'views discourse about the world not as a reflection or map of the world but as an artifact of communal exchange' (Gergen, 1985a: 266).

The function of language, and thus of our theories, is not that they refer to the world at all; they have no truth-value. The basic function of language, according to Shotter, 'is *not* the representation of things in the world. . . . It works to create, sustain and transform various patterns of social relations.' And he adds that if some words stand for things, 'they do so only *from within* a form of social life already constituted by the ways of talking in which such words are used' (Shotter, 1991: 70).

These arguments are being put forward in the context of a critique of the prevailing categories, concepts and views in (social) psychology by which one gains understanding of personal and social actions and interactions. Topics and concepts such as gender, aggression, person, self, emotion, schizophrenia, child, mother's love are *social artefacts*, products of historically situated interactions among people. Social constructionists challenge the supposedly objective and universal basis of this knowledge; they are sensitive to cross-cultural psychological or ethnographic studies which reveal that such psychological conceptions differ among wide-ranging cultures because they are produced by and sustain the social, moral, political and economic institutions. Forms of psychological understanding are not directly dependent on the nature of things but on the vicissitudes of social processes, such as communication, conflict, negotiation; they are forms of *negotiated understanding* and as such tools for praising or blaming, assigning or diminishing responsibility, rewarding or punishing, and exercising censure.

One of the main problems social scientists encounter is the identification of *actions* (Gergen, 1980). Empirical evidence does not help to understand what is going on when, for instance, 'Ross reaches out and momentarily touches

Laura's hair'. We cannot identify any given action in itself, because what it means is embedded in an ever-unfolding context. To understand the meaning of the action, we have to rely 'on a network of interdependent and continuously modifiable interpretations' (ibid.: 242).

Social constructionists think that there is no such thing as objective under-standing in psychology: 'reality is negotiable'; what there is depends on what society agrees about. They endorse an interpretative social science, chiefly concerned with 'conceptual transformations of social life', the theories of which are not 'mapping devices for a pre-existing reality', but 'render experi-ence intelligible' and 'give meaning to such experience' (Gergen, 1980: 258).

From these considerations about the construction of knowledge of social activities and relationships, the social constructionists infer that there are no empirical grounds of scientific knowledge at large and that the epistemo-logical question, what are facts and what is true or false, is constituted in the lap of communities.

> Scientific formulations would not on this account be the result of an impersonal application of rigorous and decontextualized method, but the responsibility of per-sons in active, communal interchange. (Gergen, 1985b: 13)

To conclude, social constructionism radicalizes the social component to the extent that science is nothing but social activity and social construction; and it thus ends in all-out relativism.

Rhetoric

According to the social constructionists science, wrought as it is in language, is not meant to map the world; it is *discourse*, that is, a social interchange. In this light, Michael Billig (1987) concentrates on the character of discourse. The most important element in this human activity is *argumentation* and it is Billig's intention to promote this argumentative aspect of thinking. Since ancient times, rhetoric has had a bad press; it is degenerated grandiloquence and stylistic conceit used merely to impress the audience. But this rhetoric of adornment is not the argumentative rhetoric which concerns Billig.

Following in the footsteps of the Greek philosopher Protagoras, Billig draws attention to the social-psychological principle of science, the funda-mental two-sidedness of thinking. Because there are no fixed truths and no fixed laws, it is useless to try to discover the fixed essences of truth, as was Plato's vision. 'Plato may have dreamt of an end to argument, but in Protagoras's philosophy there is no escape from rhetoric' (Billig, 1987: 44). Knowledge is not absolute but is the interim product of debates between adversaries, a never-ending dialogue. In this context of argumentation, it is possible to argue both sides of a case. Contrary statements can each be reasonable and justified, and both can be open to criticism. Western philoso-phers have assumed that truth is one; that thinking is, or should be, reducible to logic, and that, therefore, contrary statements cannot be both true and reasonable. However, this would end argumentation, and that is, in fact, an illusion, according to Billig.

Emphasis upon the argumentative context of discourse has a number of theoretical implications for cognitive psychological issues. Billig refers, for example, to the problem of meaning (1987: 90 ff.). According to social constructionism words do not refer to the world and do not possess fixed meanings; they take their meanings from communal exchange. That being so, argues Billig, one must understand words in relation to the argumentative contexts in which they are being used. One should examine them in terms of the contest between criticism and justification. 'Without knowing these counter-positions, the argumentative meaning will be lost' (ibid.: 91). One cannot properly understand an argument if one fails to grasp what it is arguing against: 'Thus, if one is puzzling over an extremely difficult piece of intellectual work, whose meaning seems too abstruse to grasp, one should ask oneself, not "What is this about", but "What is this attacking?"' (Billig ibid.: 92)

Another example, taken from cognitive psychology, to which Billig applies his rhetoric theory, is the problem of *categorization* (ibid.: 120 ff.), the placing of a particular stimulus or object within a general category. To see Billig, for example, as a representative of scientists who approach science exclusively from a social-psychological point of view, is making a categorization, sorting him into a group. Cognitive psychologists, whom Billig sees as heirs to objectivism, assume that categorization is an essential function of organisms because it is based upon the need to reduce, simplify and distort the infinite variety of information. This assumption of biological necessity, however, expresses only 'one side of the many-sidedness of human nature', according to Billig (ibid.: 123). Categorization as used by cognitive psychologists is linked with prejudiced thought because it shuts out complexity by the imposition of stereotypes, or group schemata. By categorization the particular is robbed of its particularity. By defining categorization as a biological necessity the cognitivist overvalues the inflexible aspects of thought and reduces a perceiving person to a bureaucrat who processes the messiness of the world into orderly categories. Categories and schemata determine the information process – what will be coded, what retrieved from memory. The categorizing thinker appears as a rather dull person, being inherently prejudiced and programmed to bureaucratically pigeonhole. The 'cognitive miser', limited in his capacity to process information, must take cognitive 'shortcuts', and 'consequently, errors and biases stem from inherent features of the cognitive system' (Fiske and Taylor, 1984: 12). The implication that stereotyping is merely an instance of normal cognition is 'not just depressing it is also one-sided' (Billig, 1987: 126), leading to a one-sided image of the person, as a routine- and rule-follower, without tolerance, flair, wit or sagacity which 'seem to have been edged out by the demands of organization and stability' (ibid.: 129) .

By his rhetorical approach Billig opposes objectivism and challenges the scientist's quest for law and order. He argues in favour of the versatility of life, the particularity of individual cases and the contestability of points of view. He attempts to establish 'the primacy of rhetoric over logic' (Billig, 1990: 50), because logic or mathematics cannot supply a higher realm of discourse, in which truths have an absolute status. He recommends ordinary discourse rather than scientific methodology.

> Science is . . . an intrinsically rhetorical, or persuasive, activity, and, consequently, a rhetorical analysis of science is not so much an exposé, but an analysis which looks at the way that scientists argue and discuss their scientific cases. (Billig, 1990: 50)

Conclusion

After a survey of classical empiricism, its quest for demarcation and certainty, and its demise, we have sketched the reintroduction of human, subjective and social concerns as essential components in the practice of science. In the work of Kuhn, and in hermeneutics, prejudices are indispensable factors in research, rather than corrupting influences. However, it seems that these subjective influences detract from the realism of scientific theories: they seem more about us than about the world.

So, having rejected the idea of detached objectivity, the question becomes how to escape all-out subjectivity, the view that the truth becomes relative to the viewpoint of a particular observer. Such relativism would undermine science; if there is no external yardstick, no demarcation criterion to distinguish between scientific and pseudo-scientific, and between progressive and degenerating programmes, if 'anything goes' and voodoo is not, by any rational criterion, inferior to conventional medicine, why spend time and money on research?

2.7 Problems of realism and relativism

A major problem that faces us, as a result of the failed quest for universal criteria for scientific objectivity, concerns the question: How realistic is science? or: How relativistic? Is science at the mercy of subjectivity because objectivity is not attainable? Let us rehearse some arguments for and against both pictures of science: realism and relativism.

The first problem for realism or objectivism, heavily stressed by anti-realists, is the *failure of empiricism* as a theory about perception and the fixing of concepts and beliefs, already dealt with in this chapter. There are no neutral data which we reproduce, as in mirrors, in our concepts and which we could use in a justification of theories. We should give up the view that the terms of our observations, scientific or not, are given in sensations and are causally dependent on natural information, and that the physical flow of natural information (at a particular moment) is necessary and sufficient for conceptual observation and theory formation. Neither will it do to suggest that we receive neutral data from the world, after which we switch to the interpretation mode. Our judgements about what there is and what we see are theory laden from the outset and are coloured by wide experience, beliefs and practices.

From this follows, secondly, that there are *no indubitable foundations* for

knowledge. 'There is no special subset of the set of human beliefs that is jus-
tificationally foundational for all the rest.' (Churchland, 1979: 41). There are
no free-floating truths we have to grasp, no knowledge we have to pluck from
the air. What we think and say, what we know about the world, is known by
us; and this knowledge is not part of the objective world itself, but is the set
of beliefs about the world wrought by us as participants in cultures, sharing
languages, worldviews, theories, hopes and expectations, practices and institutions, and reflecting a rich matrix of intersubjective relations.

These two problems for objectivism lead to the third one, the *fallibility* of
scientific theories. History teaches us that no theory is immune to alteration
and even complete rejection in the course of time. Every science has its exemplars of broken theories in the attic. Psychology's well-known example is
phrenology and its gadget cranioscopy, the measurement of skulls in pursuit
of the bumps of psychological qualities, much in vogue during the nineteenth
century. Whatever the value of theories or knowledge, their truth and the sup-
porting evidence cannot be absolute. Truth and objectivity, if philosophy of
science can still use these terms, appear to be limited qualities. Though much
science was successful, the standards by which the success was measured, the
standards of rationality, were also local and historical. After positivism many
philosophers have brought home to us that we have to give up the illusion that
there is a permanent set of ahistorical standards of rationality (Bernstein,
1983).

Do we, then, have to give up realism? Do we have to choose the relativistic
alternative that truth has indefinitely many faces? Is science nothing but a
matter of rhetoric, is it nothing more than arbitrarily endorsing one set of
beliefs rather than another? Many scientists, especially social scientists, and
the wider intellectual community have come increasingly to suppose that science cannot claim objectivity and therefore is not reliable.

There are, however, also many scientists who think that there are no reasons to consider ourselves 'cut loose from the anchor to reality' (Churchland,
1979: 41). The philosopher of science Larry Laudan writes:

> The displacement of the idea that facts and evidence matter by the idea that every-
> thing boils down to subjective interests and perspectives is – second only to
> American political campaigns – the most prominent and pernicious manifestation
> of anti-intellectualism in our time. (Laudan, 1990: x)

Before we come up with reasons and suggestions for different versions of realism and our own opinion let us first indulge in some bad news for relativism.

In a sense relativism is *self-defeating*. To declare that no utterance can be
true because it is a product of the one who utters it, is devastating for the
statement itself. 'Notoriously, there is no room for the assertion of relativism
itself, in a world in which relativism is true' (Gellner, 1982: 183). Nobody
would take this absolute form of relativism seriously, so we should perhaps
not overstress this. Nevertheless in relativistic circles one tries to overcome
this problem of 'reflexivity'; we will come back to this in Chapter 3, p. 89, on
the sociology of science.

It is a relativist claim that 'we' ourselves provide the criteria for what is true or false, for what is rational or not. The question is who 'we' might be? How do we delineate the relevant subject who is responsible for a particular viewpoint? Few relativists would designate the individual as the relevant subject, because it would lead to solipsism (I am the only reality), not very popular among the '-isms'. More popular is the notion that what I think is true, is true for me, and what you think is true, is true for you. But it does not take much imagination to see that the notion kills every communication. More serious is the relativist idea that it is language that is responsible for viewpoints, language games, forms of life; and that language is not private, but a social medium (cf. Wittgenstein). Therefore, rationality is relative to at least groups. But which groups? Classes, determined by socioeconomic factors, as a relativist of Marxist leanings would have it? Scientific communities as in Kuhn's paradigms? Cultures, communities, nations, tribes?

> Matters are clear if we deal with geographically separated tribes or nations. In a modern society, however, there are so many cross-currents of agreement and disagreement that specifying who "we" might be is difficult. (Trigg, 1993: 43)

Apart from this problem of identification of the subject, however, the notion that truth depends on the group I happen to be in is not a comforting one. A truth valid for me and my friends only must be parochial and uninteresting, and sometimes even dangerous.

This central relativist idea that what is true for one group might not be true for another, is incoherent (Newton-Smith, 1982). Suppose we encounter some social group who produce a sentence *s* in a context in which we would hold a sentence *s'* to be true. We may be saying the same thing or we may be saying different but complementary things, or we may be saying incompatible things. How do we establish that? 'We cannot adjudicate between these alternatives without a translation of *s* in our language.' And this is not a viable option for the relativist. 'There is no question of coherently saying that *s* is true for them and its translation, *s''*, is false for us' (Newton-Smith, 1982: 108).

This brings us, again, to the notorious *incommensurability* thesis, put forward by Kuhn and Feyerabend (see section 2.5). Different theories or different systems of thought, separated by scientific revolutions, are said to be incomparable, because the meanings of the descriptive terms used will vary from theory to theory. There can be no question of translating the claims of one into the language of another. But how can we claim a difference without forwarding an opinion about the alien theory, that is, as we saw in the previous objection, without some kind of translation? In line with Wittgenstein's thesis that understanding a way of life cannot be separated from adopting it, Kuhn held the view that it is impossible to understand a theory without subscribing to it (Trigg, 1973: 101). But in order to make a comparison between meanings and theories one cannot but pretend to take a neutral standpoint and claim objectivity (a 'God's eye view') while it is not possible for a relativist, by definition, to do this. It seems that for relativists all theories are equal and that they cannot provide us with criteria with which to sift good theories from bad ones.

Another, less formal, objection is that relativists tend to view science or knowledge as a mere *language game*. Relativists claim that all our knowledge is a matter of language and communication only. The world, they think, is only an interpretation, a human construction, and there is no way to step out of your interpretation. Actually, they go on, it makes no sense to talk about *the* world because we only have interpretations; and there are so many, according to time, place and culture and depending on tradition. Therefore all we can do is try to understand each other's language games.

So, relativists seem to assume that our relation to the world consists only in language, that our access to the world is through language alone, or that there is 'nothing outside the text'; that statements and theories are not about the world and can refer only to each other. However, is language the only game in town? Of course, our theories, opinions and beliefs are wrought, expressed in language, though it remains to be seen if they are themselves linguistic.

According to Suppe (1977: 221 ff.), among others, theories are not collections of propositions or statements, but are extralinguistic entities which may be described or characterized by a number of different linguistic formulations; and he suggests that a theory 'qualifies as a model for each of its formulations'.

Knowledge will usually be *expressed* in language, but, we think, it is not *identical* with language: it refers to the world; it is our (active) relation to the world. Stating that a chair is something to sit on is expressing knowledge about a segment of the world, and expressing our (possible) active relation to it. Knowledge can be expressed in language, or without language – to sit down is also a token of the knowledge that a chair is something to sit on. Our active contact with the world, our handling of things and participation in events contribute to our knowledge. Sure, it is *our* knowledge, hence fallible and never certain, but it does pertain to the world.

Relativists tend to ignore this *subject–object* relatedness and seem to replace it altogether with *subject–subject* relations, that is, by convention, discussion, mutual understanding and negotiation, or persuasion. They see knowledge and science exclusively as a social practice or a social institution. The unwarranted step in their reasoning is to conclude that there is nothing beyond socially constructed knowledge, and that science cannot refer to a mind-independent world; that everything matters, except the world. Many relativists acknowledge the importance of practice, but by turning this into an exclusive *social* practice they still ignore the object-relatedness or what could be called the role or the constraints of the world in the production of knowledge. Let us illustrate this with a quotation from Steve Fuller:

> Knowledge exists only through its embodiment in linguistic and other social practices. These practices, in turn, exist only by being reproduced from context, which occurs only by the continual adaptation of knowledge to social circumstances. (Fuller, 1989: 4)

One of the relativist's main targets is the *correspondence theory of truth*, held by positivist realists. How can we ever be so sure about the relation between a belief and reality, or between a proposition and a state of affairs in the world, if our only access to the world is via beliefs, and we are not in the position to check our beliefs independently? Traditional realists, writes Gellner (1974: 74) scornfully, 'compare their own ideas with their own ideas and find, much to their satisfaction, that they match perfectly'.

The problem with the correspondence theory, however, is not only that one opts for a mysterious function of beliefs and language, consisting in mirroring or copying something as reality. Another problem is that the correspondence theory of truth is language ridden: we mirror the world only in thoughts. In their attack relativists, unwittingly, side with (old-fashioned) realists. Relativists suggest that the best we can do is to care for coherence between beliefs or to opt for a criterion of consensus. So it seems that in both, the realist's and the relativist's suggestions lurks the notion that our relationship to the world is only mediated by language, beliefs, theories.

However, as we suggested before, knowing, expressed in language or not, is not an exclusively theoretical or intellectual, but an active relationship to objects or aspects of the world. We believe that this active relationship shows a pragmatic way out of the realism–relativism, or objectivism–subjectivism, quagmire (Bem, 1989).

In the next section we will review the characteristics of a moderate, sophisticated (scientific) realism or pragmatism.

2.8   Alternatives to positivism 2 – scientific realism and pragmatism

One way to define realism is that it holds that science is a *representational* activity, in that it attempts to represent the world, to produce models of the world; or put more strongly, that science represents the world as it really is. There are several anti-realist options. The first is that of constructionists and other relativists, whom we have already met. They deny that there is a world independent of our theories and concepts; and that theories and concepts do refer to, or represent, a world out there. 'Reality' is a social construct, in their view. Every concept, theory, observation, method, experiment, measurement, etc. is determined, defined or constituted by the contingent theoretical tradition in which the scientist takes part; they are not objectively given by 'reality'.

Another branch of anti-realists are *instrumentalists* who think that scientific theories are not claims to truth and do not refer to the world at all; that they are nothing more than convenient instruments or tools for describing the world. Instrumentalists are mostly empirically working scientists; and many scientists who are not interested in general philosophical or ontological questions are perfectly happy with an instrumentalist conception of their theories.

Another, related, way to define realism, is to say that it traditionally creates a dichotomy between everyday perception and the 'real' underlying nature of reality. This problem is known in one form as Eddington's 'two tables': the manifest table we see and chop our vegetables on, versus the table as described by quantum physics, a void filled with subatomic particles. The objectivist line holds that only physical properties (the 'primary qualities' as the empiricist Locke called them) are real. Sellars (1963; see also Chapter 1), for instance, relativized the manifest image and preferred the scientific image. At first sight, objectivism seems to vindicate naive realism, the belief in the reality of everyday objects, through science; science tells us that the world really exists and that it is no figment of our imagination; it dispels the idealist, anarchist, relativist doubts about the reliability of our knowledge of the world. However, it undermines in fact the legitimacy of everyday experience (Putnam, 1987) by correcting and replacing it with scientific concepts.

Scientific realism is a more sophisticated kind of realism; it is sensitive to some post-positivist/empiricist criticisms, but it denies constructionist or instrumentalist ideas. A prominent defender of scientific realism is Richard Boyd (1984) who formulated four central theses of scientific realism. We reproduce them here; the characteristics of realism we have already mentioned can easily be recognized within these four.

1. *Theoretical terms* in scientific theories (that is, nonobservational terms) should be thought of as putatively referring expressions; that is, scientific theories should be interpreted 'realistically'.
2. *Scientific theories*, interpreted realistically, are confirmable and in fact are often confirmed as approximately true by ordinary scientific evidence interpreted in accordance with ordinary methodological standards.
3. The historical *progress* of mature sciences is largely a matter of successively more accurate approximations to the truth about both observable and unobservable phenomena. Later theories typically build upon the (observational and theoretical) knowledge embodied in previous theories.
4. The *reality* which scientific theories describe is largely independent of our thoughts or theoretical commitments. (Boyd, 1984: 41–2; italics added)

The problem is that probably almost every modern realist would modify one or more of these tenets.

Many philosophers of science who are sceptical about traditional realism, but who are not entirely sympathetic to relativism either, try to overcome the dichotomy (Bernstein, 1983; Margolis, 1986). Pragmatism, which avoids a strong a-priori ontological commitment and an epistemology that takes mirroring of reality by language as its hallmark, seems to be a way out, though not everybody has the same picture of pragmatism, as we shall see. There is a strain of pragmatism in scientific realism. In this section we will discuss Putnam's revision of realism, Van Fraassen's version of anti-realism, and Churchland's plea for scientific realism. Finally we offer some explicitly pragmatic conceptions of knowledge.

Putnam on 'internal' realism

Hilary Putnam's (1981, 1987) *internal* or *pragmatic* realism tries to overcome the dilemma of realism versus relativism, of the correspondence ('copy') theory of truth versus the view that the mind makes up the world. His slogan is 'The mind and the world jointly make up the mind and the world' (Putnam, 1981: xi).

Traditional realism holds that the terms of scientific theories correspond to real things in the world (for instance, subatomic particles really exist). The major problem with realism is that any theory about the relation between theoretical entities and the world is, well, a theory: the problem just multiplies like Chinese boxes. Put more formally, there is no theory-independent way of assessing whether a theory corresponds to reality. One of Putnam's targets is the classical realist notion of intrinsic, mind-independent properties that is assumed in the traditional realist view that such properties should fit with theoretical terms.

Putnam (1990) argues that it is not possible to describe the world in an absolute way, independent of a human perspective. That such a 'God's eye view' is inaccessible, however, does not necessarily lead to relativism.

> [O]ur image of the world cannot be 'justified' by anything but its success as judged by the interests and values which evolve and get modified at the same time and in interaction with our evolving image of the world itself. . . . On the other hand. . . the world is not the product of our will – or our dispositions to talk in certain ways either. (Putnam, 1990: 29)

Putnam's internal realism then parts ways with traditional objectivist realism, and allows for conceptual relativity. There is no such thing as a ready-made world; rather it depends on the knowing subject. Reference, the correspondence between mind and world, is interest-relative, and cannot be objectively or intrinsically determined. The concept of truth is redefined along the lines set out by the American pragmatist philosopher C.S. Peirce: truth is a kind of limit; it is what we would accept in ideal circumstances, that is, when we knew all. This means that the correspondence idea of truth as correspondence with external pre-existing reality is rejected, and naive or metaphysical realism is replaced by a pragmatic criterion. Rationality, the seeking for truth, is a human activity, guided by values that cannot be reduced to objective states of affairs.

Putnam's account of natural kinds underscores this. The taxonomies science creates (like the periodic table of the elements, or classification of the animal kingdom) are on the one hand discoveries of the real, ontologically necessary nature of things, on the other hand dependent on historical and subjective conceptual frames. They can be revised without entirely rejecting or eliminating previous views. The medieval proto-scientist, who thought that the nature of gold was that it was yellow, and the modern scientist who defines it by its atomic number are both talking about the same reality. However, the way they talk about it is interest-relative and determined by historical context. There are no things, or causes, in themselves; what words refer to, or what counts as a cause depends on the interests of the investigator. In this way the world is the joint product of the mind and the world.

Empiricism revisited

One of the most prominent anti-realists is the American philosopher Bas van Fraassen. He does not at all side, however, with relativists; instead he tries to reinforce empiricism. He rejects scientific realism, formulated by him as follows: 'Science aims to give us, in its theories, a literally true story of what the world is like; and acceptance of a scientific theory involves the belief that it is true' (Van Fraassen, 1980: 8).

The addition 'literally' is important, to rule out as realist positions such as those which imply that science is true if 'properly understood', but is literally false or meaningless. Instrumentalism, for instance, contends that scientific theories do not convey literal truths, and that concepts do not refer to real things in the world; that they are nothing more than useful tools or instruments for describing and predicting phenomena. Whereas the scientific realist genuinely believes that his statements refer to (correspond to) and describe things in the world.

Van Fraassen rejects realism as well as instrumentalism and defines his own position, which he calls '*constructive empiricism*', as follows:

> Science aims to give us theories which are empirically adequate; and acceptance of a theory involves as belief only that it is empirically adequate. . . . [A] theory is empirically adequate exactly if what it says about the observable things and events in this world, is true – exactly if it 'saves the phenomena'. (Van Fraassen, 1980: 12)

He calls this 'constructive' because he contends that the aim of scientific activity is to construct models that must be *adequate to the phenomena*, observable things and events. It is not the task of science to discover literal *truth* concerning the unobservable, theoretical terms (such as an electron, a muon, or a mental script). Thus, he trusts observables, empirical phenomena, but has no ontological faith in unobservables: these do not exist, but are just concepts in models.

This anti-realist position is as sceptical as David Hume's (1711–76) empiricist position. We cannot demand more of theories and statements than that they be empirically adequate; and we can accept a theory as empirically adequate, but not believe it to be true. A scientist's major concern, according to the sceptical empiricist, is to answer factual questions about nothing more than regularities in the observable phenomena. If the phenomena are saved, according to Van Fraassen, the theory or model can be accepted, even if not necessarily true. The scientist could not care less about truth.

A theory, says Van Fraassen (1980: 87 f.), is accepted, however, for more features than empirical adequacy alone. We have mathematical elegance, simpleness, great scope, completeness, usefulness in unifying our account of hitherto disparate phenomena, and explanatory power. Also, it would be a mistake to overlook the ways in which the appraisal of scientific theories is coloured by contextual factors. 'These factors are brought to the situation by the scientist from his own personal, social, and cultural situation.' These features are what he calls 'pragmatic virtues'.

Thus, empirical adequacy, the most important virtue of a theory, as well as the pragmatic virtues provide reasons to prefer one theory to another, independently of questions of truth. To accept a theory is to make a commitment to the framework of that theory, the research programme, and even a world picture. It means also that you immerse yourself fully in a language which is 'thoroughly theory-infected' (ibid.: 81). After all, 'all our language is thoroughly theory-infected. If we could cleanse our language of theory-laden terms . . . we would end up with nothing useful' (ibid.: 14). But, again, commitments are not true or false; 'they are vindicated or not vindicated in the course of human history' (ibid: 88).

The recognition of the importance of this pragmatic dimension of theory acceptance, involving context-dependent features of persons and circumstances, highlights an anti-logical positivistic strain in Van Fraassen's philosophy of science. However, though he may not be a logical positivist, he nevertheless continues the 'positivist antipathies', such as anti-metaphysics, pro-observation, anti-cause, and anti-theoretical entities (Hacking, 1983, 44 f. and 50 f.).

Scientific realism

In presenting his version of scientific realism, Paul Churchland attacks Van Fraassen's claim that 'empirical adequacy', or observational excellence, is the primary epistemic virtue for the acceptance of theories. The reason is Van Fraassen's unwarranted faith in the integrity of observables. If all concepts are theory laden, as Van Fraassen concedes, why then should he pay tribute to observables and downplay unobservables? In fact, 'our observational ontology' is rendered exactly as dubious as our nonobservational ontology' (Churchland, 1985b: 36). Van Fraassen wants to save the observable phenomena, the empirical facts, but, according to Churchland, they are not 'read off' the world directly; they are part of theories, speculative assumptions included and thus no more privileged than the unobservable parts of the theory. Churchland inverses the hierarchy: the pragmatic virtues, listed by Van Fraassen as we have seen, such as simplicity, coherence and explanatory power, are more fundamental values than is empirical adequacy, 'since collectively they can overthrow an entire conceptual framework for representing the empirical facts' (ibid.: 42). These pragmatic – or global, or superempirical – virtues, as Churchland calls them, guide the evolution of our theories and consequently our belief in what we observe.

What about truth? We have to reconsider truth as the aim of science; Churchland grants Van Fraassen that science is construction rather than discovery.

> The notion of truth is suspect on purely metaphysical grounds, anyway. It suggests straightaway the notion of The Complete and Final True Theory. . . . Such a theory would be, by epistemic criteria, the best theory possible. But nothing whatever guarantees the existence of such a unique theory. . . . It may be that, for any theory whatsoever, there is always an even better theory, and so *ad infinitum.* (ibid: 46)

This sounds like relativism, or perhaps instrumentalism; why, then, continue to call this position 'scientific realism'? Because, Churchland says, he remains committed to the idea 'that there exists a world, independent of our cognition, with which we interact and of which we construct representations' (ibid.: 46). Global excellence, instead of Van Fraassen's observational excellence, 'remains the fundamental measure of rational ontology. And that has always been the central claim of scientific realism' (ibid.: 47).

Churchland's realism, thus, moves in the direction of *pragmatism*: not a naive version of realism, but one which endorses the post-positivistic criticism of empiristic epistemology and foundationalism, and favours the use of science as a guide to practice.

More views of pragmatism

According to Richard Rorty (1979) a major consequence of pragmatism is that it avoids the metaphysical dichotomy of appearance versus reality. The traditional view that science addresses the eternal reality behind appearances, which is supposedly independent of human interests, that science unveils things as they are in themselves, is what Rorty calls the *spectator theory of truth*. This theory sees the whole mental apparatus of beliefs and representations as reflections of reality. The pragmatist alternative is that beliefs are tools for dealing with reality. They represent nothing, so that no correspondence theory of truth and no account of the mapping between representation and reality is necessary or even possible. Pragmatism is, according to Rorty, *anti-representationalism*; truth is not a correspondence between language and reality, because there cannot be such comparison between them: truth is relative to a given language system, and cannot be elevated out of the linguistic realm. Knowledge derives from language only and the world emerges in *discourse*. Therefore conversation is 'the ultimate context in which knowledge is to be understood' (Rorty, 1979: 389). It remains to be seen if Rorty's pragmatism has anything to do with scientific practice or investigation (Diggins, 1994: 416 f.).

Ian Hacking (1983), on the contrary, claims that *experimental work* provides the strongest evidence for scientific realism. Experimental physicists are generally realists about the theoretical entities they use; and why not? Using these entities, for instance electrons, means manipulating them, building new kinds of device and exploiting the causal properties of the entities to explore nature further. Entities are tools not for thinking but for doing. Hacking distinguishes realism about *entities* and realism about *theories*. Realism about theories is perhaps less central to the concern of the active scientist; it is a belief in the aims of science, a value, and perhaps a matter of psychology. Anti-realism is popular among onlooker-philosophers, endorsing the 'spectator theory of knowledge' (Hacking, 1983: 274). But the lesson is: 'think about practice, not theory' (ibid.: 274). So, Hacking's pragmatism is, indeed, practice, intervention.

Rouse (1987) argues, in the same vein, that truth and reality only figure within a background of scientific and everyday *practices*. The idea of knowledge as tool for action rather than a mirror of mind-independent reality tallies with the rejection of representations and sense-data as the stuff knowledge is (entirely) made of. This relational view of knowledge, reality and truth, which we also encountered in Putnam, is characteristic of the pragmatists. As Rouse (1987: 211) puts it:

> '[W]hat there is cannot be intelligibly separated from what we can encounter through the successes and failures of specific practical engagements, where scientific theorising is among these practices.'

Deflating the empiricist copy theory of truth in pragmatism

Interestingly, in the philosophy of science attention has shifted recently from a view of knowledge as (linguistic) representations, to knowledge as *skills and practices*, that is, it has shifted from representation to manipulation. Scientific knowledge is a matter of actively disclosing the world rather than merely picturing it. This suggests a more pragmatic, interactive view of reality, as dependent on practical exploration, than is implied in the classical realist tenet of a mind-independent reality: 'science [is] a pragmatic exploratory coping with the world' (Rouse, 1987: 149). This view avoids the extremes of subjectivism and vulgar instrumentalism: the pragmatic success of science is not a matter of a theory or mental representation corresponding with a mind-independent world, but is grounded in pre-reflexive practice: the real is what we manipulate (Hacking, 1983; cf. Von Wright, 1993).

Rouse argues that Kuhn's notion of paradigm involves such shared skills, and shared instruments – a field of practices rather than a logical edifice built out of propositions. Rouse connects this with what he calls practical hermeneutics (inspired by Heidegger); it holds that skills ('knowing how') precede theoretical knowledge ('knowing that'). The implications of this view are that all knowledge is local, situated, from the perspective of an embodied agent, and rooted in practical daily activities. Analogously, the Kuhnian picture suggests that research is first and foremost a matter of using research tools, and of learning to extrapolate from concrete cases (exemplars).

Hacking emphasized the original contribution of the laboratory to science – empirical success, the creation of new phenomena depends on technical innovations, not only on new theories. The laboratory is a micro-world, the only place where data are created, so in this sense research is local, not universal: data are not everyday phenomena, but are created in a specific practice, not to be found anywhere in the world outside the laboratory. That data are created in specific domains by specific skills does not mean that they are unreal fictions.

On the contrary, Rouse argues, when we abandon the traditional idea of truth as a correspondence in the sense of a 'copy' relation between theory and reality, and acknowledge that reality is only grasped in dealing with the world through practical skills (the real is what we manipulate), then it becomes clear that practical hermeneutics does not make the world as it is (that is, in an idealistic or relativistic sense), but allows it to show itself the way it is. There is no such thing as uninterpreted reality, apart from human practices; the world is what shows up in our practices.

Engineering, not theorizing, is the best proof of scientific realism, is Hacking's thesis. As Rouse puts it, the world reveals itself under humanly created conditions; laboratory practices are in his view grounded in the ordinary pre-reflexive practices of the kind Heidegger and Dreyfus described in their criticism of the Cartesian theatre of the mind. Thus, in recent views on the philosophy of mind, as we will show in Chapter 4, p. 140 ff, the focus is on interaction, and on information-for-action rather than on picturing the world. The interaction of environment and exploration constitutes reality.

Information is information for action, embedded in exploratory practices which are a precondition for any talk about reality or environment.

Another development emerging from the failed quest for a universal criterion for scientific rationality is the *naturalistic turn* in the philosophy of science. Philosophers have to some extent turned away from the a-priori specification of universal standards, and have started looking at how the actual practice of science is done (see next chapter; see also Callebaut, 1993). Instead of trying to lay a-priori foundations, on which science has to build, it is argued now that philosophy is continuous with science, and has to elucidate and systematize its results a posteriori.

Finally, the bogeyman of relativism has disappeared. It is realized that the absence of a universal criterion for rationality is not the same as the absence of rational discourse.

Suggested reading

A collection with topics related to this chapter:
    Boyd et al. (1991)
Main currents (Marxist, deconstructionist, structuralist, phenomenological, analytical, etc.) in philosophy and their relevance for the social sciences:
    Anderson et al. (1986)
Good introductions:
    Bechtel (1988a)
    O'Hear (1989)
Philosophy of science from a historical perspective:
    Losee (1980)
    Gower (1997)
Conversations with the present ('third') generation philosophers of science:
    Callebaut (1993)
A good collection on 'scientific revolutions' with articles by Kuhn, Putnam, Popper, Lakatos, Laudan and Feyerabend:
    Hacking (1981)
On how to defend social constructionism without relativism:
    Greenwood (1994)
A thorough collection with arguments for and against scientific realism:
    Leplin (1984)
A lively and amusing dialogue between a relativist, a realist, a pragmatist and a positivist:
    Laudan (1990)
On positivism and relativism:
    Laudan (1996)
Journals:
    Philosophy of Science
    British Journal for the Philosophy of Science
    Philosophical Review
    Philosophy of the Social Sciences

3

Sociology and Psychology of Science

3.1   Introduction

In Chapter 2 we saw that in the philosophy of science concern for the purity of science and demarcation of science from non-science yielded to the study of the (pragmatic) relation between the knower and his or her world. Can we claim objectivity for our statements or theories, or are the subjects themselves the measure of things and are they somehow dominantly present in what they assert? Is knowledge only related to the observer and the knower and the group he or she belongs to, or does it refer to the observer-independent world? Philosophers of science have developed arguments for either realism or relativism, but they have also tried to overcome the dichotomy. Most philosophers of science have come to understand that somehow the time and the community make a difference, although the extent of subjective influence is under discussion.

The arguments of philosophers boil down to the thesis of the underdetermination of theories by the evidence (Duhem, Quine) or, put differently, the thesis of the theory-ladenness of observation (Hanson, Kuhn). These theses do not immediately prove that social factors *completely* explain scientific claims; if no evidence is conclusive for the acceptance of a theory, the door is in principle open to *all* kinds of evidential support, not only social factors (Laudan, 1990: Ch. 6). On the other hand, we no longer have grounds to exclude social studies of science, as happened under the regime of positivism. For the positivists carefully distinguished the *justification* from the *discovery* of theories and assumed that the context of justification was the same at all times and places. As contrasted with the positivist's ideal, however, it is held nowadays that we cannot make a sharp distinction between two contexts or domains with their own independent stories, one in which the methodology of rationality and logic brings about true scientific knowledge, and one where cultural, social, political and economic interests and events generate possibly erroneous and partial beliefs.

Philosophers of science have entrenched themselves in the domain of epistemology, working on theories about the nature of knowledge in general. In this chapter we will present the ideas of *sociologists* of science, who take the relativity of scientific knowledge as their point of departure. They investigate the historical context and determinants of scientific theories or, more radically, the 'socially constructed' character of science. The ideal is to explain science and knowledge sociologically. Attention is paid to the social factors that produced them, rather than to the truth and justification of these beliefs.

The next section of this chapter will deal with the concept of ideology, proposed by Karl Marx, which was meant to designate the societal character of science and culture in general. For Marx 'ideology' referred to the false ideas of the opponents of the working class; he was convinced that those ideas were determined by the socioeconomic position of those who held them. Mannheim, however, gave the concept a general epistemological interpretation and eventually preferred the concept of 'sociology of knowledge'.

The concept of ideology inspired leftist social scientists to criticism of established ideology, which the Frankfurt School developed into a 'Critical Theory'. Kuhn's and Feyerabend's work triggered a flood of studies in the sociology of science proper, mostly historical studies of episodes in the development of different sciences. In section 3.3 we will introduce this work.

Some philosophers of science took a more radical stand and formulated theses of a markedly relativistic persuasion, as in the so-called 'strong programme'. These will be dealt with in section 3.4.

In section 3.5 we will see that the earlier tradition of sociology of science which stressed macro-factors, broad cultural and socioeconomic influences on the development of science, was supplanted by the study of micro-factors at work in the manufacture of scientific beliefs and practices, so to say, right down to the laboratory bench. Once again the reader will be confronted with a radical relativistic thesis claiming that even the sociology of science has failed to push relativism far enough, and that the core of epistemological presumption, the 'ideology of representations', has remained unchallenged.

In the last section of this chapter we consider psychological aspects of scientific knowledge. The psychology of science is psychology's contribution to the so-called 'science of science'. This section can also be seen as a stepping stone to the next chapter about the philosophy of mind which will be presented as a naturalized epistemology, being of fundamental importance for the understanding of the mind–world relationship and the development of (scientific) knowledge.

3.2   Ideology and the sociology of knowledge

The German revolutionary and political economist Karl Marx (1818–83) did not invent the term *ideology*. He took it from French philosophers of the eighteenth-century Enlightenment who criticized the residue of religion and superstition in scientific thought. Marx introduced the term in 'Die deutsche Ideologie', a critical study of the German social and political situation at the time. He held that the socioeconomic structure of a society determines its legal and political organization and institutions, its art and literature, and its moral, religious and scientific ideas. Ideology, the production of ideas, reflects the material basis of a society. What a person thinks, how he judges and what motivates him to act, stems from his ideology, which is a reflection of his social and economic position. And because ideology conforms to a certain social position, it is partial, it distorts the truth, in brief it is *false consciousness*. Individuals and socioeconomic groups are unaware of their partiality, and believe that their moral and political views are objectively and universally true and right: they have false consciousness. Only in a classless society, the ideal of the working class, will the right worldview be gained.

This notion of false consciousness allowed the Hungarian-German sociologist Karl Mannheim (1893–1947) to make the distinction between the 'particular' and the 'total conception of ideology' in his famous 'Ideology and utopia' (in Mannheim, 1936). The first conception was intended to expose certain ideas of opponents. These were stamped as lies, distortions or half-truths, to be interpreted in the light of, and as a function of, the social position and interests of those who proclaimed them.

Within the 'total conception of ideology', however, ideas are interpreted as a function of the 'life situation' of the subject. Here we are not interested in specific ideas but in the whole worldview of the subject. This may seem only a slight difference, but Mannheim had a deeper distinction in mind: not so much the content of certain ideas, but the form, the way in which knowledge in general happens to develop as a function of the life situation. What he intended was a broadening of the original concept of ideology in the direction of a *sociology of knowledge* (*Wissenssoziologie*), a 'method of research in social and intellectual history' (Mannheim, 1936: 69) which is concerned with the mutual relationships of the two. The general basic assumption is that 'the thought of every group is seen as arising out of its life conditions' (ibid.).

Sociology of knowledge should be non-evaluative, according to Mannheim. It does not aim at exposing specific lies or distortions but conducts a search into the ways in which, in general, cultural and scientific knowledge is interwoven with life conditions, defined by social and historical circumstances. The subjective, local and changeable nature of every knowledge claim, even of the scientist's own research, is unavoidable. Thought is 'a particularly sensitive index of social and cultural change' (ibid.: 74). (Scientific) thought has no history and domain of its own, apart and independent from its socioeconomic determinants. The sociology of knowledge aims at explaining theories from social factors.

Though Mannheim proposed, in 'The sociology of knowledge' (in Mannheim, 1936), to avoid the concept of ideology as much as possible, the term is still in existence. It has been used, however, rather ambiguously; sometimes it refers to Marx's critique of society and to the false ideas of the class-interested establishment; sometimes it is used merely as a descriptive term to denote some complex of social and political ideas as a whole, such as the Marxist, the liberal, socialist, or Christian-democratic ideology; and sometimes it is even used to refer to a philosophy or a vision about anything whatsoever. In all these shades of meaning the notion of unmasking ideas as subjective has been more or less preserved.

3.3   Critical Theory and the sociology of science

In Chapter 2 we saw that many philosophers of science came to doubt the basic ideas of positivism. One of the results of their criticism was that the history of science gained central importance in the new understanding of science. But the historiographic approach also changed. Previously the assumption was that science developed in a continuous and natural trajectory towards progress and enlightenment and that the production of true (scientific) knowledge is beyond and without social explanation. In the light of this assumption history was considered of no great importance because the latest state of the art always carried more truth than before; and the history of science could be no more than a set of anecdotes of superseded theories. According to this so-called *internal* history, science is an autonomous enterprise above and beyond the petty social interests of the scientists; it develops apart from the general history of society, it has its own progress and its own rules. Science *is*, and *has to be* (normatively) a pure, value-free, detached and rational search for truth.

The Frankfurt School and Critical Theory

In the wake of Marx and Mannheim neo-Marxist students took exception to this 'neat image' of science. They claimed that science is a social enterprise and, as such, is part of general history, reflecting interests, and social and cultural change. This was part of the philosophy of the so-called Frankfurt School, the Institute of Social Research in Germany, which gave its name to a movement. In this Institute the philosophy of Hegel, Marx and other idealist and materialist philosophers and their importance for social theory was much discussed. The staff of this avowedly Marxist organization, among whom Max Horkheimer, Theodor Adorno, Herbert Marcuse and Erich Fromm were the senior and the most famous members, was almost exclusively of Jewish descent and had to emigrate when Hitler came to power in 1933; but despite dispersion the Institute managed to remain more or less intact (Jay, 1973). *Critical Theory*, as their social philosophy was called, adopted Marx's critique of Hegel's idealist philosophy, that there is no abstract spirit as such, apart from material circumstances, but that the thoughts of people were rooted in their socioeconomic conditions. Their target was the closed systems of thought they saw emerging around them, such as Nazism and Stalinism. Concern for the 'open society' also guided Popper's study of science; his conclusion was rather that science could and should withdraw from the political scene. In the view of the critical social scientists, it was possible to be socialist without being totalitarian, and sociology can and should contribute to social change.

Many of the themes of Critical Theory, popular among the generation of the 1960s, were reiterated and elaborated by Jürgen Habermas, a post-war student of the Frankfurt School, in his famous essay 'Technik und Wissenschaft als "Ideologie"' (Technology and science as 'ideology': published in 1968, see Habermas, 1971) and in other influential work. In his view, the expansion of the state and bureaucracy in capitalist society and the increasing predominance of economic and technological thinking have killed independent thought and rational discussion of values and goals. Critical reason is reduced to *instrumental reason*, the search for the best (technical) means for the attainment of a given end (e.g. economic growth); this goal itself, however, is no longer rationally criticized or reflected upon. Values are merely subjective, a matter of taste, beyond rational debate. Social problems are defined as technical problems, the solution to which is best left to experts (technocracy). By mainly offering technical solutions, science and technology constitute instrumental rationality pre-eminently. They have become the leading forces in the economic progress of society and the only accepted forms of legitimation. In this way, instrumental reason has reached social life and has become the 'background ideology' of the depoliticized mass of the population.

A central theme, especially in Habermas' later work, is the interaction of people. Interaction is symbolically mediated, that is, by language. In this Habermas was influenced by the American pragmatists, especially George Herbert Mead (1863–1931) who defended the thesis that the individual mind emerges only in relation to other minds and that this interaction involves shared meanings and communication. Mead's ideas were first of all adopted by Herbert Blumer (1969) in the sociological theory of 'symbolic interactionism'. Things in the world are mediated through their symbolic content, their meaning. They are not inherently meaningful; they become meaningful by the way people act towards them. In their communicative interactions people share meanings or symbols. And so reality and the social order of norms and rules become the creations of actors, and every language user internalizes them. To understand the life of a group you have to identify its world of objects, that is, its symbols. Kindred ideas can be traced in hermeneutics and social constructionism. Habermas is especially interested in the problem of rationality. For him the kernel of sound rationality is *communicative action* (Habermas, 1984), a way of life in which undisturbed communication, unforced agreement and mutual understanding are possible. The goal of knowledge and science is not to search for correspondence with reality. On the contrary, there is no independent reality to catch in value-free theories. Habermas advocates a consensus theory of truth and his view of knowledge and science is that they guide communication about the world. One should arrive at consensus and shared opinion, which is made possible in a communicative community in which individuality and intersubjectivity, knowledge and morality, tradition and critical reflection are combined. This contrasts sharply with instrumental reason, which places discussions about values outside rational discourse.

Sociology of science

The social origins of science and knowledge already studied by philosophers and sociologists, more or less of Marxist leanings, became a central issue after Kuhn's seminal *Structure of Scientific Revolutions* of 1962. Though the concept of paradigm did not at first carry a socioeconomic meaning, in the ensuing debate on changes in scientific knowledge the social aspects of the production of knowledge and the concept of ideology or sociology of knowledge became central notions. The new Anglo-American critics of the positivistic picture of science (Quine, Hanson, Kuhn) and the elder, mostly German, critics of empiricism and positivism (Marx, Mannheim and other sociologists) joined hands; they all agreed that scientific knowledge cannot be simply 'read off' from the world, but is a socially conditioned phenomenon.

The sheer mass of studies presented as social studies or sociology of science is so overwhelming – in the words, not without irony, of critic Mario Bunge (1991–92), 'it has become a growth industry' – that we cannot hope to do justice to all the differences in approach, emphasis or selection of problems. For the sake of some ordering we will briefly set out two broad categories, and in due course some subcategories in both. The first class consists of historical studies of social or cultural influences on the development of scientific institutions, ways of thinking, concepts, methods, etc., in short, the *macroscopic* approach. The other category contains the more recent interest and studies in the production of scientific knowledge, the practice and content of scientific work, in short, the *microscopic* approach.

Social history of science

The external or contextual history of science is the oldest tradition in the sociology of science. This consists of studies of science in relation to wider social changes and refers to external factors as the explanation for scientific development. In the 1930s Robert Merton discussed in his famous doctoral dissertation, 'Science, technology and society in seventeenth century England' (1970), the modes of interplay between society, culture and science. It is, he stated in the original preface, 'an empirical examination of the genesis and development of some of the cultural values which underlie the large-scale pursuit of science' (1970: xxxi). In the 1970 preface he paraphrased the main sociological idea of the book, stating that 'the socially patterned interests, motivations and behaviour established in one institutional sphere – say, that of religion or economy – are interdependent with the socially patterned interests, motivations and behaviour obtaining in other institutional spheres – say, that of science' (ibid.: ix). And because the social structure is such that the same individuals have multiple social statuses and roles, scientific and religious, economic and political, it makes for the interplay of seemingly autonomous institutional spheres. Merton's study grapples, for instance, with the much debated question of the interplay of science and religion (Puritanism) in the seventeenth century, the thesis that the new Protestant religious ethos sanctioned natural science with its rationalism and empiricism, assuming that the study of nature enables a fuller appreciation of God's works. Merton stresses that the different institutional spheres, in this case religion and science, are indeed interdependent, and warns against the doctrine that there are universally dominant 'factors' in social development which result in claims to 'the economic determination of historical change', or its technological or political determination (ibid.: x). So he seeks answers to such questions as: 'How does a cultural emphasis upon social utility as a prime, let alone an exclusive, criterion for scientific work variously affect the rate and direction of advance in science?' And, once science has evolved forms of internal organization: 'How do patterns and rates of social interaction among scientists affect the development of scientific ideas?' (ibid.: ix).

Merton was the founder of the sociology of science in the English-speaking world, and numerous studies of the social or cultural history of science followed his example, especially after Kuhn's (1962) work. For instance, studies about the importance of hermeticism and alchemy for the development of science in the late sixteenth century (Yates, 1964, 1972); the social and cultural background of the development of mesmerism (Darnton, 1968); eugenics (Allen, 1976); phrenology (Shapin, 1975; Cantor, 1975); the use of social science in American industry (Baritz, 1960) and its application to other social problems (Napoli, 1981) to name only a few.

Other subcategories within this historical branch of the sociology of science tradition are the historical studies of scientific institutions, such as Hahn's study of the French Académie des Sciences (1971); and histories of the scientific professions, such as Geuter's history of the professionalization of psychology in Nazi Germany (1992).

Merton also made a sociological analysis of the norms of scientific conduct, an ethos of science – how to keep the community of researchers together.

3.4   The Strong Programme in the sociology of knowledge

While studies of the social circumstances and influences on the development of scientific theories, institutions and professions continued to appear abundantly, some sociologists of science began to focus their attention on the construction of scientific knowledge itself, and this can be seen as a shift in the sociology of science. In his analysis of the development of sociology of science Steve Woolgar (1988) has contended that the old sociology of science – the work of Merton and others – placed emphasis on science as a social institution and on the social relationships between knowledge producers, their social roles and the norms they followed. By doing this such studies adopted a view which was essentially a 'sociology of *scientists*' and neglected the very relationship between *scientific knowledge* and what is still seen as 'the objective, natural world'. In Woolgar's eyes the old sociologists of science were not radical enough. More recent work, he continued, 'emphasizes the relativity of scientific truth, calls for a sociological analysis of technical content' (1988: 41). What has to be studied is the way scientific knowledge is constructed and how what is considered true or untrue is the outcome not of a neutral and rational endeavour but of a *social* process: the very content of scientific theories, not only the organization of research, is studied as a function of social circumstances.

So whereas Merton and others concentrated on the institutions or group processes, a new sociology of science endeavoured to explain the very content of scientific theories as products of social factors.

Though Kuhn's and Mannheim's work can be regarded as steps in this direction of what is called 'sociology of scientific *knowledge*' rather than 'sociology of science' (in the sense of a community and its institutions), the breakthrough in this social epistemological research was brought about by the so-called 'strong programme' in the sociology of scientific knowledge launched by Barry Barnes, David Bloor and Steve Shapin (at the University of Edinburgh).

In his *Knowledge and Social Imagery* (1976) Bloor stated that the sociologist of scientific knowledge employs a definition of knowledge that is rather different from that of the philosopher:

> Instead of defining it as true belief, knowledge for the sociologist is whatever men take to be knowledge. It consists of those beliefs which men confidently hold to and live by. In particular the sociologist will be concerned with beliefs which are taken for granted or institutionalised, or invested with authority by groups of men. (Bloor, 1976: 3)

Not the questions of what truth is, or how we can arrive at true knowledge – these are *philosopher's* questions, but questions such as: 'How is knowledge transmitted; how stable is it; what processes go into its creation and maintenance; how is it organised and categorised into different disciplines or spheres?', are the *sociologist's* questions.

Bloor formulated four tenets which define what he baptized 'the strong programme in the sociology of knowledge' (ibid.: 4–5).

1. The sociology of scientific knowledge should be *causal*, that is, concerned with the conditions (social, economic, political, cultural, psychological) which bring about knowledge (claims).
2. It should be *impartial* with respect to truth and falsity, rationality or irrationality, success or failure.
3. Therefore it should be *symmetrical*, that is, the sociologist should invoke the same causes for success and for error in science; he should not credit rationality and logic for success stories and blame social factors for failures, as the standard image of science would have it. In a joint article Barnes and Bloor (1982: 22–3) define this requirement as an *equivalence postulate*, meaning 'that all beliefs are on a par with one another with respect to the causes of their credibility'. So, the sociologist must search

for the causes of a scientific belief, regardless of whether s/he evaluates the belief as true or rational, or as false and irrational.

4. The sociology of scientific knowledge should be *reflexive*; the patterns of explanation should be applicable to sociology itself; sociology is not immune to sociological analysis.

In other words, the sociologist of science must not only investigate the beliefs of other scientists, but must also attend to his/her own beliefs. So, the problem for the sociologist of science is how to avoid the danger of self-refutation. It seems that Barnes and Bloor think to escape this danger by their neutral standpoint on matters of truth and rationality, required by the third tenet. According to this they need neither to claim nor to negate the rationality of their own sociological theory; hence they get the chance to circumvent the danger of self-refutation (Derksen, 1985: 122).

The importance of the strong programme lies in the renewed attempt to ground relativism and the social construction of all (scientific) knowledge. The concept of truth is essential here. The process of judging a theory is an 'internal' one, according to Bloor – not a correspondence of the theory *with reality* but of the theory *with itself*. We never have independent access to reality: 'all that we have, and all that we need, are our theories and our experiences of the world'. And by 'experiences' he means 'our experimental results and our sensori-motor interactions with manipulatable objects' (Bloor, 1976: 34).

We think, however, that this brings him near to a refined, pragmatic realism, as becomes clearer when he contends that we cannot altogether abandon the concept of truth. The concept does a number of jobs (ibid.: 35–6). First there is what he calls the discriminatory function – we cannot but order our beliefs. Second there is the rhetorical function – the labels 'true' and 'false' play a role in argument, criticism and persuasion. The third job of the concept of truth is its 'materialist function', the 'obligatory character of truth' (as one of the fathers of sociology, Durkheim, called it): 'all our thinking instinctively assumes that we exist within a common external environment that has a determinate structure'. And Bloor adds: 'in practice the existence of an external world-order is never doubted' (ibid.: 36).

In our opinion, these ideas are remarkable for their slight undertone of realism, as in the following passage where Bloor opposes the anti-relativist 'assumption' that if something is a convention then it is 'arbitrary'. He replies that conventions are not arbitrary at all. The acceptance of a theory by a social group doesn't make it true, because the relation of a belief 'to the basic materialist picture of an independent world precludes this' (ibid.: 38). This seems to ring a realistic bell, indeed. Is there still a distinction between subject and object, between the scientist (knower) and things and events in the world? Does not the social construction of scientific knowledge preclude such a distinction? Apparently, even Bloor cannot avoid acknowledging the object side of scientific knowledge. And what about the object of the sociology of science itself? One critic, Roger Trigg (1993: 155), writes that the sociology of scientific knowledge takes as its focus 'the work and assumptions of scientists' and therefore is 'as dependent as any other form of intellectual activity on the idea of truth, and on the separation of subject . . . and object'.

On the other hand the strong programme presents itself as radically subjectivist. Already in the first of Bloor's four requirements, causality, he claims that there is no question of mere social influences, but that social factors *cause* scientific beliefs; that all knowledge, even mathematics – Bloor's case study – is shaped by society. A basic argument is that because 'what we count as scientific is largely "theoretical"' and because theories are not 'given in our experience', but 'give meaning to experience by offering a story about what underlies, connects and accounts for it, . . . this theoretical component of knowledge is a social component' (Bloor, 1976: 12–13). It is, however, far from clear that the underdetermination of theories by data, as the premiss suggests, leads to the conclusion that what is added should be social by nature. Behind this claim is the ubiquitous argument that because science is a social activity, which nobody would deny, science can only be understood in sociological terms. But, as Laudan writes: 'science is a multi-faceted process'.

> To argue that because science is a social activity we should view sociology as the primary tool for its investigation is like arguing that because syphilis is a social disease it is only or primarily the sociologist who can have scientific knowledge of syphilis. (Laudan, 1981: 194–5)

The strong programme rests on 'a form of relativism', writes Bloor in the conclusion to his book (Bloor, 1976: 142). We saw in the previous chapter that one of the criticisms of relativism is that a relativist cannot discriminate among different theories or knowledge claims. The recipe is – in the words of Gellner (1974: 48) – 'when in Rome, do (and above all, think) as the Romans do'. And Gellner adds that the recipe is empty: 'It is like the injunction "meet me at the town entrance" when the town has countless entrances, or none' (ibid.: 49–50).

According to Bloor, however, his relativism does not mean that 'anything goes'. His 'methodological relativism', summarized in the symmetry and reflexivity requirements, is the opposite of absolutism; no knowledge, not even sociology which designates the determining social factors, is absolute and final. Knorr-Cetina and Mulkay (1983: 5) call this 'epistemic relativism', which asserts that knowledge does not just mimic nature but is rooted in a particular time and culture. It should be distinguished from 'judgmental relativism' which claims that all forms of knowledge are equally valid and that we cannot discriminate among them, a position the authors reject.

Nevertheless, there is reason to be concerned about the consistency of Bloor's strong programme. It is strange, to say the least, to claim that the sociology of knowledge is a contribution to scientific knowledge, and at the same time to define that knowledge as 'whatever men take to be knowledge' (Bloor, 1976: 2). We think that knowledge, however fallible, is in principle a claim to universality (not in an absolute sense) and deserves to be called knowledge if it is 'properly' grounded; science requires that those grounds should be open to public scrutiny and rational debate.

3.5   The sociology of scientific practice

If one is convinced that the content of scientific knowledge is a product of social creation, the step towards direct examination of scientists at work follows naturally. A precursor of this kind of sociological analysis can be found in a book by the Polish bacteriologist Ludwik Fleck (1896–1961), *Genesis and Development of a Scientific Fact* (1935). This book is in the first place a study of the origin of the concept of syphilis. But that case study also grounds epistemological claims about the origin and nature of *facts*, and about the working of 'collective thinking' (*Denkkollektiv*) and 'style of thought' (*Denkstil*). Fleck argues that the scientist shares in an exchange of ideas and that his/her thoughts are socially constrained by the existing preconceptions and the stock of knowledge of the research group in which he or she participates. Facts do not exist a priori and are not extracted from or found in the world but are the social and historical products of collective understanding. Kuhn, in *The Structure of Scientific Revolutions* (1962), acknowledged his debt to Fleck's book.

Since the end of the 1970s more studies in the sociology of knowledge show a preference for the *empirical* study of scientific *practice* itself. What is investigated are the judgements, interpretations and activities of the scientists, the practice of the scientific enterprise. Besides preference for the 'microscopic' study of the production of science, these studies tend to give 'priority to the question HOW rather than to the question WHY' scientists act as they do; and they adopt a *constructivist* perspective (Knorr-Cetina and Mulkay, 1983: 7), that is, they take social processes as 'constitutive of the production and acceptance of knowledge claims' (ibid.: 9).

> Whereas we now have fairly detailed knowledge of the myths and circumcision rituals of exotic tribes, we remain relatively ignorant of the details of equivalent activity among tribes of scientists, whose work is commonly heralded as having startling or, at least, extremely significant effects on our civilisation. (Latour and Woolgar, 1979: 17)

This ethnographic analogy is chosen deliberately. What these studies do, especially *Laboratory Life* by Latour and Woolgar, is share the daily life of scientists in the laboratory, in this case the Salk Institute for Biological Studies, a private laboratory in California. The focus of *Laboratory Life* was the 'routinely occurring minutiae' of the work carried out there, for instance the daily encounters, the working discussions, the production of papers and the culture of publication. They called the project an *anthropology of science* for a number of reasons (ibid.: 27 ff.).

First they provided, just as an anthropologist would do, a body of observations presented as a preliminary research report about the 'belief system and material production' of one specific group of scientists. Secondly, in order to retrieve the 'craft character of scientific activity', they collected and described the observations in a particular setting, because understanding of science had been dogged by the problem that the reports of the scientists themselves are silent about the ways and the circumstances in which science is done and 'conceal the nature of the activity which typically gives rise to their research reports'. The prolonged immersion of an outside observer in the daily activities of scientists was regarded as one of the better ways to answer such questions as, 'How is it that the realities of scientific practice become transformed into statements about how science has been done?' Thirdly, in order to reduce the mystery which surrounds scientific activity they adopted, paradoxically, the anthropological notion of strangeness, that is, they bracketed their familiarity with the object of study and did not take too much for granted. Because 'there are no a priori reasons for supposing that scientists' practice is any more rational than that of outsiders', they made the activities of the laboratory seem as strange as possible, by approaching it in as unprejudiced a way as possible. By framing their methods in this way Latour and Woolgar intended to comply with the requirement of *reflexivity*: to subject their own sociological methodology to the same rigour as they did the objects of their scrutiny.

The constructivist perspective of the book is clear. In order to demonstrate the 'idiosyncratic, local, heterogeneous, contextual, and multifaceted character of scientific practices' (1979: 152) the authors want to show the micro-processes at work in the constitution of phenomena such as 'having ideas', the way beliefs are created and adopted in a 'group's thinking process'. They point to the use of logical arguments and proofs, suggesting that the logical character of reasoning is only part of a complex of interpretation which comprises 'local, tacit negotiations, constantly changing evaluations, and unconscious or institutionalized gestures' (ibid.). One of the conclusions of the work is that 'facts' are socially constructed:

> The construction and dismantling of the same statement can be monitored by direct observation, so that what was a 'thing out there' can be seen to fold back into a statement which is referrred to as a 'mere string of words', a 'fiction', or an 'artefact'. (ibid.: 180)

Because of the epistemological assumptions this genetic and microscopic approach within the sociology of knowledge is called 'the programme of *constructivism*' by Karin Knorr-Cetina (1981; Knorr-Cetina and Mulkay, 1983). In opposition to the notion that scientific investigation is descriptive, and that it concerns the factual relations between its products and an external reality, the constructivist interpretation considers the products of science 'as first and foremost the result of a process of (reflexive) fabrication'. Accordingly it involves an investigation of 'how scientific objects are produced in the laboratory rather than a study of how facts are preserved in scientific statements about nature' (Knorr-Cetina, 1983: 119). Elsewhere Knorr-Cetina says that 'the world as it is, is a consequence rather than a cause of what goes on in science' (In Callebaut, 1993: 180). Nowhere in the laboratory, she writes, do we find 'nature' or 'reality'; on the contrary, scientists operate upon and within a 'highly preconstructed artifactual reality' and their 'instrumentally accomplished observations intercept natural courses of events' (Knorr-Cetina, 1983: 119) – scientific reality is an artefact. The network of decisions and selections of methods, measurements, formulations and interpretations contribute to this artificiality and invest scientific products with a 'decision-impregnated character'. In short, scientific consensus is not fully based on evidential considerations and not fully accounted for in terms of technical rationales.

Because language is of the utmost importance in the sociological constructivist and in the social constructionist approach (see Chapter 2), discourse analysts came to highlight the importance and even the priority (Mulkay et al., 1983) of their methods for the micro-genetic study of scientific investigation. *Discourse analysis* is a method of analysis of all kinds of discourse, of the government, the police, the classroom, the media. Analysis of scientific discourse shares with the sociology of science, of course, the epistemological conviction that scientists' data, methods and products are a result of social construction. It contends that not only are the conversations and discussions about professional organization, publicity, fund raising, etc. social by nature, but the discussions in learned journals and during congresses, constitutive of scientific knowledge itself, are also social and contingent. Behind the formal scientific literature lie personal and social contingencies. Therefore, a systematic investigation of the social production of scientific discourse is 'an essential preliminary step in developing a satisfactory sociological analysis of action and belief in science' (Mulkay et al., 1983: 194).

In *Science. The Very Idea* (1988) Woolgar reiterated in a radical way his critique on the assumptions of traditions in the history, philosophy, and even (old) sociology of science: namely, the view that science is 'something special and distinct from other forms of cultural and social activity', whereas in Woolgar's view, scientific beliefs and products are 'rhetorical accomplishments'. The traditional idea was 'that the objects of the natural world are real, objective and enjoy an independent pre-existence', whereas Woolgar thinks that the contents of scientific knowledge are social by origin. And he criticizes what he calls 'the persistent notion of knowledge as an individualistic and mentalistic activity', 'the enduring respect for the work and achievements of "great men"', and the complete failure 'to take up the relativist themes' (1988: 26).

Underlying these assumptions, according to Woolgar, there is a basic *fallacy* – the supposed distinction between 'representation' and 'object', such as the distinction between knowledge and facts, between voltmeter reading and voltage, between documentary evidence and the historical situation, between image and reality, between questionnaire response and respondent's attitude (ibid.: 31, his examples). The problem that follows from this fallacy is 'the adequacy of connection' between the two. What he means, of course, is the epistemological idea of truth as correspondence: first there is the object which, then, is represented; and this representation is understood as corresponding to the object. But, says Woolgar, there is an 'intimate interdependence' of representation and represented object, such that 'the sense of the former is elaborated by drawing on "knowledge of" the latter, and knowledge of the latter is elaborated by what is known about the former' (ibid.: 33). This ideology of representation is the kernel of *objectivism* and even sociologists of knowledge, who should know better, sometimes commit this fallacy. Therefore, Woolgar thinks, the fallacy should be deconstructed; we should invert the order: the representation precedes the represented object; and we should resist 'the persistent construal of science as a distinct topic for study, an object "out there", beyond us *qua* observers/inquirers, and essentially separate and distinct from our own writing practices' (ibid.).

But the world 'talks back'

Accepting that knowledge is never absolute, that the prejudices of knowing subjects are involved in the determination of what there is, does not preclude independent counterpressure from the world, constraining the interpretations, measurements, methods and local decisions scientists may invent. We do not meet the world in ideas and theories only: we do not live in the world only as theorizing and talking creatures, sooner or later we also act upon our beliefs so that in this sense we cannot arbitrarily and with impunity believe what we want. It is no naive realism to suppose that knowledge is to be seen as a subject–object relation and that this epistemology need not be replaced by one in which a subject–subject understanding is all there is. Knowledge is fallible, but beliefs and theories help us to get a picture and a grip of the world and enable us to live in it. Concepts and conceptual systems are held by humans, but they always have referents, are always about something outside the subject, the existence and nature of which can be a source of disagreement. We need knowledge about the world that is properly grounded and can be trusted; we have to discriminate between true and false, between the trustworthy and the dubious, in order to be able to act. The very *raison d'être* of science is information about the world – 'securing answers to our questions about how things stand in nature in terms of description, classification and explanation' (Rescher, 1987: 36).

Though humans have a firm hand in how the 'external' world looks these days, and pure nature, untouched by humans, is nearly extinct, we do live in a world which is not altogether a human or scientific creation and of which we too are in part the products. Despite the artificiality of much scientific investigation, we do not live in a reality that is altogether artificial. And even when nature and culture are merged, even when nature is almost 'acculturated', humans find themselves in that world and need knowledge about that reality. Scientists allow themselves to construct virtual realities for a while, but sooner or later their products as well as the scientists themselves have to face reality of which they, like everybody else, are inhabitants. That scientists 'are strategists, choosing the most opportune moment, engaging in potentially fruitful collaborations, evaluating and grasping opportunities, and rushing to credited information' (Latour and Woolgar, 1979: 213) is probably a correct empirical description of modern scientific enterprise. Scientists are human and do not live in a social vacuum, but it is a wholly different matter to draw fundamental epistemological conclusions, like saying that knowledge is whatever people take to be knowledge (Bloor, 1976: 2).

To sum up, it is natural, we think, that the overall purpose of knowledge and science, and therefore of scientists as well as of non-scientists, is to know what there is and how things work, however they might be distracted by local interests, however they might be part of the social mechanisms of communication and interaction, and however they might be wrong in their beliefs. Sociologists of knowledge pretend to replace epistemology, but, by their own admission, they cannot do this in the name of truth, since they consider truth to be local – so, one could say, why should we worry about those theories? Though Bloor tries to ward off this danger of self-refutation by staying neutral in matters of truth, he appears not to escape the quagmire of relativism. As for ourselves, we do take sociological analysis of science and knowledge seriously, but we disagree with its epistemological pretensions. Social studies of science are highly relevant to the understanding of the processes and development of science, but we take them as contributions in the same way as psychological studies of science and knowledge investigate certain aspects of the development of scientific knowledge.

3.6 And what about a *psychology* of science?

Though the investigation of psychological aspects of science and scientists seems to be in a less advanced state than the sociological approach to science and knowledge, the concern for the social genesis of scientific knowledge is in part a psychological, a social-psychological, concern. There are, however, many more psychological aspects and objects of overall science that can be studied in the context of *science studies* (or the 'science of science', or 'meta-science'). In fact there is already a considerable psychological literature pertaining to science studies, but the field is not well structured and the many studies of psychological aspects of science are scattered (see for many titles the bibliography in Fisch, 1977; for a more recent reader and many references, Gholson et al., 1989). The psychology of science can be seen as the fourth 'core discipline' of science studies, next to the philosophy, history, and sociology of science (Houts, 1989). Adopting the definition of the psychology of science given by Gholson et al. (1989: 9), 'the scientific study of scientific behaviour and mental processes', we suggest for the sake of some ordering and to give an impression of the field the following broad categories:

1. *Social-psychological studies of the scientific enterprise*, the scientific community, and the receiving public. In this category we find historical studies about, for example, the religious background of scientists; culture of publication; political influences; institutional mechanisms; career patterns; the peer review system; studies on the reception of scientific beliefs and concepts; the making of psychological society, etc. In fact, many studies in this category have been started and developed within the sociology of science.
2. *Social-psychological studies of the acquisition of scientific knowledge*, that is, social influences on cognitive processes, such as mechanisms of socialization into a scientific belief system; psychological accounts of

theory change; the social basis of scientific discoveries (Brannigan, 1981); scientific networks; and many of the so-called ethnographic laboratory studies (the behaviour of scientific communities) we became acquainted with in the previous section.

3. *(Cognitive) psychological studies of scientific knowledge*, that is, concerning the structure and processes of the generation and fixation of scientific beliefs; studies about scientific thinking (Tweney et al., 1981) and reasoning (Faust, 1984), creativity (Gruber, 1974; Amabile, 1983), the genius (Simonton, 1988), scientific discovery (Kantorovich, 1993; Shrager and Langley, 1989), conceptual change (Thagard, 1992). Studies in this category can have a general approach, or can be person-oriented (by means of case studies).

It will be clear that the psychology of science will in fact overlap with studies of science from the other disciplines, the philosophy, history and sociology of science; take for instance the psychohistorical case studies of scientists, such as *A Portrait of Isaac Newton* by Frank Manuel (1968); or the cognitive historical case studies, such as Ryan Tweney's work on Faraday's thought (1985, 1989).

Perhaps one will feel a tension between the second and the third category. The social constructionist approach denies the importance of individual cognitive processes, because beliefs, reasoning and facts are supposed to be social by nature. On the other hand, traditionally, the other disciplines of metascience, especially philosophy, had a distaste for psychological inquiry, as we saw in Chapter 2. As one of the tenets of positivist philosophy of science was to divorce epistemological questions from psychological questions, many authors 'ridiculed or explicitly dismissed the psychology of science as an undesirable flirtation with subjectivism, irrationality, and relativism – those legendary foes of the Western philosophical tradition' (Houts, 1989: 50).

However, appeals to extrahistorical foundations of scientific rationality, to the independence and autonomy of logical laws and criteria, being the general laws of science, and to the notion of the 'proper' study of science (the philosopher's ideal science) are undermined and at least some subjectivity in the scientific enterprise has to be considered. One of the early authors on psychology of science, Mahoney (1976), contends that we cannot separate (scientific) knowledge from the knower, nor epistemology from psychology. The social psychologist Kruglanski (1991) asserts that because of the nonunique character of science, as well as because of its unique aspects, science is highly amenable to study from the social science perspective. The relevance of psychological inquiry derives from the assumption that scientists as humans abide by the regularities of social behaviour and cognition. In this sense, science shares its modes of knowledge acquisition with everyday practice. And in so far as 'Western science is a unique societal institution that is committed to a unique set of values, subscribes to a unique set of assumptions, interacts in unique ways with other societal agencies, and regulates its own internal affairs (allocations of funds, publication and communication) in its own unique ways' (Kruglanski, 1991: 226), the sociological and the psychological perspective are highly relevant.

Cognition

The third group of psychological studies of science, mentioned above, borders on the study of cognition, which is in part the business of psychology: for example research on observation, thinking and reasoning, problem-solving, experimentation, etc. In the last decades it has become clear that cognition is a multidisciplinary phenomenon. It began as a chapter of philosophy, namely, the study of knowledge or epistemology. Understood as the groundwork for science it became the most significant part of orthodox philosophy of science. However, in post-positivistic philosophy it has been acknowledged that epistemology is not the concern of philosophy alone but that it has to be continuous with science. This is sometimes called the *naturalistic turn*: epistemology should be naturalized (Quine, 1969; Kornblith, 1994; see also Chapter 1, p. 13).

Kantorovich (1993), for example, 'naturalizes' the epistemological concept of discovery by applying the evolutionary model to it. One of the most important kinds of creative discovery in science, he contends, are 'serendipitous discoveries'. These discoveries are made when scientists unintentionally solve a problem while intending to solve a different one. In his book he demonstrates that a serendipitous discovery, like a biological mutation, 'can be explained as an "error" which infiltrated a routine procedure – a research program' (Kantorovich, 1993: 7). In this way he borrows the element of chance from the natural selection model and applies it to the concept of discovery, a facet of scientific creation which he labels 'tinkering', adopting the notion that the French biologist François Jacob (1977) uses for characterizing the evolutionary process. The generation of novelty in science is not a matter of sheer chance, however; serendipitous discoveries contribute to the adaptability of science, making science a major tool by the use of which the human species 'does not wait passively for environmental changes to occur but creates the changes by its own activity' (Kantorovich, 1993: 208).

Experimental research

Problem-solving and the reasoning process are among the favourite subjects in empirically based and experimental cognitive psychology, and it stands to reason that an interest in scientific discovery and the scientific reasoning process should appear on the agenda. Klahr and Dunbar (1988) developed a model of the scientific reasoning process. They propose that scientific reasoning requires search in two problem spaces: a hypothesis space and an experimental space. They placed subjects in a simulated scientific discovery context by first teaching them how to use an electronic device and then asking them to discover how a hitherto unencountered function worked. The subjects had to formulate hypotheses based on their prior knowledge, conduct experiments, and evaluate the results of their experiments. The general model of Scientific Discovery as Dual Search (SDDS) shows how search in two problem spaces shapes hypothesis generation, experimental design, and the evaluation of hypotheses. Computer programs play a major role in this

kind of research (Shrager and Langley, 1989), because the idea is that thinking is a computational process and Artificial Intelligence research is
concerned with designing models of information processing. Kulkarni and
Simon (1988) developed a program, KEKADA, which models the heuristics
Hans Krebs used in his discovery of the urea cycle in 1932, an important
event in biochemistry.

Paul Thagard (1992) deals with conceptual change. Since Kuhn (1962) we
have been acquainted with the concept of scientific revolutions. But how
exactly do conceptual revolutions occur? What *are* the conceptual systems
whose transformation is so fundamental to scientific development?
Conceptual change is of general psychological interest, since people other
than scientists also experience it, writes Thagard (1992: 4). 'Children's acquisition of knowledge is not simply a matter of accretion of new facts. Rather it
involves an important restructuring of their conceptual systems' (ibid.). His
approach to the thinking process in the history of science and in developmental psychology is, as with the other experimental cognitivists we mentioned
before, computational. But, whereas Artificial Intelligence (AI) researchers
have concentrated on cases of learning by accretion of knowledge, Thagard
wants to extend AI and machine learning research to revolutionary replacement of complexes of concepts. He offers a theory that explains cases of
conceptual change in the history of science, and tries to answer questions
such as: Why did the oxygen theory of combustion supersede the phlogiston
theory? Why is Darwin's theory of evolution by natural selection superior to
creationism? For this reason he examines, among other reasoning processes,
how we in general infer to explanatory hypotheses, and how we determine the
explanatory coherence of a hypothesis, that is, how we assess the credibility of
hypotheses, their fit with the evidence and other hypotheses; in short, how we
infer to the best explanation (see Chapter 1, p. 12).

These are only a few examples of the research that is carried out in the field
of the psychology of science. There is more, but the work is scattered; the field
is still in need of a framework.

Philosophy of mind, the subject of the next chapter, is the philosophical contribution to the multidisciplinary science of cognition and it raises important
theoretical issues in its own right. However, philosophy of mind can also be
understood as a contribution of philosophical psychology to the study of
knowledge and the 'science of science', in so far as it helps us to understand
how we – or scientists, for that matter – make sense of the world, by observation, interpretation and intervention. Thus this concern can be seen as
part of the psychology of science.

Suggested reading

On relativism, pro or contra (see also Chapter 2):
Hollis and Lukes (1982), a reader with important texts.
Laudan (1990)
Jarvie (1993), a review of some recent titles.
On Mannheim:
Kettler et al. (1984)
On the Frankfurt School and Critical Theory:
Jay (1973)
Held (1980)
A discussion of Habermas:
Thompson and Held (1982)

Studies and cases in the sociology of science:
Mendelsohn et al. (1977)
Krohn et al. (1978)
Knorr et al. (1980)
Meja and Stehr (1984)

For the psychological and cognitive view in the study of science:
Fuller et al. (1983)
Gholson et al. (1989)
De Mey (1982)

Basics of the Strong Programme:
Barnes (1977)
Bloor (1976)
Barnes and Bloor (1982)
Barnes et al. (1996)
Some critics of sociology of science, especially of the Strong Programme:
Bunge (1991–92)
Laudan (1981)
Slezak (1994)
Trigg (1993)

Discourse analysis, a journal:
Discourse and Society. An International Journal for the Study of Discourse and Communication in their Social, Political and Cultural Contexts (London: Sage)
On scientists at work:
Knorr-Cetina (1981)
Latour and Woolgar (1979)
Latour (1987)
Pickering (1992)

On scientific elites, power relations and the organization of research:
Elias et al. (1982)

4

Philosophy of Mind

4.1   Introduction: the nature of mind

Philosophy of mind

At the most abstract level, philosophy of mind is concerned with the basic notion of psychology – what is the nature of mind? – more or less in the way philosophy of physics is concerned with the nature of time and space, and philosophy of biology is concerned with the nature of life or the concept of natural selection.

Broadly speaking, problems in the philosophy of mind can be clustered into four categories.

1. What *are* mental states?
2. What is the relation between mental and neurophysiological processes (the mind–brain problem)?
3. What is the relation between mind and world: questions of representation, intentionality and meaning (semantics)?
4. What is the status of 'folk psychology'?

Apart from their relevance for psychology, answers to these questions are extremely important for the epistemological problems with which we were concerned in the previous chapters: we deal here with fundamental notions, like the relation between representation and reality, or the unity of science. In this sense philosophy of mind (philosophy of cognition) also contributes to the general science of science.

In the following, we will use these four questions as guidelines to discuss the several ideas and theories in the philosophy of mind. In section 4.2 we will set out the core concepts in the philosophy of mind. In section 4.3 the orthodox view in cognitive psychology, the computational theory of mind, will be presented. This view has been contested in the last two decades by eliminativism and connectionism. This will be dealt with in section 4.4. In section 4.5 we will discuss other views on the same issues; and in section 4.6 alternatives for the mechanist model of mind. But first we will briefly go into some answers that were given before the cognitive revolution of the 1960s.

Although contemporary views are strongly influenced by the ascent of computer models and more recently neuroscience, some important questions date back to the pre-computer era. Before, say, 1960, roughly three options were available for conceptualizing the nature of mind and its relation to the brain: dualism, materialistic reductionism (the mind–brain identity theory), and linguistic behaviourism.

Dualism

The traditional view of the relation of mind and body was dualism: the doctrine that mind and matter are different substances and should be studied by different methods. The historical culprit was René Descartes (1596–1650). He distinguished a material substance (*res extensa*) and a thought substance (*res cogitans*) which are independent. He then of course ran into the problem of how these might interact: how one's thoughts lead to movements of one's limbs; and how a blow on the head leads to a feeling of pain; how to account for the obvious interactions of bodily and mental processes, as in fatigue, alcohol effects or psychosomatic diseases. Descartes suggested that the pituitary gland was the locus where the thought substance and the nervous system interact, which leaves the philosophical problem as mysterious as it was. This position is known as *interactionism*: it holds that there must be a point of contact where the mind and the body interact. In our own time, Popper and Eccles (1977) state that through cortical modules the immaterial Self monitors and directs its brain. Of course, this only transforms the problem – how can the immaterial mind influence bodily processes? – into the question: how can the Self, the immaterial mind, act upon cortical structures? Popper and Eccles contribute little in answer to that conundrum.

Another position within the dualist mainstream is *epiphenomenalism*: it holds that mental processes are by-products of bodily processes, without any causal influences on the body, more or less like the whistle on a steam engine, which reflects the physical process, but doesn't change it.

Cartesian dualism is routinely ridiculed in philosophy textbooks. However, until quite recently it seemed inconceivable that material systems could possess consciousness and intelligence. Therefore the view held by most psychologists was something like *property dualism*: it was conceded that there is no independent mental substance, that mental processes are properties or products of the brain, although it was deemed practically impossible to study them by neurophysiological methods, and psychologists were free to go about their business without paying attention to physiology. Therefore, it is arguable that, obligatory references to the brain notwithstanding, theoretical psychology has until recently been methodologically (or epistemologically) dualist.

Identity and reduction

The second option consisted of a number of materialist or reductionist theories. The most explicit in the 1960s and early 1970s was the so-called *mind–brain identity theory* (Feigl, 1967; Borst, 1970). It held that mental states like pain or seeing a yellow after-image could empirically be identified with neural events like the firing of certain nerve fibres. The standard example is the supposed identity of pain and the firing of C-fibres; interestingly, every one of the dozen or so philosophers who recycled the example at the time apparently failed to notice that it is neurophysiological nonsense, since C-fibres are characterized by myelin sheaths and conduction velocity, and some C-fibres do subserve pain, while others have different functions.

Much ink has been spilled over logical questions associated with such identifications. For example, can mental properties like pain which have no physical location be considered logically identical with events that take place in specific locations in the brain? At least, there seems to be a difference in location, so they cannot be considered identical, it was argued.

The death blow for the identity theory was the doctrine of *functionalism* (see also Chapter 1, p. 27 ff.), first put forward in a paper by Hilary Putnam (1961). Putnam suggested that functionally identical mental processes can be realized in different ways in different physical or physiological systems, where these realizations have little or no physical properties in common. We might say, for instance, that a computer 'thinks' about a chess move in about the same way as we do, although it has a physical make-up completely different from ours. This so-called *multiple realizability* effectively precludes identification of mental and physical events. The idea can be illustrated by considering a computer program, which can be run on different types of computers. The program will be functionally identical, will work in the same way, independently of differences in the computer chips. Analogously, mental processes like being angry or thinking about chess can be functionally identical in beings with completely different nerve systems or processors. We will come back to this in section 4.2.

Linguistic behaviourism

Linguistic behaviourism was the third view on the nature of mind; it was initiated by the later Wittgenstein, and by Ryle and Malcolm.

The linguistic focus comes from Wittgenstein's conceptual analysis, which explores the rules of commonsense discourse. Philosophical psychology is about exploring the 'logical geography' of our mental concepts, not about discovering facts in the mind.

Gilbert Ryle (1949) launched a devastating attack on the Cartesian myth of the Ghost in the Machine, the idea that the mind is an inner realm of ghostly events (sensations, thoughts, pains, intelligence), which reside in a 'second theater' alongside the real life theatre of physical events and public behavioural acts. His thesis is that this myth rests upon conceptual confusion, more precisely, on a *category mistake*.

Suppose you show a visitor around Oxford. You point out the buildings of the colleges, and when you eventually sit down exhausted in the Bear over a pint of Hall's Bitter, she asks which of the buildings you have shown her is Oxford University. She makes the category mistake of assuming that the university is a building among the others, rather than the collective of the colleges. Likewise, assuming that *the* mind is a thing like the body; that mental events are events like physical ones, only in a non-physical realm, are category mistakes, according to Ryle.

Ryle goes on to expose the confusion that results from juxtaposing mind and body, as in: 'We have a body *and* a mind', and mental to physical events; and treating mental events as if they were immaterial causes and effects in a 'mental theater'. If you think that you can explain seeing something as the having of an internal mental ghostly event (mental recognition), then you have to explain a whole internal chain of ghostly causes and effects. If you think that acting consists in having a mental event (an intention) that causes your limbs to move, then you are stuck with the 'wire and pulley question': how an immaterial event can interface with, and cause a physical movement.

Ryle's way out of the confusion caused by 'inner realm' explanations of external behaviour has been dubbed *linguistic behaviourism*. It holds that mental concepts refer to *behaviour* and behavioural *dispositions*. A disposition is a tendency to behave in a certain way in certain circumstances; for instance, glass being brittle is a disposition, meaning to shatter when hit. Referring to someone as intelligent means that she will behave in certain ways under certain conditions; for instance, that she will score high marks in mathematics, that she will win a game of chess, etc. The concept of intelligence as we use it in daily life does not refer to an inner mechanism of immaterial cogs and wheels, but it serves to describe and predict behaviour. No reference to the inner life of a ghostly Cartesian mind-substance is needed.

There are, however, objections. The reason that linguistic behaviourism is out of fashion these days is that it cannot go beyond what is implicit in commonsense knowledge. It aims at describing the 'logical geography' of our concepts; as a philosophical approach, it tries to dissolve conceptual confusions by exposing traditional metaphysical problems as conceptual fallacies, and thus to solve or dissolve metaphysical problems. Ryle's classic is a philosophical delight to read, but having done so, one knows little more about mind than before. Linguistic analysis is a great way to undermine 'bad habits of thought', but does little to increase our knowledge. Reflecting on the use of daily language and its rules, straightening its fabric, showing where it goes off the track is hardly likely to produce new knowledge and compete with new discoveries in the age of neuroscience. The enterprise of linguistic analysis has been likened to restricting astronomy to a painstaking analysis of what is meant by the statement that the sun rises in the east and sets in the west.

4.2   The explananda: consciousness, intentionality, representation

Consciousness

Before discussing some prominent authors it is useful to take stock of possible answers to the first main question: what is, at core, the nature of mind?

As mentioned, since Descartes consciousness has been seen as the essence of mind; and any philosophical story of mind had to account for consciousness. Whereas the continental tradition saw consciousness among other things as an *activity*, to some extent creating itself (Van Rappard, 1979), the Anglo-Saxon tradition has confined consciousness to so-called *qualia*, pure experiences or sensations: how it feels to have pain, or to see red (see section 4.5, p. 137 ff.).

Until recently, consciousness was more or less absent in the philosphy of mind, where attention was focused on *intentionality*. Those who wanted to tell a story about it usually construed it in a functional way, as somehow derived from the information-processing capacities of the mind/brain (e.g. Lycan, 1987; Dennett, 1991; Flanagan, 1991). That is, notions like cognition, mental content and information are seen as primary, and consciousness as secondary.

Recently, Searle (1992) has tried to reverse the tables. He argues that conscious experience logically precedes cognition: cognitive processes are either conscious or can be brought to consciousness. The brain processes that cannot be conscious are not cognitive but brute neurophysiology (section 4.5, p. 131 ff.).

Intentionality

Whereas traditionally consciousness was considered the characteristic of mind in contradistinction to matter, nowadays philosophers concentrate on the particular property of mind that goes by the somewhat technical term, intentionality.

The Austrian philosopher Franz Brentano (1838–1917) is usually credited with the definition of intentionality as the 'mark of the mental'. The *locus classicus* is Brentano's *Psychologie vom empirischen Standpunkt* (Brentano, 1924). According to Brentano, the defining characteristic of mental states, distinguishing them from physics, is their property of being *directed* towards an object, or having some content.

> Jedes psychisches Phänomen ist durch das charakterisiert . . . was wir . . . die Beziehung auf einen Inhalt, die Richtung auf ein Objekt (worunter hier nicht eine Realität zu verstehen ist), oder die immanente Gegenständlichkeit nennen würden. [Every psychological phenomenon is characterized by something we would call a directedness towards a content, an object (here not a thing in reality), or something immanent.] (Brentano, 1924: 124–5)

Thus a mental state, unlike a physical state, includes an object or content within itself: the intentional object. This implies that *aboutness* is a criterion for the distinction between mind and matter. Intentionality, defined as the ability of the mind to refer to something outside itself, to be about something, distinguishes the mental from the physical. Your thoughts represent things, a cup of coffee or the mountain Fujiyama, whereas the cup of coffee and the Fujiyama are not about anything.

It will be clear that notions like representation, meaning and mental content are closely related to intentionality. They all refer to the ability of mental or cognitive states to indicate something beyond themselves. Incidentally, one might argue that some non-mental things or states have meaning or content; that this book is about or represents theoretical issues in psychology or that traffic signs mean something. However, you will agree that these have only *derived intentionality*, they depend on some original intentional system that can interpret them (Searle, 1992).

Naturalizing intentionality

Brentano himself presented his concept of intentionality in the context of the demarcation between mental (*psychische*) and physical (*physische*) phenomena (Brentano, 1924: 111–24). In this view, the entire world can be divided into the two mutually exclusive categories of mental and physical phenomena (ibid.: 109). And for many philosophers of mind a definite 'mark of the mental' is important because it provides a last line of defence against the attempts to reduce the mind to physical or physiological processes (see e.g. Bechtel, 1988b; Flanagan, 1992).

A major issue in modern philosophy of mind is whether and how intentionality in physical systems (brains or computers) is thinkable. This project is called 'naturalizing' intentionality. Since most contemporary philosophers of mind are materialists, who believe that physical processes are all there is, they feel compelled to give an account of the phenomena of intentionality in natural mechanistic or physical terms. Descartes' and Brentano's position, that mind is an irreducible entity apart from nature, is seen as unscientific, invoking mysterious unexplainable entities.

The ideal is to understand intentionality as a property of natural systems, something that at least biological organisms can have, and perhaps machines and computers too; and to explain it in mechanistic, computational or biological terms.

Mental content and imaginary objects

A further aspect of Brentano's theory is that the intentional object is not necessarily identical with a real object outside the mind. It can be imaginary or non-existent: one can think about a unicorn or fear a werewolf. This concept of intentionality and more precisely, the notion of non-existent intentional objects, captures some important aspects of mind – abstraction and imagination. Being aware of objects not present in the visual field, and goal-directed activity, planning to realize a goal that is not yet present, are typical mental capacities.

Even those who think that Brentano's philosophical concept of intentionality with its metaphysical implications is a red herring, accept that some degree of independence from the directly given is an important characteristic of mentality (Rorty, 1993; see Looren de Jong, 1991), that is difficult to explain in naturalistic terms or mechanisms.

Propositional attitudes and folk psychology

Another way to express the property of intentionality and to say that mental states have content, is to explain mental states linguistically. A proposal dating back to Bertrand Russell (1988) is that a mental state takes the form of an attitude to a proposition. Mental content can be expressed as a proposition (it is raining), a kind of sentence in the head, to which the subject takes an attitude (belief, desire, hope, fear). You can hope, fear or believe that it will rain, that the earth is flat, that interest rates will fall, etc. Such mental states are known as *propositional attitudes*. Thus, the essence of mental life is that it consists of a host of *representations* in a sentence-like format, plus the mental attitudes to them. In this view, beliefs and desires, and representations are the stuff the mind is made of.

So-called *folk psychology* refers to (supposed) commonsense explanations of our fellows (and of ourselves) using beliefs and desires; something like: he leaves his office because he desires a cup of coffee, and believes that the canteen is open; a politician cuts taxes because she desires to be re-elected and believes the voters will reward their benefactor. The point about these examples is the 'because': beliefs and desires seem to explain the behaviour of humans in the same way gravity explains the falling of objects. Such commonsense explanations are interpreted by (linguistic) philosophers like Jerry Fodor (1981) as being in line with their ideas on intentionality, cognitive science and the nature of mind. Fodor thinks that folk psychology necessarily assumes propositional attitudes, that therefore we must literally have propositions in our heads, and that these can be thought to cause our behaviour as in a natural law. Cognitive science is in the business of finding the intentional laws that explain our behaviour as a result of the knowledge and goals we have (Bechtel and Abrahamsen, 1993).

Fodor's central thesis is that propositional attitudes are not only essential in a philosophical reconstruction of folk psychology, but that they are also central notions of an adequate cognitive science. In his view that is no coincidence: cognitive science vindicates the naive notions about mental processes in more or less the same way as physics vindicates naive commonsense notions about the solidity of matter and falling objects. He takes beliefs and desires to be real in the most literal sense, as entities literally existing somewhere, somehow in the mind. Behaviour is literally caused by entities in the head (beliefs/desires, propositional representations): your taking an umbrella is caused by your belief that it is raining and your desire to stay dry. Thus, causal scientific explanation is compatible with commonsense psychology taken literally. This is roughly analogous to the way a computer program exists and drives the behaviour of the computer. Fodor's *Computational Theory of Mind (CTM)* buttresses this claim.

Churchland (1989) on the other hand wants to eliminate both, folk

psychology and the CTM, and replace them with neurophysiological concepts (see section 4.4, p. 114 ff.). Others, like Clark (1989), contend that while
neurophysiology may change the face of cognitive science and displace the
CTM, this might leave folk psychology untouched, where it belongs: with
commonsense experience and communication (see section 4.5, p. 125 ff.).

Representations

In cognitive science the concept of representations is supposed to play a pivotal role (Fodor, 1981; Sterelny, 1990; Cummins, 1989). The mainstream in
the philosophy of mind (also called the 'orthodox' or the 'classical' view of
cognitivism), led by Fodor, has joined the topics of intentionality, mental
content, folk psychology, beliefs and desires, representations, cognition, functionalism and computation into one coherent view. The idea is that mental
representations and mental computations constitute the machinery of the
mind. Between stimulus and response, a series of information-processing
transformation processes takes place that is characterized in terms of information rather than in mechanical terms. This is suggested by the fact that
behaviour is not influenced by the physical features of the stimulus, but by the
semantic content of the message. When someone tells you the house is on fire,
your behaviour is controlled by the meaning of the information, not by the
physical way the message is delivered (by speech or writing or whatever) and
your subsequent behaviour equally cannot be captured in a physical description. For the explanation of your behaviour (flight from fire) it is irrelevant
whether you walk in wooden shoes, in sneakers, or on all fours: your behaviour differs from the response of, for instance, a microphone to sound waves
or the trajectory of a vehicle.

The important conclusion, then, is that intentional generalizations rather
than physical ones are the mode of explanation in psychology (cf. Pylyshyn,
1984). In the classical view cognitive science needs the concept of mental
representations to account for intentional intelligent behaviour.
Representations provide a way to classify typically human behaviour in distinction from physical responses. Perception, reasoning, goal-directed
behaviour, rational decision-making all presuppose representations in this
view. You will see how cognition and hoary philosophical issues are brought
together here. More precisely, Fodor and his partisans conflate Brentano's
problem of intentionality and mental content with the explanation of rationality. Behind this is a deep, rigorous, comprehensive, interesting and rather
counterintuitive vision: the computational theory of mind.

4.3   The orthodoxy: the computational theory of mind

Origins

The computational theory of mind has, broadly speaking, three sources. First,
there was the cognitive revolution in psychology. It made the notion of internal mental processes as causes of overt behaviour respectable again.

Behaviourism had eliminated all references to internal processes from scientific psychology, and had substituted the study of overt behaviour (Gardner, 1987). Mentalist terminology was considered speculative and unscientific, and could only be legitimized if it was directly linked to, or translatable into, observed behaviour. The cognitive revolution made a case for independent internal processes that are only indirectly linked to behaviour, and consist in information processing. Whether this constituted a new paradigm remains to be seen: the term 'cognitive' seems to apply to approximately anything.

Secondly, on close scrutiny, many problems in the philosophy of mind resemble traditional issues in the philosophy of language that had dominated Anglo-Saxon philosophy since the days of Gottlob Frege, Bertrand Russell, and Ludwig Wittgenstein, in the early twentieth century (see Devitt and Sterelny, 1987; Harnish, 1994). These philosophers were interested in questions concerning intentionality, reference, meaning, propositional mental content – that is, questions like: how does language relate to the world? How is it possible that words or thoughts somehow reflect reality? How can sentences or thoughts be about things in the world? *Mental representation* is the label under which such problems are now usually summarized (e.g., Fodor, 1981; Silvers, 1989; Sterelny, 1990). The having of internal representations in the form of propositions is supposed to explain or at least to be compatible with the properties of mental processes that go under the label of intentionality – in other words, mental processes are modelled on linguistic ones. The notion of linguistic expressions as expressing some state of affairs is transplanted to mental content, as representing the subject's environment, in Jerry Fodor's (1975) (in)famous *Language of Thought* hypothesis that thinking is manipulating sentences in a kind of logical language in the head. It is interesting to note that such notions hardly play a central role in cognitive psychology textbooks, and if they do, it is usually with quite a different emphasis (compare Palmer, 1978 and Fodor, 1981). Recently, doubts have arisen as to whether the concerns of cognitive science dovetail as nicely with philosophical ones as, for instance, Fodor (1981) thinks (Stich, 1992; Rorty, 1993).

Thirdly, the rise of the computer and the promise of *Artificial Intelligence* boosted the idea that thinking is symbol manipulation (see p. 112 ff.), and that the computer can be used as a tool for studying thought. Within AI, two approaches can be distinguished: weak and strong AI. *Weak AI* just tries to write programs that can do tasks that require intelligence, such as making a medical diagnosis, playing chess, translating and summarizing texts (e.g. a news bulletin). *Strong AI* claims to write programs that exactly simulate human thinking, and as a consequence it claims that programmed computers can literally think. Obviously, only the strong variety is relevant for CTM.

Functionalism and the cognitive revolution

The cognitive revolution required some idea of mental processes that would be independent of neurophysiology, because neurophysiologists had next to nothing to say about cognitive processes like thinking; and for cognitive science to grab its share of the Defence money it had better have its own identity.

Against this background, Putnam (1961) and Fodor (1981) advanced decisive arguments against both the identity theory and linguistic behaviourism (see section 4.1, p. 102 ff.). The problem with *linguistic behaviourism* is that it is not a real theory about mental processes, and has nothing to say about inner mental processes that cause behaviour. It does not explain anything about the underlying mechanisms, only about commonsense labels for what we already know. The problem with the *identity theory* (IT) on the other hand is that it identifies mental states with neural states. Although this means that in contrast to behaviourism, mental states are seen as real and causally effective, it also abandons cognition as an independent field of study, leaving it to neurophysiology.

Functionalism is intended as an improvement on both the identity theory and linguistic behaviourism (see also section 1.5, p. 27 ff.). Mental processes can be considered in their own right, apart from overt behaviour, unlike behaviourism. Also in contrast with behaviourism, mental states are not just labels, but they are ontologically real and mental causation can be taken seriously. Against the IT, the one-to-one correspondence of mental and physical processes is abandoned. IT assumes type identity of mental and physical processes, so that a whole class of mental events can systematically be identified with a class of neural events (such as, pain is the firing of C-fibres).

Functionalism has been the cornerstone of the view of mind as a symbol manipulator, the orthodox view of cognitive psychology. It implies that empirical identification of the mental and the physiological is no longer an interesting option; no lawlike generalization is to be expected between our neuronal events and our thinking. On the one hand, functionalism implies that mental processes are instantiated in material processes, there is no such thing as non-physical thought, no metaphysical dualism of mind and matter. On the other hand, mental processes are irreducible to neurophysiology. This is an interesting achievement for a philosophical idea, because it legitimizes the autonomy of psychology, while being impeccably scientific, materialistic and anti-Cartesian. In the same way as you can know about the way a computer program like, for instance, WordPerfect works, without knowing anything about the machine(s) it works on, a psychologist can study mental processes without looking at neurophysiology. Since the hardware is essentially irrelevant, cognition can be studied in computer simulations (Artificial Intelligence) rather than in human 'wetware', functioning human brains doing cognitive tasks.

More precisely, one might distinguish two kinds of identity. *Type identity* refers to identity of kinds or categories (types); all instances of a certain type of mental state, for example pain, are identical with a type of neurophysiological event, such as firing of neurons in the hypothalamus. *Token identity* is a much weaker claim: it holds that every instance (token) of a mental event is a token of a physical event, but the connection may be different in different species or on different occasions or in different individuals – say we may call ant behaviour aggressive, and ascribe causal powers to their aggression in roughly the same way as in human or monkey behaviour, while ants have a completely different physical make-up from ours. So, although there is no such thing as non-physical thought (mental and physical processes are token-identical), there are no laws connecting classes of mental and neural events (no type-identity).

Hence, the categories of psychology cannot be type-identified with those of neurophysiology. This is because the way a mental state is realized in some physical substrate, may be different in different cases. An animal with a different nervous system from ours can be considered to have the same mental states; a computer which has nothing physical in common with us can be assumed to think; and Mary's love of the policeman has not the same neurophysiological realization as Harry's love of the same policeman.

This is known as multiple realizibility of mental states. If the possibility of multiple realizibility is granted then obviously the identification of mental and physical categories is hopeless. An autonomous domain has thus been carved out for cognition, and cognitive psychologists can safely ignore neurophysiology as merely a matter of implementation.

The question then becomes: what characterizes mental processes? Here Fodor goes beyond functionalism; in his view mental processes consist in symbol manipulation. Functionalism's mechanical realizibility is guaranteed by the Turing machine concept. A program is in a sense a causal force. If intelligent behaviour can be executed by mechanical procedures (programs), then, it seems, the 'homunculus', one of the major problems of orthodox cognitivism and its conception of representations, is exorcized.

The notion of computation

The theoretical foundations of such a claim lie in the notions of a *Turing machine* and effective procedure. A Turing machine, named after the mathematician Alan Turing (1912–54), is a general-purpose symbol manipulator: it reads a symbol, performs an elementary operation on it, and writes it back. A universal Turing machine is a Turing machine that can simulate the input–output function of any other Turing machine. The interesting thing about symbols is that they can be combined according to strictly formal rules: the progress in mathematical logic in the late nineteenth and early twentieth centuries has proved it possible to formalize deductive reasoning. Frege talked about 'eine der mathematischen nachgebildete Formelspräche des reinen Denkens' (a formal language of pure thought, modelled on mathematic language). *Effective procedures* are mechanical procedures that can be executed without any insight. This means that any activity that can be specified in a series of mechanical operations, an *algorithm*, can be executed by a universal Turing machine. The empirical hypothesis is that such a universal symbol manipulator (Newell, 1980, called them 'physical symbol systems') can exhibit intelligence, in the sense that they can be said to possess goals, plans and knowledge. Symbol manipulation is instantiated in a physical system, a computer, and the existence of a mechanism that embodies logical operations, namely, symbol manipulation, made the notions of information and symbol manipulation palatable to materialists. Logic is put to work, and

AI shows 'how . . . rationality [is] mechanically possible' (Fodor, 1987: 20); or in Newell's words: 'mind enters into the physical universe' (1980: 136).

Language of thought

Jerry Fodor's CTM holds that the mind is a symbol manipulator, that representations are symbol strings, formulae in some canonical notation, the language of thought (LOT); this is not a real language as spoken, but a group of formulae as in formal logic or computer languages. Thinking consists in transforming these symbol strings according to formal, purely syntactical rules. According to this picture, we have a head full of logical formulae, and symbol crunching is the essence of cogitation. Mental representations are symbol strings; transforming them according to formal rules into new symbol strings is thinking. Below we will discuss arguments pro and con such a counterintuitive hypothesis. In a nutshell, defenders of the view that we have 'sentences in our head' argue that thinking must be very much like language, since it can be expressed in words and must have a comparable logical structure to make reasoning possible.

Empirical evidence

It must be emphasized that this is an empirical hypothesis: there is no compelling logical reason to assume that symbol manipulation adds up to intelligence. Fodor and other orthodox cognitivists, like Zenon Pylyshyn, think that CTM rests on an inference to the best explanation: although the theory transcends the facts, it is the story that is the most compatible with the facts. Usually, his arguments take the following form: given the properties of human thought and language, nothing less than a LOT would explain them: how could it be otherwise? The LOT is the only game in town (we will see something of this in Fodor's attack on connectionism, in section 4.4, p. 118 ff.). More direct empirical evidence, showing that cognitive systems are symbol crunchers, is surprisingly scarce.

Pylyshyn (1989) proposed some criteria to decide whether a computational simulation exhibits what he calls 'strong equivalence' to a real thinker; and these criteria seem to allow considerable leeway. In fact, strong AI is said by some critics (Dreyfus, 1979) to be all but defunct by now (although weak AI is big business). Copeland (1993) cites the CYC project (the name comes from 'en*cyc*lopaedia'), which tries to build the basic categories of our common sense into a large encyclopaedia-like system, as the last surviving (serious) attempt to build a cognitive system within the framework of a LOT, that is, as symbol manipulator.

Fodor is fully aware of this, and is downright pessimistic about the success of building a mind in the foreseeable future, but maintains that the CTM is the only theory that is not dead in the water from the start. Other attempts, like connectionism (see p. 116 ff.), are sure to fail, he thinks.

Let us now have a closer look at the philosophical aspects of the CTM. A key feature is that mental states are computational relations to syntactically structured representations. This brings together a number of philosophical and psychological issues.

Mechanical rationality

The grand scheme of the CTM is: naturalizing *intentionality*, showing how rationality is mechanically possible (Fodor, 1987). Basically, the argument is that intentionality requires symbols, because symbols are the only bearers of meaning we know. Symbol manipulation can be arranged so that the semantics follows the syntax (Fodor, 1994); the syntactic engine mimics the semantic engine (Haugeland, 1981). Roughly, the idea is that a formal program behaves in an intelligent way, as if it tracks referents, things in the world. A key concept here is 'truth preserving': the formal program is so arranged that true input symbols lead, after a lot of symbol crunching, to true output symbols. If that sounds like magic, recall that this is what happens in mathematics and formal logic too; even the lowly desk calculator is designed so that it infallibly comes up with the true answer to a mathematical problem. Likewise, formal logic provides a formal mechanical recipe in reasoning: how to get to true conclusions from true premises.

Importantly then, a mechanical formal structure can exhibit logical, semantic and truthful behaviour. Hence, mechanical rationality is possible in computational symbol-manipulating systems.

Intentional realism and folk psychology

In contrast with linguistic behaviourists, Fodor believes that intentions are real entities, not only convenient labels for describing behaviour, and that the CTM supports this claim of 'intentional realism', that is, the real existence and causal efficacy of intentional states like beliefs and desires. The CTM vindicates folk psychology, the use of beliefs and desires as explanations, and abandoning intentional idiom would be a cultural catastrophe since all our daily predictions and explanations of our fellow beings' behaviour implies it. We simply have no other way of explaining and predicting what our fellow beings do, other than in terms of what they believe and what they think.

It should be realized, however, that in this picture both the computer metaphor and folk psychology have been extensively reconstructed to make *rapprochement* between them possible. The man in the street does not usually assume propositions in his head, nor mental causation; and functionalism is not committed to a linguistic construal of mental states. Churchland manages to abandon the sentential (propositional, or linguistic) model and to eliminate folk psychology in one fell swoop.

Formality and solipsism

A somewhat peculiar consequence of the claim that thinking is symbol manipulation according to formal, purely syntactical rules is that *semantics* can play no role in psychological explanations. Whatever the mental system's symbolic formulae are *about* is no part of its functioning. To see this, consider a program that produces medical diagnoses: it transforms a series of inputs (which the user knows are symptoms) into some output (which the user understands as a description of a disease) through the application of a set of formal rules. The program does not know what its inputs and outputs stand for, that is, it does not know what symptoms are, what a disease is, and it could not answer even the simplest question about human physiology. Hence, explaining its workings, knowing what its symbols are *about*, would not help you; you need to know the rules it uses and the symbols it stores.

Fodor (1981) has transformed this somewhat embarrassing result into a methodological principle: *methodological solipsism*. This follows from the formality condition: symbols and the rules according to which these are manipulated are formal and syntactic. Only the *form* of a symbol string determines what can be done with it. As in mathematics and formal logic, only the formulae determine what operations can be applied, not the *content*, not what x, y and z stand for.

If the mind is a purely syntactic engine, then, reference to its environment, its semantics, is beyond the explanatory power of cognitive science. Cognition is about the internal economy of the system and nothing more. Of course, this is a methodological principle: Fodor does not deny that environments are important, but only that they can enter into explanations in cognitive science.

Another related, but distinct, argument is what in philosophy of mind is called *individualism* (Burge, 1986). This is a metaphysical argument (recall that the LOT and its formality condition is an empirical hypothesis), built upon the notion of *supervenience* (see Chapter 1, p. 35). In essence, it says that every mental event must have some physical correlate (otherwise there would be disembodied thought, thinking without brains, which is metaphysically unacceptable for materialists). It follows that the environment is only relevant in so far as it causally affects the body, like causal events in the sensory systems, so that we only have to look at the individual system, and not at its environment. So, individualism holds in essence that only processes *inside* the organism can be studied. In this view, psychology 'ends at the skin'.

However, one could also be interested, of course, in the way an organism functions in its environment, how processes within the skin can be understood as adaptations to an environment (for a critique of individualism, see Burge, 1986; Baker, 1987). Therefore individualism is a rather unfruitful prescription, for example, for the psychology of perception, where the function of perceptual systems, what they accomplish in terms of reconstructing the environment, is an essential part of the explanation (see Marr, 1982; Looren de Jong, 1995). It seems reasonable to allow that interesting generalizations can be made using adaptive functional considerations (see section 1.4, p. 25 ff.), that go beyond narrow causal impact on the senses (Van Gulick, 1989). Individualism and methodological solipsism seem at variance with sound psychological research.

CTM: intentionality and rationality

Fodor sharpens the functionalist intuition by connecting it with the idea of a language of thought, introducing the apparatus of the philosophy of language into the philosophy of mind. More precisely, Fodor (1987) combines the cognitive-psychological problem of the nature of mental processes with the philosophical problem about the semantics of propositions. The LOT carries in its wake a lot of problems of semantics. However, Fodor (1981) is also clear that he is in fact taking on two problems in one theory: intentionality and mechanical rationality.

The former refers to Brentano's problem: how is it possible that some (mental) states are about something? How are meaning and representation possible? The second refers to AI and the problem of giving a naturalistic theory of intelligent behaviour (that is, as computation). It is quite conceivable that the former does not contribute anything to the latter, and vice versa.

Fodor (1994) tries to reconcile the two distinct claims – that the laws of psychology are intentional, that is, that they explain behaviour by citing mental content, the goals and desires an organism has; *and* that these are implemented in computational mechanisms. The problem then becomes: how can we be sure that the mechanisms run in harmony with the semantics? Fodor's answer is that there is no necessary relation between them; the connection is contingent: the computational mechanisms have a causal history of interactions with the world that generally connect the current outcome of the syntactic mechanisms with the right behaviour in the environment, that is, preserve the meaning or content of a belief or desire over a series of formal computations.

The beauty of Fodor's theory is that CTM has a story for both the philosophical problem of intentionality and semantics, and for the problem of the mechanisms of intelligence and rationality. However, it is also possible to have a purely syntactical idea of cognition, without intentionality, aboutness or semantics (Stich, 1983, see section 4.5, p. 122 ff.).

4.4   The competition: eliminativism and connectionism

The crux of Paul Churchland's attack on the Fodorian orthodoxy is the rejection of *propositions* as the basic material of cognition, and the proposal that *folk psychology* might eventually be eliminated. Recall that Fodor argued that a sentential (propositional) model of thought vindicates folk psychology. Both these theses are fleshed out using connectionist (neural network) models to demonstrate that non-propositional intelligence is possible, and that our knowledge of ourselves and our fellow beings can be radically reconstructed. Interestingly however, Churchland advocated these ideas before the advent of connectionism.

Churchland (1979) has presented an integrated naturalist philosophy of mind, of science and psychology in one. Three interconnected issues stand out: (1) the theory-ladenness of all observation which precludes recourse to some 'given' empirical foundation; (2) a non-sentential (non-propositional or non-linguistic) view of knowledge (*contra* the conception of the LOT); (3) the rejection of folk psychological categories as obsolete theories.

Theory-ladenness and eliminativism

Churchland's (1981) original proposal started with the thesis that folk psychology is a real theory, and should be judged like any other theory – whether it is progressive (comes up with new knowledge and new research directions), whether it fits with the rest of science, etc.

An essential assumption of Churchland is that *all observation is theory laden* (see Chapter 2, p. 45 ff.). There is no such thing as pure observation: our mental make-up (our 'theories') determines what we see, and when our theories change (that is, when we learn) our experiences and observations change with them.

Equally importantly, he rejects the classical view of a theory (elaborated by the positivists as an edifice of propositions, statements, sentences, in short: the doctrine congenial with the notion of language of thought. In his view a theory is something like a cognitive capacity to recognize and discriminate rather than a body of statements. This means that folk psychology is also a theory – and possibly a false one. Changing our outlook might thus dissolve or radically reconstruct deep-rooted convictions in our self-image – our intuitions that we all have beliefs and desires and thoughts and feelings. That folk psychology (being a theory) has no privileged status in terms of certainty is a controversial claim: many people think they know their inner life directly and infallibly, unlike the (indirect and fallible) knowledge they may have of the external world. They just know that they act upon their beliefs, and think their fellow beings are just as rational and intentional. When your dentist tells you that you do not feel pain, you will tell him that you know better. Churchland (1981) argues that our folk-psychological intuitions are not directly evident or 'given', but depend on theoretical presuppositions. His arguments derive directly from Sellars' 'Myth of the Given': our concepts of mind are 'plastic', malleable, and even our introspective judgements are theory laden.

Where Brentano and others considered intentionality the mark of an indubitable ontological distinction between mind and matter, Churchland (1981) argues (like Sellars' Jones) that intentionality is more a fact about the language in which we frame our views of the world than an ontological distinction in the world itself – and therefore entirely fallible and revisable. Hence, folk psychology with its assumptions of irreducible beliefs, desires, intentionality, etc., may be replaced by new scientific theories.

In his 1981 paper Churchland could only offer some science-fiction-like speculation on the ways the theoretical framework of folk psychology could be eliminated and replaced by new ways of understanding. However, in the mid-1980s connectionism came up, and provided Churchland with a vehicle for the overthrow both of sentential models of cognition (the CTM), and of its commonsense counterpart, 'belief-desire' psychology.

Neural networks

A connectionist network consists of nodes and connections between them; activation spreads through the network, and the connections have weights that determine to which extent nodes influence each other (pass on activation). This is vaguely analogous to signal transmission between the neurons in the nervous system, hence the adjective 'neural'; though some warn us not to take this too seriously (Shepherd, 1990).

Learning occurs through adjustment of weights according to some rule by the network itself; thus it learns to produce the correct response (activation of the output nodes) for a given problem (activation of the input nodes). A network can learn to recognize and discriminate between different kinds of input; for example, a network in a submarine can learn to distinguish between the sonar signals belonging to rocks and mines. To perform adequate discriminations, a three-layer network (a layer of input nodes, a layer of output nodes, and a layer of hidden nodes in between) is required. Usually the weights are set in a training period in which feedback about the right response is provided. The knowledge of the network is in the weights, which determine the response to the input (that is, the flow of activation through the network).

In a certain sense, the network has created this knowledge on its own account, because it has organized itself to tune in to its environment. This learning process can be visualised as a trajectory through a kind of space of all possible weights, so that error, the distance between desired and actual response, is minimized. Pattern recognition by a network is the activation of a recognition vector: the network 'sees' a solution when activation is spread in the right way over units.

In practice, real networks, as they exist today, need a lot of help to do anything interesting. The researcher has to provide a highly structured situation, and all sorts of constraints are put upon the task, the size of the network, the nature of the problems to be presented, etc. Of course, the explosively growing research in network design is about ways to find learning rules and network designs for a variety of cognitive tasks.

The knowledge of the network is usually distributed over many connections; unlike the so-called classical approach with its discrete symbols and data structures, the content of the system's beliefs cannot be localized in discrete symbol structures or program statements.

Churchland (1995) proposes that consciousness is realized in recurrent networks, that is, networks that feed back information from hidden nodes to output nodes.

The contrast between the *classical* and the *connectionist* approach will be clear. Fodor's language of thought uses discrete symbols, connectionist models go by diffuse activation patterns; or, in mathematical terms, the former uses logical means, the latter uses numerical means.

The classical approach holds that logical reasoning and language-like structures and processes (sentences in the head) are the stuff that mind is made of. Connectionism thinks it is holistic neuron-like activation patterns.

The classical approach has to assume an inborn cognitive structure, analogous to the programmer who sets up the system with a database and a set of rules for reasoning and induction (cf. Holland et al., 1986). Whereas the classical approach is *pre-programmed*, the connectionist challenger claims to have a means of *self-organization*. For this reason classical cognitivism has been compared to Cartesian rationalism, for Descartes presupposed inborn ideas: the most important ingredients for knowledge were wired in from the start. Fodor (1975) is a self-confessed nativist.

The connectionist approach also claims to be more biologically plausible, more in tune with the neural nature of the mind/brain. The latter claim is pushed vigorously by Churchland to substantiate his ideas on elimination of psychological categories, and their replacement by neuroscientific discourse.

Naturalism

An essential part of the naturalist story is that philosophy, including philosophy of mind, is not an a-priori enterprise. The influence of Quine and Sellars (see Chapter 2) is easily detected in Churchland's work. Philosophers have to give up their one-time dream of laying down a-priori methods, epistemological criteria, ontological statements about the furniture of the world, according to which empirical research can proceed. On the contrary, philosophy is continuous with science and extrapolates and clarifies empirical results.

In this way, Churchland and Sejnowski (1990) set out to elucidate representation from a connectionist (neurophilosophical) perspective. Their point is that if you want to know what representations are you should not primarily consult philosophers and linguists like Frege, Brentano and Chomsky, you should look at what the nervous system does in keeping track of the world, or at least at what a neural network does.

Patricia Churchland and Paul Churchland (1990) restate the old Brentano question, 'How is aboutness possible?', into, 'How can the brain be a world representer?' And how are these representations used such that intelligent and purposeful behaviour ensues? The functionalist and rationalist strategy, followed by Fodor and others, is to consider representations as symbol strings, and thinking as transformation of symbol strings. The first major problem here is to explain how such symbol strings hook on to the world. Secondly, the functionalist Fodorian style expressly ignores the brain.

The naturalist approach treats representation as a function developed in evolution; cognitive processes lie on an evolutionary continuum, ranging from pattern detection in lower animals to complex forms of thought and language. Thus, it looks for the basis of human cognition not in language and logic, but in elementary perception and action in animals. We are epistemic engines for the extraction, production and control of information in the service of survival.

Neuroscience then will suggest how the brain represents. It is clear that it does not do so by way of sentences in the head. For a model of cognition we should look at pattern recognition, for example the recognition of mice by a rattlesnake. Churchland buttressed this model using the results of the modelling of connectionist networks, which can be said to tune in to their environment, and adapt their internal structure to respond adequately to input. Network models are capable of learning, are sensitive to the world and mature through an active engagement with their environment. In contrast, *rationalist*, classical symbolist models are pre-formed and pre-programmed, bringing with them from the start everything that is psychologically important, such as rules for cognition and a language of thought.

The confrontation: propositional representations versus network activation

The question of symbolic versus connectionist views of mind is the backdrop of Fodor's rather extensive criticism of the feasibility of the connectionist enterprise, and the capacities of neural networks. Although the Churchlands hardly entered this debate, we will nevertheless discuss it here, since it bears upon the first issue mentioned above: are networks powerful enough to produce systematic thought?

Not surprisingly, Fodor thinks that non-propositional representations are insufficient as 'architecture' of human cognition, and that, whatever the successes of connectionism, a language of thought is still needed (Fodor, 1990; Fodor and Pylyshyn, 1988; Fodor and McLaughlin, 1990). The test case is that of the properties of systematicity and productivity. *Productivity* means that in principle an infinite number of complex propositions (sentences, thoughts) can be generated from a limited number of simple constituents. This is a typical feature of languages: with a limited number of words in a dictionary, an unlimited number of sentences can be made. *Systematicity* means that you cannot have a thought without the ability to have or understand another thought that is semantically close to the first one. If you know what 'John loves the florist' means, then you will also inevitably understand a sentence like 'The florist loves John.' Fodor argues that to get productivity and systematicity in a cognitive system, you need a language-like medium with a constituent structure, that is, discrete elements (words, symbols) which can be concatenated using standard connectives, such as 'and', 'therefore', 'or' and 'if . . . then'.

Note that Fodor (e.g. Fodor and Pylyshyn, 1988) does not hold that it is impossible for networks to exhibit logically structured behaviour. The point is that a LOT-like medium has productivity and systematicity intrinsically, it comes along with the classical architecture of cognition, and that the same is true of human language and thinking; however, structure is not intrinsic to networks and has to be hand-crafted. Fodor and Pylyshyn think that networks are similar to associationist psychology, where everything can be connected to everything else (think of Pavlov's dogs). Thus, they interpret the debate as a return to the controversy between Skinner and Chomsky on language acquisition. Chomsky showed that children cannot learn how to construct grammatical sentences just by listening to the way their parents put one word after another, as Skinner proposed, since sentence structure often requires long-distance connections, as in embedded clauses, such as: 'The woman who the janitor we just hired hit on is very pretty.' They need an inborn *language instinct* to unpack such structures, and learning to associate words won't help (Pinker, 1994: 207).

Fodor and Pylyshyn (1988) and Fodor and McLaughlin (1990) conclude that connectionism might be a theory of the way cognitive structures are *implemented* in the nervous systems, but not of the architecture of cognition itself: no cognition without systematicity and productivity, and no systematicity without constituent structure. The only viable solution to date is the language of thought. Connectionist networks are in their view interesting as an implementation, a physical, neural realization, of essentially serial rule-governed symbolic cognitive processes in the parallel network of the brain: it is no viable proposal for a new architecture of cognition. In fact, as a proposal for the architecture of cognition, it is hardly an improvement on the associationism of Hume and Skinner.

Connectionists counter in different ways (Bechtel and Abrahamsen, 1991). One answer is *compatibilism*: some connectionists admit the need for explicit rules, and try to build hybrid systems including *both* classical rules and connectionist activation patterns.

Smolensky (1988) gives an example of another answer which Bechtel and Abrahamsen (1991) call *approximationism*: he argues that compositionality, how complex representations or sentences can be constructed from simpler ones, is also attainable by connectionist networks. Connectionist networks can provide structured representations and structure-sensitive processes as a kind of by-product of pattern activation (Smolensky, 1988, 1991). In his view, the real medium of cognition is what he calls the 'intuitive processor'; mental representations are vectors, and mental processes are differential equations governing the development of the system. Thus, in reality, the causal mechanisms governing cognition are activation patterns and vector transformations, and compositionality is an epiphenomenon of them, more or less in the same way as the underlying reality of physics (atoms and molecules) has as macro-features chairs and tables.

Smolensky then proceeds to prove that networks can exhibit constituent structure in the form of ordered vector transformations; his example is that the representation 'a cup of coffee' can be thought of as consisting of a vector with a number of elements (hot, brown, liquid, contained in white porcelain, etc.), and proper transformations can preserve a plausible degree of constituent structure. Such a system has *weak compositionality* where the meaning of the elements depends on the context in a holistic fashion, unlike *strong compositionality* in Fodorian fashion where the constituents are independent of each other, as 'meaning atoms'. Note that this is a middle course between the distributed and holistic nature of representation in networks, on the one hand, and functionally discrete, fully compositional, classical architecture, on the other. Smolensky has the best of both worlds: the network is said to be structure-sensitive (like classical architecture), and at the same time context-sensitive and holistic (the forte of connectionism). However, the real, causally effective work is done by the connectionist activation patterns;

the (classical) structure-sensitive properties are epiphenomena and only approximately true. Whereas in the CTM discrete symbol structures are the rock bottom of the system's working, Smolensky thinks that cognition really works through vector activation.

Fodor and McLaughlin (1990) are not convinced; their major criticism is that structure sensitivity is not a necessary part of the system, unlike language and thought. Furthermore, Fodor and McLaughlin ask, somewhat sophistically, why Smolensky takes the neural level as more real and causally effective than the cognitive (LOT) level; why should the causal buck stop there; and why does not Smolensky proceed to abandon the neural level and take the molecular, or the atomic, or the subatomic level as more real than the neural?

It is, of course, difficult to assess the future successes of connectionism with respect to compositionality. The consensus seems to be that cognitive systems must be able to represent complex structured items (Van Gelder, 1990: 356). Fodor demands that the structure of the representations must be the same as the structure of the represented items; that a cognitive system able to think systematic and productive thoughts and sentences must have an internal Language of Thought. Fodor's classical construal of this structure is modelled on formal logic; it consists of concatenating symbols into formulae, such that the symbols themselves are preserved in the concatenated expressions, just as words are still recognizable in a sentence.

Van Gelder (1990) argues that a system can be compositional without being classical; there is also something called *functional compositionality*. This obtains when there are general rules for putting together a complex expression, and for decomposing it again into its constituents. It is conceivable that the representational medium is merely functional, but not classical (of course classical compositionality is always functional). Perhaps cognition can be explained by neural networks which are only functionally compositional. Smolensky's vectors, mentioned above, would be an example of functional compositionality.

Another example of non-classical decomposability is the connectionist architecture RAAM (Recursive Auto-Associative Memory), which implements a stack structure in a network, and extends this to a tree structure (Clark, 1993: 119–21). Hence, the rather uncontroversial claim that representation requires complex structures does not support Fodor's strong claim that compositionality must be classical. Connectionist networks have been built that instantiate a fair amount of functional compositionality.

Recapitulation

Having conveniently divided the field into two opposing camps – the Fodorian orthodoxy and Churchland's more recent alternative – and having reviewed the main empirical bone of contention between them, let us wrap up the deep philosophical disagreements. We will then go on to other views on these issues, and introduce a few other actors on the scene.

Let us emphasize that both Fodor and Churchland consider mental processes as computation; only their views on the nature of that computation are opposed. Fodor thinks that cognition (symbol manipulation) is an autonomous level of description relative to its implementation in silicon chips or neurons. Fodor's paradigm of mind is language and formal logic, 'sentences in the head'. Churchland looks for alternatives for language-based models of cognition, and has found them in pattern recognition skills, exemplified in connectionist networks. It is highly implausible that the brain has a language of thought.

Fodor thinks that the CTM vindicates folk psychology, and its vocabulary of beliefs, desires, intentionality, propositional attitudes and mental content as a genuine (causal, lawful) explanation of behaviour. Churchland proposes elimination of folk psychology and its replacement by a new neuroscientific idiom, presumably in terms of neural networks. The disagreement over the autonomy of functional classical architectures of cognition is interpreted by both Fodor and Churchland as having consequences for the status of folk psychology: can intentionality, mental content, etc. be salvaged in cognitive science, or will they be eliminated?

Churchland (1981) argued in the spirit of Sellars (1963) that mental events are dependent on the concepts and theories in which they are expressed. Churchland (1979) called it the plasticity of mind; mind is malleable. Hence, there is no such thing as knowing your own mind directly, and all mental reports are, in principle, as theoretical as statements about external perception. Folk psychology is a theory, and therefore revisable, for example by neuroscience. Other aspects of common sense have been replaced by science, such as the phlogiston theory of combustion in the nineteenth century. Churchland argues that the apparatus of folk psychology is as useless, trite and stagnant as alchemy, and deserves to be eliminated and replaced by a new neuroscientific idiom for our self-image and concepts of mind. Functionalism is in Churchland's view a conservative and a cheap explanation; anything can be a functional state, and declaring the analogues of beliefs and desires functional states tends to preserve obsolete theories; an alchemist might have called his phlogiston a functional state.

Note that Churchland's ideas about the elimination of folk psychology, theory-ladenness, and neural networks, his naturalism and the rejection of symbolic models in cognition and propositional (logical positivist) views of scientific theories, are of one piece.

Since the way perception and recognition works is determined by the weights in a network, perception is always interpretive and discriminative (theory laden). The knowledge a network has is embodied in its weights and determines its response to input. Network-like models are a good alternative to proposition-based views of scientific theories. The neural plausibility, and the commonality with organisms lower on the evolutionary ladder of such networks make them for the naturalist more plausible as mechanisms of cognition than language, which came only very late in the evolution.

Churchland advocates network-style processing as an alternative to linguistic models across the whole range of cognitive activity, from perceptual categorization to scientific theorizing. Explanation in science can thus be understood as activation of a prototype vector: recognizing, interpreting and amplifying events in terms of scientific knowledge is an extension of the discriminating power of a network in perceptual recognition.

Folk psychology is for the naturalist a candidate for elimination, since its intuitions cannot have an undubitable ('given') status, but are determined by theories, and hence revisable and replaceable by neuroscientific views; the latter are better integrated in successful scientific developments.

So, comparing Fodor and Churchland on some important points in the philosophy of mind, we see that: (1) they have different views on the stuff the mind is made of: symbols in canonical formal language versus activation patterns in neural networks; (2) they disagree on the relation between mind and brain: autonomy versus elimination; and (3) the relation between mental representation and reality is conceived in opposite ways: individualism (or solipsism, or rationalism) versus naturalism, the biological, adaptive view of the genesis of representations (Bechtel, 1990; Churchland and Churchland, 1990).

4.5   Other views, same issues

Folk psychology revisited

The orthodoxy considers folk psychology to be vindicated by the computational theory of mind. Propositional attitudes tally with the language of thought, and support explanations in terms of beliefs and desires: we have discrete, causally active symbol structures in our heads that produce our behaviour, and we are literally right in invoking these as explanations (cf. Haselager, 1995).

It is probably not Fodor's thesis that the CTM, in itself, necessarily entails folk psychology; rather, by some happy coincidence convergent notions emerged in commonsense psychology, in philosophy and in cognitive science, so these are probably true (Fodor, 1981).

Pure syntactical psychology and folk psychology   It should be mentioned that at least one proposal separates folk psychology from the CTM. Stephen Stich (1983) suggests that all semantic and folk-psychological idiom should be deleted from cognitive science, so that a purely syntactic (computational) theory of mind can exist without folk psychology. The difference with Fodor is that the latter wants to keep intentional explanation, in a naturalized form, tied up with computation. Fodor would consider it a major cultural disaster if we had to abandon folk-psychological discourse, and considers the conjunction of computational implementation and intentional explanation the essence of his work (Fodor, 1994).

Stich (1983), on the other hand, happily sacrifices the intentional, meaningful idiom of folk psychology, the explanation in terms of beliefs ('She goes to university to get a degree, because she wants to be rich and famous, and thinks a degree helps to achieve that') have no place in cognitive explanations.

Stich's 'case against belief' (the subtitle of his book) is that cognitive psychology should only advert to formal and syntactic processes, since the intentional and semantic idiom of belief talk is hopelessly vague and full of connotations and ambiguities, and depends on context; it misses relevant generalizations; and too many fine-grained distinctions get in the way of useful explanations. Furthermore, folk psychology cannot explain the behaviour of the mentally retarded and disturbed, but is limited to the psychology of 'people like us'. Cognitive science has, in order to be rigorous and respectable science, to get rid of all the vague connotations; has to restrict itself to formulae; and has to generalize and explain on the basis solely of syntactic relations, without reference to content, but only to uninterpreted symbols.

This programme seems to come close to Churchland's eliminativism, with syntactic rather than neurophysiological replacements for beliefs and desires. Stich (1992), however, considers them different pursuits, and different knowledge interests. Looking at the debate on cognitive science and folk psychology he takes a rather sceptical view of the claim that representations are the foundation of cognition.

Fodor's project is an attempt to vindicate folk psychology by identifying it with computational mechanisms; his adversary, Churchland, proposes to eliminate it and replace it by neurocomputational concepts. Stich argues that eliminativism is a less clear and radical proposal than it seems. To specify exactly what the elimination of folk psychology implies, we need a theory of reference, that is, a specification of how its terms relate to mental processes. It is only natural that naive theories are to some extent corrected by new ones, in psychology as elsewhere, but we don't usually say that the naive theory is eliminated. For example, we agree that some caveman who referred to gold as a yellow metal and had no idea that it has atomic number 79, had a concept of gold that is now entirely eliminated by modern physics, although he was talking about the same reality; in contrast, a concept like 'witches' did not refer to anything (cf. Kripke, 1980).

Analogously with the commonsense notions of mental life: without a clear definition of when a concept is eliminated, that is, ceases to refer to anything, the elimination of folk psychology by cognitive science may be a rather gradual and commonplace affair. Churchland's eliminativism is less revolutionary than it seems. Science has always adjusted its theories to fit new discoveries about its referents and it is not obvious that this really means the dramatic massacre of common sense that Churchland suggests.

As to the alternative, Stich deems Fodor's project – to make the mind respectable within the framework of natural science by reducing mind to computation – quite hopeless. We do have reliable intersubjective concepts for behavioural and mental phenomena, and there is no need either to naturalize them or eliminate them. Common sense and sciences such as ethology can work with broad functional descriptions (see Chapter 1) of behaviour, which are difficult or impossible to translate into some physical language, but which are good enough as they are.

To sum up then, Stich (1992) deflates the notion of representation as the foundation of cognitive science, and concludes with a kind of *pluralism*. This is consistent with his pragmatic view of cognition: there is no single best way of going about the business of cognition (Stich, 1990). There is nothing intrinsic or special about beliefs and truth, it is just that they are instrumentally useful.

Dismantling the notions of folk psychology   From a historical perspective, Richard Rorty arrives at an even more radical conclusion. He thinks that the concept of mind is a turbid mixture of two concerns, the knowing subject and the moral agent (Rorty, 1982). Rorty thinks that philosophy of mind has been the victim of seventeenth- to nineteenth-century ideas, which consider *consciousness* and *intentionality* as irreducible, and mind as a kind of substance. He has sympathy for the Ryle–Dennett tradition that dismantles the notions of inner theatre of which we, supposedly, have intuitive direct knowledge. He suggests that we should abandon these ideas of mind as a thing, and be content to let 'the subjective realm float out of ken'. We may forget about intractable consciousness and keep only what can be accounted for in science. In his view Searle (see p. 131 ff.) and Nagel (see p. 137 ff.) are like medieval essentialists who think that the mind has an intrinsic essence, in more or less the same way as medieval philosophers were interested in the essence of material things.

Rorty thinks that philosophers have now all but dispensed with consciousness – they may now start to sacrifice intentionality and meaning. Fodor's intentional realism (representations and intentionality, the beliefs and desires of folk psychology, really exist) is now 'fading out', he thinks, as consciousness has faded out before. Connectionist modelling is the first sign that all things psychological become the subject of physiology, and that there is little left for philosophers to do here.

The idea of mind will 'float out of ken', disappear as medieval substances have disappeared from our conceptual framework. Consciousness, and subsequently intentionality, will become untractable, philosophy of mind shrinks to nothingness, and psychology itself, the study of consciousness and rationality, disappears in biology. Mind as an entity does not exist, and psychology may become a pseudo-discipline.

Rorty compares this sorry story of the demise of consciousness and intentionality with the Galilean outlook on science: explanation is about useful terms, not about intrinsic natures. Searle and Fodor are partisans of an intrinsic view of intentionality, Dennett and Davidson have seen the pragmatic Galilean light. Mental concepts are not about 'what there really is', but depend on the context of the questioner, on the needs of the current empirical inquiry, on the uses to which we put them. Mind is not, or has not, an intrinsic, internal structure, but is a set of concepts whose cash value has something to do with describing and relating a kind of behaviour – namely, that kind of behaviour which has a certain freedom from the direct coupling of behaviour and environment. It is not some independent inner place.

Thus, the whole philosophical debate about representations and intentionality is dissolved in pragmatic considerations; how to describe the brain in action in the most useful way. Mind, intrinsic intentionality, beliefs and desires, representations and consciousness are unfortunate residuals of outdated philosophies according to Rorty's radical disavowal of the central notions of the philosophy of mind.

Connectionism and folk psychology   Connectionists say that since a network has no such things as identifiable beliefs and desires, no discrete states that can be identified with propositions and attitudes, the realist view of folk psychology is incompatible with connectionism (Ramsey et al., 1991). Note that this is a somewhat preciser analysis than Churchland's rejection of the LOT and the promissory note of elimination by future neuroscience. If folk psychology is defined as (minimally) the asssumption of functionally discrete states, causing behaviour, and connectionism implies distributed representations, then folk psychology is out, when connectionism is in. To the extent that neural networks are a good simulation of our cognitive life, we do not have beliefs and desires, and explaining our fellow beings in these terms cannot be literally correct. Folk psychology then is relegated to an *intentional stance* (Dennett, 1978), not more than a convenient fiction, or more respectably a 'job description' (Bechtel and Abrahamsen, 1993), which roughly describes what people can and should do in a normal environment, not what the inner structure and causes of that behaviour are. Here, the Fodorian identification of descriptive viewpoint with underlying mechanisms is abandoned: beliefs and desires are not what cause our behaviour, they are just convenient labels for describing and predicting behaviour.

But is folk psychology a scientific theory?   Andy Clark (1989, see also 1993) wants to preserve folk psychology as practical utility, but not as a description of a causal mechanism. His main argument is that folk psychology is not a scientific theory at all. If one understood the nature of folk psychology in the right perspective, then it should not, according to Clark, be sought as the opponent of connectionism or any neurophysiological theory. Original folk psychology does not seek to model cognitive processes *at all*. It is the classical cognitivist approach which contends that concepts and relations spoken of in natural language are mapped neatly on computationally operated and syntactically specified internal states. The mapping, the idea that there are in-the-head analogues to propositional attitudes, is in the eye of the orthodox cognitivist who endorses a language of thought.

Churchland (1989), therefore, is wrong in attacking folk psychology as a bad *theory*. Remember that Churchland thinks that folk psychology is stagnant and infertile and hopelessly backward compared to the sophisticated science we now have; and because it does not carve up nature at neurophysiologically respectable joints. According to Clark, this is not its purpose at all, folk psychology is not playing the same game as scientific psychology; it is not a scientific theory. It should not be identified with classical cognitivism, nor with any other physical theory of cognition. The primary purpose of folk-psychological talk is to make intelligible and predictable in a convenient way *to us* the behaviour of fellow agents acting in the world. If I have a forged rail ticket to Scotland, is his example, and I want to sell it, I am not interested in the fine-grained details of anyone's neurophysiology. 'All I want to know is where to find a likely sucker', irrespective of his neurophysiological make-up. 'Folk psychology is *designed* to be insensitive to any differences in states of the head that do not issue in differences of quite coarse-grained behaviour' (Clark, 1989: 48).

But what is more, because of its purpose, folk psychology defines what cognitive science has to explain in the end: people's behaviour and not simply mechanisms and bodily movements. Therefore cognitive science '*must*, of course, rely on a folk-psychological understanding at every stage, for we need to see how the mechanisms we study are relevant . . . to our performance in various cognitive tasks' (ibid.: 53). And these tasks have to be specified in folk-psychological terms. Psychology, Clark seems to say, is more than a theory about the brain. He pleads for the autonomy of psychology in its full-blown intentional idiom (compare this with our discussion on reasons and actions in section 1.7, p. 37 ff.).

Another of Clark's theses is that the classical approach and the connectionist approach need not be uniformly regarded as competing paradigms of cognitive architecture. The mind, he says, is best understood as a multiplicity of *virtual machines*. A virtual machine is not the hardware machine, but the different systems of rules and procedures which can be run on a physical machine in order to perform different sets of basic operations; compare them with your word processor, or different word processors and the spreadsheet you can run on your PC. Some of our cognitive virtual machines could be adapted to symbol-processing tasks (the classical approach) while others could be adapted for subsymbolic processing (the connectionist approach). Clark suggests that the connectionist approach is ill suited to higher, more abstract tasks, such as the serial reasoning tasks of logical inference and the temporal reasoning tasks of conscious planning; but that it seems to be 'nature's gift' to pattern recognition tasks, low-level vision and motor control (ibid.: 127).

An alternative? The simulation theory   The view assumed by Churchland and Fodor is the 'theory theory': folk psychology is a theory, and judging behaviour in terms of beliefs and desires is applying theoretical notions to phenomena, assuming that they refer to (presumed) laws (like: when someone desires a drink, she will go to the fridge). Such laws explain acts as caused by mental contents (thoughts). This is not to say that application of such generalizations occurs explicitly or must be conscious; on the contrary, we know them only tacitly and implicitly. Nor is it assumed that these laws are interesting as new discoveries in physics are – mostly they sound like platitudes. Nevertheless, Fodor thinks, it is a major cultural feat of the CTM to vindicate such laws, and Churchland is equally eager to eliminate them.

However, there is another possible interpretation of our predicting and explaining other people's behaviour through beliefs and desires than the 'theory theory'. Folk psychology might be a kind of *simulation*; we might just put ourselves in other people's shoes and imagine, 'simulate' what we would do, think or feel ourselves. Sigmund Freud called something like this 'projection' – of one's own mind on to someone else's. Quine allows that we 'dramatize' even the state of mind of, say, a mouse in terms of its beliefs and desires. This is a kind of imaginative or dramatic skill, not the application of a *theory* of what causes behaviour. Compare: we causally explain the behaviour of falling stones as according to the laws of gravity (the analogy of the 'theory theory'), not from dramatizing our own experiences when diving (as in the 'simulation theory'). Although Churchland has built his attack on folk psychology on the theory theory, the simulation theory is also compatible with eliminativism: if we abandon appealing to beliefs and desires, we can also forget about the mental realm as a really existing entity. Talk of beliefs and desires requires in that case no more than assumptions about our behavioural dramatic simulating skills, not about inner causes (Crane, 1995).

Representations abandoned?

Dynamical systems theory More recently, the Churchlands' radical anti-orthodox position seems to have been overtaken by an even more radical development in computational modelling, which abandons representations in the traditional sense entirely.

Recall that the classical, or orthodox, view assumes syntactically structured representations in a linguistic format. As we saw in section 4.4, Churchland (1989) and Smolensky (1991) and Van Gelder (1990) tried to demonstrate that compositionality can also be achieved by other than symbolically structured media, such as *distributed representations* with functional decomposability. That is, they argue that distributed representations can do the job that the classical view requires. The main difference between these connectionists and the classical view is how this inner computational structure is built.

A far more radical challenge to the classical agenda is the criticism of internal representations *tout court*. A first attack came from work on mobile robots ('mobots'), which are claimed to exhibit *intelligence without representation* (Brooks, 1991a, 1991b). Hence, it is argued, the reliance of classical cognitive science on the notion of representation is misguided, to say the least. Brooks has however a somewhat peculiar definition of intelligence. The main point of his argument is that the roots of intelligence, and the most important component of it, is the ability to move around in a dynamic environment. After all, it took evolution billions of years to get that right, and only a few hundred years to create human expert knowledge. Brooks' work is building mobile robots that can locomote in the real world (well . . . in his own office for the time being), doing smart things like picking up cola cans in the office and dropping them in the recycle basket. His methodology is that robots must be able to maintain multiple goals, change these, depending on circumstances, that is, adapt to the environment and capitalize on luck; they should be robust, not collapse with minor changes in the environment.

The 'boxology' common in classical information-processing accounts, where a system is specified in subsystems with distinct functions (like feature analysers, feature integrators, long-term memory, short-term memory, motor control, motor execution, etc., in linear succession), is rejected by Brooks. He wants no distinction between the peripheral (motor and sensory) systems and central representations. Rather, he builds layers of independent behaviour-producing systems, each of which may have its own goal and provides a complete perception–activity connection. Successive new layers are then added, pursuing different goals in parallel, data-driven by the environment: for example avoiding, wandering, and exploring, which can inhibit each other (for instance, the mobot wanders, when not busy avoiding things). This is called subsumption architecture. Rumour has it, however, that in Brooks' laboratory new generations of robots are not layers upon existing older models, but have to be built from scratch – that is, no subsumption seems to be realized.

Brooks argues that no internal, in fact pre-programmed, representations mirroring the world are necessary, since the world is used as its own representation. There is no symbolic interface coding and decoding input and outputs to and from an internal medium, but each layer is under local environmental control. The layers (behaviours) inhibit and suppress each other, but there is no central controller or goal representation. The device has to seek its own way in its environment, and not to follow internal models, put in by the programmer and representing the way the programmer sees the world (see also Keijzer and Bem, 1996; Bem and Keijzer, 1996).

The 'Watt governor' as a non-representational framework   Van Gelder (1995) argues that cognition in neural networks should not be analysed as a new answer to the old question of how a system mirrors the world, but as a trajectory through a series of states. Cognitive processes are evolving in an abstract space of possible states rather than (classical or connectionist) computation. His example is the 'Watt governor', which controls the throttle valve of a steam engine so as to keep power output (rotation of the flywheel) constant. The computational approach to this problem would be to divide it into a number of subtasks, specified by algorithms. A computational governor would compute the change in valve position by discrete and sequential symbol-manipulating operations according to rules; it would involve symbolic representations (for instance a number standing for engine speed), and a kind of bureaucracy of interacting agents (homunculi).

In contrast, the real Watt governor simply uses the angle of a rotating weight attached to the flywheel to control engine speed. This is not really a representation, and hence not computation: there are no processing steps, algorithms or sequences of discrete operations or subtasks. Rather, it can be mathematically described as a dynamic system, in terms of equations that describe the changing of its states in numerical values. Van Gelder's claim is that cognition is better seen as such a dynamic system, rather than as a computational system. Cognition is evolution through state-space.

Elman (in Bates and Elman, 1993) argues that such dynamics (somewhat more precisely, the trajectory of a cognitive system through a multidimensional space of possible states), are the most appropriate way to approach cognition rather than symbolic or activation patterns. The interesting thing about Elman's empirical work is that he implements the temporal aspect of cognition by copying back activation from hidden nodes to the input nodes; thus he manages to get a handle on context and achieves interesting results on the prediction of word sequences in natural language. Hence, the network is able to track sentences without internal representations of grammar and syntax. Elman emphasizes that instead of static representations it is the trajectory of the system through states (activation patterns) that is the proper level of analysis for this particular aspect of cognition. How the new dynamics will develop is too early to judge.

Thus, cognition is no longer seen as having symbols in the head that somehow represent (mirror) the world, and manipulating these is no longer supposed to be the stuff that thinking is made of. Although connectionist networks are also instances of dynamic systems, the traditional networks are set up to transform static input representations into static output representations (Van Gelder, 1995). Recall Churchland and Sejnowski (1990) who analyse the knowledge and representations a neural network possesses in terms of the frozen image of weights and activation pattern after training, and it will be clear that Van Gelder has a point in describing traditional connectionism as a 'half-way house' between classical and genuinely new, dynamic models.

Van Gelder (1995) draws some philosophical conclusions from this new, non-representational framework. Cognition is basically skilfull coping with the world, which can be done without explicitly representing it. As such, it contrasts with the Cartesian framework which considers mind in itself. Furthermore it is temporal, because of this interaction with the world, rather than static representional structures mirroring nature. Hence, these new views on cognition are more naturalistic than the classical view and the conservative connectionist view. Emphasis is on continuity between lower forms of life and human cognition ('Today the earwig, tomorrow man,' as Kirsh, 1991, put it somewhat ironically), and the connection with the environment is emphasized. What is slightly disturbing however is the rather lowly definition of intelligence put forward by dynamic systems theory aficionados: the Watt governor is certainly not everyone's idea of a cognitive system in the full sense of the word, and Brooks' claim that locomotion is almost all of intelligence is somewhat exaggerated.

Are representations really dispensable? Van Gelder (1995) and Brooks (1991a, 1991b) conclude that cognitive systems do not need internal, symbolic representational structures. Rather, like the Watt governor, an agent is coupled to its environment, and both co-evolve in real time, without the need for inner representations. As an example of a psychological theory in line with this metaphor consider the modelling of decision behaviour as push and pull by desires and opportunities (say, hunger and the availability of food) in a quasi-gravitational way; approach and avoidance can be seen as a continuous trajectory through state-space (Van Gelder, 1995). Thus, cognition can better be described as the realization of a dynamical system, proceeding through state-space, than as a system computing symbolic states so as to keep track of the world. Therefore, Van Gelder concludes, intelligence does not need representations.

Clark and Toribio (1994) reply that such wholesale rejection of representations rests on a mistake. Brooks and others think that representations are unnecessary because certain kinds of complex intelligent behaviour can occur without explicit internal representations that intervene between input and output. However, in some situations intelligent behaviour requires more than continuous coupling of agent and environment. Clark and Toribio (1994) argue that there are what they call 'representation-hungry' contexts: when the agent needs to refer to absent or counterfactual situations, or situations involving distal, non-existent or highly abstract properties; or where the agent has to be sensitive to 'parameters whose ambient physical manifestation are complex and unruly' (Clark and Toribio, 1994: 419). There, coupling between agent and environment obviously breaks down, and some kind of internal representation seems indispensable.

However, in accounting for representation-hungry contexts, we do not have to re-introduce the whole Fodorian apparatus of symbolic, syntactically structured representations. We may define representations as stand-in for features of the environment that are not present, and that guide behaviour in their stead (Haugeland, 1991); these are not necessarily explicit, symbolic and computational. Clark and Toribio assume a continuum of representations, ranging from mere input coding and input interpretation, to the creation of abstract and counterfactual representations. Typically, the notion of representation is invoked as an explanation when organisms react to objects or situations that are not present in the environment (when, for instance, Claire is hoping that Count Dracula will pay her a visit tonight and she thinks that opening her window will make it easier for him to come in).

It can be concluded that Brooks' mobots and Van Gelder's governor fail to prove the general radical anti-representational case, because these are just not representation-hungry enough. Representations as internal information-bearing states emerge as products of filtering, recoding and transforming inputs, and this is not the case in the latter examples. Whenever dynamical systems realize such strategies, and a 'gap between the dimensions of the relevant state space and bare, easily available input parameters' (Clark and Toribio, 1994: 424) exists, they can be considered as representational. Clark and Toribio not only suggest that dynamic systems theories have not yet proved that representations are dispensable in representation-hungry situations; they also claim that dimensions of state-spaces are sometimes best conceived in terms of representations.

Clark and Toribio's (1994) liberal notion of representations suggests a way out of the representation debate. They emphasize that connectionists and Fodorians agree about the central role of the notion of internal representations and only disagree on their format. Anti-representationalists like Van Gelder reject Churchland's approach, as well as Fodor's, and consider the former at best a 'half-way house' (Van Gelder, 1995) between classical (Fodorian) and dynamical approaches: both focus on the transformation of static input patterns into static output patterns. Van Gelder's Watt governor is an illustration of the general idea behind the alternative: a mathematical description of a system's trajectory through abstract space of possible states is the way to explain cognition. The notion of representations, considered as stand-in for some aspects of a complex, unruly or imaginary environment, without strong commitments to the (symbolic or connectionist) internal format of these, is still an indispensable explanatory construct for explaining full-blown cognitive systems.

To sum up: although the strict Fodorian construal of representations and even the connectionist view of representations as activation patterns might have to be rejected, the notion of representation is still indispensable for those situations where the behavioural repertoire is really cognitive.

Our preliminary conclusion is that the anti-representationalists are too rash, and have based their case on too simple and selective cases – situations where a tight coupling of organism and environment exists. Intuitively, real cognition involves some distance from the environment, and that is where some kind of internal representation of abstract or absent properties is indispensable.

Probably the most promising approach to reconciling representations with a naturalistic view of mind will employ the notion of *internalizing*: higher organisms acquire the capacity to do some of their cognitive activities, somehow in their head, rather than in the real world, and to use tools in a more or less decontextualized way, that is, not directly coupled to the current ambient environment. (For some suggestions on how this might work see Bechtel, 1993.)

Intrinsic or instrumental intentionality

Real consciousness and intrinsic intentionality

The Chinese Room   John Searle (1990b) became famous for his attack on the central thesis of the CTM, a *Gedankenexperiment* known as the 'Chinese Room'. Imagine the following: a speaker of English is put in a room and is given two batches of Chinese characters, plus instructions in English. His task is to produce a set of Chinese characters by way of output, when given a batch of Chinese characters (input), according to the instructions. For the Chinese who provide him with questions in Chinese and read his answers in Chinese, the Englishman seems a Chinese-story-comprehending system; however, all he does is manipulate uninterpreted symbols according to some instruction (program). That is, the Englishman plus his instructions are imitating a computer program. The inspiration for this story came from Schank's computer program that could answer questions about simple stories, thus presumably instantiating understanding. The English speaker/understander without knowledge of Chinese takes the place of the program. So, the crux is: 'What would it be like if my mind actually worked on the principles that the theory says all minds work on?' And the conclusion is: 'The computer is me . . . the computer has nothing more than I have in the case where I understand nothing.' Obviously, the Englishman, in his role of computer program, does not understand Chinese; hence, a computer program cannnot be said to understand anything.

This means that the famous *Turing test* for intelligence (does the system give the right anwers to difficult questions, such that it is indistinguishable from human answers) is irrelevant; the system can give the right answers without understanding.

It has often been argued that Searle's thought experiment is unrealistic and misleading. One objection is that the complexity of a working expert system is not comparable with the sheet of instructions and the stack of symbols that Searle provides the Englishman with – and from that complexity might emerge genuine understanding.

Probably the most powerful objection is the 'systems reply', which holds that the Englishman is only a component of the system. Searle's misleading trick is to make the English symbol manipulator human; no one would ask whether understanding resides in a particular neuron or chip anywhere in the system – and this objection applies to the Englishman as well. The systems reply is that understanding can be attributed to the whole system (input, output, program, processor); the Englishman is only the analogue of the central processor, and the argument that his lack of comprehension of Chinese proves that comprehension is beyond any computational system as a whole, is about as silly as concluding that you do not understand this text because some neuron in your parietal cortex does not understand it.

We do not want to force an interpretation on the reader, but we feel that thought experiments are inconclusive evidence. What computational (connectionist, dynamic) systems can do is ultimately an empirical question.

What is really at stake: intrinsic intentionality John Searle (1992) thinks that there is something fundamentally wrong with the CTM, and with the philosophy of mind that produces such outrageous claims. After all, there is an essential difference between minds and machines that is intrinsic and not merely in the eye of the beholder, and a theory of mind should be able to distinguish between them. Searle argues that strong AI is a worthless theory of mind since it cannot see the difference between minds and computers. Searle has the strong conviction that the essence of mind is intrinsic intentionality and consciousness. His 1992 book suggests that many things are wrong with the philosophy of mind; that it practically ignores mind. He wants to restore consciousness and intentionality to a central place in the philosophy of mind; mind should be rediscovered.

Searle takes mind in the full *first-person* sense of consciousness and intentionality. Consciousness and its first-person events and qualia (feelings), are in his view ontologically real, are part of the furniture of the world, exist independently of observable behaviour, although intentionality can be recognized in the behaviour of fellow human beings and animals. The first-person experiences may be epistemically subjective (only observable by the subject that has them), ontologically they are objective; they really exist and are no figment of the imagination. They cannot be reduced to *third-person* (objective) events, as in Dennett's theory of consciousness (Dennett, 1991). The epistemic subjectivity implies that introspection conceived as objective observation is an error.

The mistake of contemporary philosophy of mind, according to Searle, is that it ignores these first-person phenomena and wastes its time looking for mind in third-person phenomena like computation. In his view, philosophy of mind confuses objectivity and scientific approach with a ban on subjective events. Behaviourists, identity theorists, eliminativists, computationalists, because of an almost neurotic fear of subjectivity, try to ignore or deny subjective states.

Searle opposes both dualism and materialism. Against *dualism*, he thinks that the mind is a product of the brain in the way that digestion is a function of the digestive tract. Against orthodox *materialism*, he believes that 'among the physical features of the world are the biological phenomena such as inner qualitative states of consciousness and intrinsic intentionality' (Searle, 1992: xii). Thus, mental events are on the one hand real, emergent properties, not reducible to material ones; on the other hand they are caused by the nervous system. Consciousness is an irreducible physical component of physical reality.

Rather than computation, *consciousness* is in his view the foundation of cognition. The hallmark of cognitive states is that they are either conscious or potentially conscious; states that are not potentially conscious are brute neurophysiological facts. Note that this in a sense reverses the order of explanation: others try to find the (computational) mechanisms that explain aspects of mind, such as intentionality and sometimes consciousness, while Searle puts intentionality and consciousness first, as intrinsic, and rejects proposals to consider them as somehow derived from something else.

Explanatory inversion   Against this background, Searle (1992) supplements his Chinese Room argument with the consideration that the CTM is not simply wrong; its claim does not even have a clear meaning. The central tenet of the CTM is that semantics (meaning) follows syntax (the program). Searle argues that this must be wrong; whereas semantics is real, syntax is observer-relative: it depends on how you interpret. Searle likes to rub in the fact that there is no foolproof definition of an algorithm. Anything can be interpreted as a computational state; you can consider the molecules in the wallpaper in front of you as an implementation of a program. There is no fact intrinsic to physics that makes a machine a computer. Now, as consciousness is for real, but computation is in the eye of the beholder, then computation surely cannot explain intentionality, and even less can intentionality be identical with computation.

Is there intrinsic intentionality?   Against Searle, Dennett (1990a, 1995) denies the existence of a thing called intrinsic or original intentionality. The only real intentional agent is natural selection, *Mother Nature*, who has 'designed' us to be the vehicles of selfish genes. We are in principle no more intentional than robots designed with the explicit aim to fend for themselves and survive. That is, all intentionality is derived from Mother Nature's ability to select the survivors. More seriously, Dennett thinks that intentionality is a *façon de parler*, that picks out real patterns of behaviour. These are not confined to human or animal behaviour: nothing prevents us from attributing goals to, for example, biochemical processes – as long as they yield accurate predictions. Furthermore, these do not necessarily correspond with the underlying causal story.

So, Searle differs from Dennett in his realism about intentionality, and from Fodor in his rejection of computation. That leaves him with the somewhat awkward obligation to explain how the brain produces real first-person phenomena, intentionality and consciousness. As yet, he hasn't produced anything more convincing than something like: the brain just does it.

Instrumental intentionality and derived consciousness

Intentional systems   Daniel Dennett tries to reconcile intentional explanation with neuroscience. Although his point of departure is third-person objectivism and materialism, which leaves no room for intrinsic and irreducible subjectivity, consciousness and so on, he acknowledges the value of the folk-psychological idiom. He distinguishes (1978) three stances: the *intentional stance* is the kind of explanation, prediction and description of behaviour in terms of beliefs and desires, more exactly, of goals and information. It can also be extended to artificial agents, for instance when a chess program is credited with the knowledge of openings, a repertoire of moves, and the goal of winning through checkmate.

Next is the *design stance*, which specifies the algorithms or the design that produces this intentional behaviour. The design of a chess computer, the specific subroutines and intermediate goals it has been endowed with, explain why it seems to have knowledge and plans and an apparent desire to win.

Finally the *physical stance* considers the hardware, and is only relevant for explaining the system's behaviour when something goes wrong with the electronics or the power supply.

The intentional stance employs notions that are traditionally considered bad explanations, because they seem to invoke a rational, intentional *homunculus* to explain intelligence. Dennett considers this as a loan to intelligence that has to be paid by providing explanations at design stance level. Moving thus from the intentional to the design stance means that the single intelligent homunculus is replaced by an 'army of idiots', by agents with simpler job descriptions, which can in turn also be decomposed into even simpler mechanisms until the level of physics is reached. Instead of goals and knowledge, program subroutines and properties of electronic circuits are invoked as explanations.

In principle there is no lower limit for the applicability of this type of intentional explanation; it is legitimate whenever it works, as when a thermostat can fruitfully be described as striving to maintain a comfortable temperature; or when a chess computer is considered as pondering on its next move.

Instrumentalism   Thus Dennett (1987) manages to exorcize the homunculus without throwing it away with the bathwater. *Intentionality* depends on the stance, on the concepts and perspective; briefly, it is in the eye of the beholder. Attributing intentionality, goals and information is a manner of speaking, an instrument for describing and predicting behaviour, not a reference to underlying mental mechanisms.

However, it is no illusion, no fiction, and it is not an entirely arbitrary decision whether to describe something as intelligent. The intentional stance reveals real patterns of intentional behaviour, that would not have been visible without it. If an alien from Mars could completely predict our behaviour from a physical stance (let us assume that Martians have a superior knowledge of physics), and could tell all our body movements with perfect accuracy, he would still be missing something, namely the intentional pattern in them. Compare the statement that a boxer is practising a left uppercut because he wants to win a match, with a list of his muscle contractions.

In Dennett's view being predictable by the intentional stance is all there is to being a 'true believer', that is, a system (human, animal or computer) that is complex enough to count as having beliefs, goals and representations. No real intentionality, no inner facts of mind, are necessary for such prediction and explanation of intentional behaviour.

In Dennett's instrumentalism we can see his Wittgensteinian and Rylean heritage. Wittgenstein and Ryle argued that the meaning of mental terminology depends on language games (see Chapter 2), rather than reference to inner events. Likewise, Dennett thinks that intentionality and consciousness depend on their concepts. What the weight of a stone is, is intrinsic, but what counts as love, or whether something is a bathtub or a boat depends on, and may vary with, the concepts of the linguistic community.

This marks his bitter disagreement with Searle, who considers the real first-person experience and consciousness, that is, intrinsic intentionality, a fact of life, whereas Dennett thinks original intentionality is a myth. Dennett thinks that his intentional stance nevertheless yields a robust criterion for the relative reality of intentional folk-psychological categories, such as beliefs, goals and intentions. A rich semantic system with lots of intricate representational states must correspond to a certain specific environment; this puts enough constraints on interpretations. How we usefully interpret some mental fact as a representation is implicit in the design and is restricted by the way it must fit into the environment; the aboutness that Brentano considered the mark of the mental resides in the system's connection to, embedding in, its environment.

A criticism that might be levelled against Dennett is that he seems to take the design or neurophysiological stance quite literally. It is not clear why the design stance should thus be privileged above the intentional stance, unless one already has a scientistic bias that takes folk-psychological discourse less seriously than scientific idiom (cf. Baker, 1995).

Consciousness   Dennett has put forward a theory of consciousness which in essence tries to explain it in terms of information processing. Design from subpersonal components can yield consciousness, in the same way as simple subsystems can make up complex rational behaviour, for example, in a chess computer. Dennett's proposal is that the mind is a jumble of parallel information-processing sequences, a kind of text fragments or narratives, which he calls *multiple drafts*, distributed throughout the brain and continuously revised and updated. The mind is a pandemonium of narrative fragments and goals, which compete for resources, attention and priority, dominance and influence over the rest of the brain. Being conscious is gaining cerebral 'celebrity' (Dennett, 1994); it occurs when a winning draft is known throughout the brain and attracts attention from all over the system.

In Dennett's multiple drafts model, there is no central executive, no central agent or *Cartesian theatre* where it all comes together. Thus, he tries to defuse the Cartesian heritage of a thinking substance, self-transparent, populated with ghostly mental events, a kind of inner mental theatre as immaterial counterpart to the material world.

A major obstacle to explaining consciousness is the intuition that it is essentially private and subjective, only accessible in *first-person* mode, and that it eludes objective *third-person* descriptions. How pain feels, or what it is like to win the lottery, is difficult to describe.

Mentalist philosophers concluded that mind was essentially private, subjectively experienced, and therefore beyond the grasp of objective explanations. Furthermore, mentalists thought that the furniture of the Cartesian theatre was open to observation by its owner, who had privileged access. Introspection, the observation of mental events, was the method of psychology for the last half of the previous century.

Dennett argues that what is reported is not a view of one's inner screen; he tries to deconstruct the idea of private access to one's own mental theatre. For once, he argues, there are no definite and ready-made thoughts and ideas in our heads, but a messy lot of half-finished narratives. Thoughts are in fact produced when uttered, as in response to an external probe; we only know what we think when we hear ourselves pronounce it. Furthermore, it is an error to think that there is an exact point in time where perception or recognition or a thought occurs in the mind; seeing or recognizing or thinking something is a kind of horse race between competing drafts (Dennett and Kinsbourne, 1992). This, a fortiori, applies to introspection: we do not observe our thoughts, but we construct a narrative from bits and pieces of self-observed behaviour, sometimes confabulate, more or less the way fiction is created. It should be added that there is some evidence for this counterintuitive view. Nisbett and Wilson (1977) showed that people have little insight into their own decision-making, and when asked about it, tend to make something up.

Thus, Dennett thinks that he effectively destroyed the mentalist claim that there is something mental that is seen and reported in introspection. Having demolished the Cartesian theatre, Dennett can also make short shrift of its principal tenant: the *self* or the I or the subject. The self is only virtual, not substantial. Just as the centre of gravity of the earth is only an imaginary point, not something substantial that draws falling objects towards it, the self is only the virtual centre around which multiple drafts gravitate, it is not the central controller of the mind. The brain spins a web of words and deeds, but there is no central subject to oversee it.

Recall the contrast with Searle. Dennett derives consciousness from content (information processing); Searle (1990a) puts consciousness first, and defines cognition in terms of consciousness.

Consciousness and qualia

The crux of the qualia-debate (singular: a quale) is whether the phenomenological or qualitative features of consciousness – like feeling pain, seeing red, tasting wine, hearing music – are in principle, irrespective of any future developments in neuroscience, irreducible to brain events or information processing. The idea, more formally, is that first-person descriptions, knowledge by acquaintance, cannot be translated into third-person knowledge by description; how I feel is not exhaustively describable in intersubjective terms (Russell, 1988). This intuitively plausible idea that you cannot explain how it feels to watch the stained-glass windows of Chartres cathedral at sunrise to someone who is colour blind, or why Chardonnay goes well with *suprême de volaille* to someone who subsists on pizza and hamburgers, or how it is to be depressive, has been exploited by philosophers to demonstrate that consciousness is essentially private and ineffable, and that qualia are directly experienced by the subject, the mind, consciousness, or whatever. They argue that the mental theatre is populated by subjective self-transparent things called qualia, and that the mind knows the contents of consciousness directly, infallibly. In essence, this is the Myth of the Given, discussed in Chapter 2; it is the view that Dennett's theory of consciousness tries to refute.

Nagel on the irreducibility of first-person experience   A well-known attempt to shield first-person experience (qualia) from reduction to third-person talk, for example neuroscience, is Thomas Nagel's (1980) bat story: 'What is it like to be a bat?' His argument is in essence that no amount of descriptive knowledge could possibly add up to experiencing how it feels to be a bat, and what it is like to perceive by sonar. Conscious experience is 'what it is like' to be an organism to the organism; proposals for reduction of that subjective experience must be considered unsuccessful as long as the reducing theory (for instance pain is the firing of neurons in some brain centre) is logically possible without consciousness. This is known as the *zombie problem*. A zombie is supposedly one of the walking dead, who behaves more or less normally, but without conscious experience. It seems fair to demand that a theory of consciousness should be able to distinguish us from zombies.

Nagel argues that subjective experience is connected with a single subjective point of view, a 'pour-soi' (a 'for-yourself') as the French philosopher Sartre called it, which an objective physical point of view has to abandon. His by now famous (or notorious) example is: what it is like to be a bat. This is not the same as imagining, by extrapolating from our own experience, how we would feel hanging from a beam. We may never be able to know animals' or other people's minds, and we may never have an adequate language to describe subjective experience. That does not mean that it is not real, complex, rich and highly specific in nature.

The facts of experience are accessible only to a subjective, single, first-person point of view, and not to objective third-person points of view. Nagel admits that in the latter case there is a multiplicity of viewpoints, tending to greater objectivity, less dependence on subjective and individual impressions, and hence the possibility of *reduction* to more basal physical mechanisms. In the former case, however, reduction fails. Moving from subjective appearance to objective reality does not work; the specific subjective point of view is irreducible; no sense can be made of the question of what their real objective nature is. Nagel ends with a rather disparate call for an objective phenomenology that develops concepts dealing with descriptions of subjective experiences. He argues that any solution to the mind–body problem is dependent on such an attempt to gauge, and span, the subjective–objective gap.

Consider another example (Jackson, 1990). Assume someone who can make colour discriminations nobody else can see; assume neuroscientists know everything about her nervous system, and can completely explain this extraordinary ability. Nevertheless, in a sense they would know more if they themselves could, through some brain transplant, actually experience the colour differences. Hence, physics (neurophysiology) is incomplete.

Again another example. A neurophysiologist who knows everything about colour perception but having been raised in a black and white environment has never experienced colours herself: does she know what the sensation of seeing red is? When given a colour television set instead of her black and white one, does she know something new? Churchland has tried to show that a full-blown reduction is in principle conceivable, that subjective experience can be shaped by neuroscientific concepts. In contrast with Nagel, his solution assumes that any subjective report is theory laden, concept dependent. Churchland (1985a) places his proposal for reducing qualia within a neuro-computational perspective against the background of his (1979) ideas on reduction and elimination of scientific theories. Thus, he challenges Nagel's claim that experience exists before its conceptualization. When we retrain our neural networks, our experience also changes – witness mundane examples, like learning to hear a symphony quite differently after studying musicology, or learning to appreciate real ale.

In the wake of his theory of consciousness, Dennett (1988, 1991) tried to provide a convincing argument that the philosophical notion of qualia, as observable private entities in the mind, is a bad habit of thought, a metaphysical muddle that cannot be solved, but should be dissolved – a knot to be cut rather than disentangled. He concentrates on the philosophical definition and tries to demonstrate that such a thing as a quale does not exist. Qualia are complex dispositions that have the property of producing certain effects on their owners. They are dispositions to react in certain ways to sensory stimuli: saying 'red', stepping on the brake pedal, adding a little tomato paste to the sauce, appreciating Schongauer's *Rosenmadonna*, etc. No intrinsic properties are required to explain the behaviour of a system that has the power of discriminating colours, smells, and so on.

Dennett concludes that qualia as private ineffable intrinsically conscious properties simply do not exist. The philosophical notion of qualia is a mess that is best walked away from (Dennett, 1991: 369). Philosophers' intuitions about the unbridgeable gap between subjective and objective are given short shrift: in the case of the bat and the colour-blind scientist, we simply cannot tell what it means to have all the information about the nervous system, and this lack of imagination should not be confused with a metaphysical necessity.

Not everyone is convinced that Churchland and Dennett have really done away with the mysteries of consciousness, and that they have good explanations of the phenomenological aspects of experience.

The mysterious property P A more fundamental argument against the possibility of explaining consciousness is given by Colin McGinn (1991), who introduced the idea of *cognitive closure*. A type of mind is cognitively closed to a certain property or a certain theory if the cognitive powers at that mind's disposal are unapt for grasping the property or understanding the theory.

> Minds are biological products like bodies, and like bodies they come in different shapes and sizes, more or less capacious, more or less suited to certain cognitive tasks. Different species are capable of perceiving different properties of the world, and no species can perceive every property. . . . What is closed to the mind of a rat may be open to the mind of a monkey, and what is open to us may be closed to the monkey. (McGinn, 1991: 3)

Therefore, he thinks that there are problems which human minds are in principle equipped to solve, and 'mysteries' which elude our understanding. In his study McGinn tries to show that the mind–body problem is not cognitively accessible to humans; that the nature of the connection between consciousness and the brain is and will remain a mystery to us. However, it is not a mystery because it is somehow supernatural – the property of the brain that accounts for consciousness is a *natural* phenomenon. Like life, consciousness is a biological development; we avoid vitalism and 'the magic touch of God's finger' as explanations of life, because we think there must be some natural account of how life comes from matter. Likewise there *has* to be some naturalistic explanation for how brains cause minds, but we are cognitively closed to that natural property, which therefore remains a mystery to us. Now, what reasons does McGinn have for asserting that our minds are closed to the correct theory of the psychophysical connection and that we cannot grasp the property which is responsible for the nexus (P for short)?

If we want to identify the property P, there seem, according to McGinn, to be two avenues open to us: 'we could try to get to P by investigating consciousness directly; or we could look to the study of the brain for P' (1991: 7).

As to the first avenue, we know what it is to be conscious; we have direct cognitive access to properties of consciousness by introspection. We know it when we taste something bitter or when we feel sad. But in these auto-phenomenological, first-person ascriptions we never catch the mind–brain relation, we never get a glimpse of P. Introspection of consciousness reveals only its surface, not 'the inner constitution' (ibid.: 80). The problem of the consciousness–brain connection lies outside consciousness and cannot be solved by simply being conscious.

Will neuroscience, then, be the place to look for P? Negative. All our empirical investigations to understand the workings of the brain do not lead to consciousness. The property of consciousness itself is not an observable property of the brain and cannot be found by empirically investigating the brain. You can stare into a living conscious brain and see there a variety of brain properties – shape, colour, texture, etc. – 'but you will not thereby *see* what the subject is experiencing, the conscious state itself' (ibid.: 11). The senses can only present things in space with spatially defined properties, and while the brain is a spatial object, consciousness is not. But, you would say, neither are the properties of quantum theory; many theories contain unobservables; without concepts about hidden structures, we could not achieve successful theories in many domains (ibid.: 89). McGinn maintains, however, that explanations of brain data will never disclose consciousness; we cannot know which property of the brain accounts for consciousness. 'Consciousness is as natural as anything else in nature, but it is not given to us to understand the nature of this naturalness' (ibid.: 88).

In his (1992) book Owen Flanagan critically evaluates the arguments of what he calls the 'New Mysterians', like McGinn and Thomas Nagel (the 'Old Mysterians' being the metaphysical dualists, like Descartes). Flanagan agrees with Nagel and McGinn that, of course, no description cast in the language of neuroscience 'can *capture* what it is like to be me' because only I can capture that and because the objective brain story is just a *description* (Flanagan, 1992: 116 f.). However, the fact that we have here 'two different epistemic access relations', the subjective first-person and the objective, scientific third-person access, does not undermine the 'naturalist's hope of isolating the specific properties that subserve first-person experience'.

4.6   Against mechanistic theories of mind: some alternatives

In the previous sections we sketched the mainstream in the philosophy of mind. This majority view is overwhelmingly mechanist: mind is considered as an, in principle, mechanical system, to be understood according to the laws of the physical universe (Crane, 1995). More precisely, the majority view relies on the notion of a computational system. This is characterized by the wedding of traditional issues in the philosophy of language, like meaning, intentionality and representation, to the idea of a Turing machine, a physical symbol system. It aims at a mechanistic explanation of rationality and intentionality, perhaps even of consciousness. Given its materialist and mechanicist creed, the computational model of mind and cognition is widely considered 'the only game in town', the only theory that tallies with the cognitive and neurosciences. Other approaches are usually rejected as unscientific, magic, on a par with vitalism and mysticism.

Some anti-cognitivists have made quite an impact: Searle's refutation of the computational approach, and Dreyfus' Heideggerian criticism of its central assumptions. Incidentally, both have recently expressed cautious acclaim for connectionism.

Others remain peripheral. Arthur Still and Alan Costall (1991; see also Costall and Still, 1987) collected in *Against Cognitivism* a motley crew of anti-cognitivsts, including ecological psychologists, phenomenologists, social constructionists, Hegelians, Vygotskians, and others. Still and Costall sum up the critique of cognitivism in terms of two kinds of dualism, the dualism of mind and body and of organism and environment: 'Together these make possible the abstractions from everyday activity . . . established under the constraints of laboratory psychology' (1991: 8). By 'cognitivism' they refer mainly to the classical, orthodox cognitive psychology. This approach, as we saw in the previous sections, characterized cognition as a world-aloof internalism (also called 'individualism' or 'solipsism': see section 4.3, p. 112 ff.); as a static innate system of formal rules without development; as a logical system of rational higher-order cognition, framed in a language of thought, without regard for its embodiment. Though avowed materialists, the orthodox cognitivists isolated intellectual faculties and ignored the epistemological significance of the body. They were not interested in the living context of organism–environment interactions (see also Varela et al., 1991).

We saw earlier that cognitive scientists with an interest in connectionism or neural networks expressed almost the same criticism of orthodox cognitive psychology. They disapproved of the intellectualist, formal linguistic and a-biological picture of cognition, the idea of pre-programmed representations and rules. Though these researchers stay within the tradition of a predominant materialistic and broad-physicalistic (neurological, biological) and computational approach to cognition, they share the disapproval of the orthodox cognitivists with many others, among whom are those who approach the mind from a social or social psychological standpoint. The following points stand out.

First, cognitivism is much too restricted; it only recognizes intellectual and individual aspects of mind. Cognitivism has manifestly no interest in 'mythology, history, philosophy or politics as ways in which human beings attempt to make sense of their lives', writes Bolton (1991: 105); that is, it does not concern real human existence. It justifies this abstraction by an appeal to scientific objectivity and impartiality. Bolton sees cognitivism as part of contemporary psychology, which is dominated by the influence of technology and intellectualism. It sees the life of the mind as a series of operations, such as problem-solving and information-processing, so that the success of the discipline rests upon 'our technical capacity to make explicit the structure of these operations . . . in purely intellectual terms' (ibid.: 111).

Secondly, the social aspects gets scant attention. The problem, writes Still, confronting mechanism and romanticism in history, lies in what seems to be left out altogether: the humanities; and what gets 'too limited a share of the epistemological cake': the social sciences and psychology, especially social psychology (Still, 1991: 13). What is meant, however, is social psychology which truly refers to other persons, since the dominant approach in the field today is that of *cognitive social psychology* (e.g. Fiske and Taylor, 1984; Wyer and Srull, 1984), which studies interpersonal phenomena using the 'conceptual machinery' of representational cognitive psychology (Shanon, 1993: 136). Central to this approach is a conception of 'social knowledge', which is how individuals perceive other people; a study of, for instance, the role of attitudes and stereotypes. This social knowledge is not very different from knowledge of other objects and is defined in the same classical representational manner. Hence, social-psychological behaviour is characterized by the same means of computational operations applied to representational structures (Shanon, 1993). The result is that the study of the social is part of the standard mechanist and representational framework, rather than truly referring to other persons.

It will not come as a surprise that this individual-oriented cognitive social psychology has been contested by social constructionists (Gergen, 1989; Shotter 1975, 1991) and other 'social' social psychologists. Because what is missing in this conception of social knowledge is the notion that the individual mind is constituted by social influences. Conceptual analysis of mental discourse proceeds from the philosophical assumption that mind is a social construction, and hence that the study of mind is essentially different from the natural sciences. For this assumption social psychologists take their inspiration from Wittgenstein, Vygotsky, Mead and phenomenologists, such as Merleau-Ponty, and Berger and Luckmann with their provocative and influential book *The Social Construction of Reality* (1967).

Wittgenstein on the nature of language and mind

In our opinion, the most articulate alternative to the dominant mechanist theories of mind is a broadly Wittgensteinian position. The mechanist position is that thinking is literally symbol manipulation or network activation; in any case, some form of computation. Wittgenstein denies the possibility of identifying mental content or meaning with a physical state, and by extension, with a computational state. More precisely, although he may agree with the thesis that the brain is a syntactic machine, it cannot be *ipso facto* a semantic machine. Recall that Wittgenstein (1953) contends that the meaning of an utterance is shown in the way it is used, 'meaning is use', and cannot be isolated from its context, the language game it is part of (see Chapter 2, p. 49 ff.). Therefore, meaning cannot be something in the head, constituted by syntactic patterns of neural activation, but is embedded in human customs and institutions, in a cultural context (McDonough, 1989).

Wittgensteinians strongly object to Fodor's thesis that the syntactic engine mimics semantics, that is, that semantic elements correspond with syntactic patterns, and that the thesis is incoherent; methodological solipsism cannot be true. Wittgenstein himself later rejected his earlier picture theory, where a similar correspondence between language and the world is assumed. McDonough (1989) identifies some kind of picture theory of meaning as a precondition for a mechanist model of mind: meaning elements must correspond with elements of a syntactic structure. In the later Wittgenstein, however, meaning is holistic, part of a wider cultural context; therefore, mechanistic models of mind, which assume that meaning elements can be isolated and subsequently correlated with language tokens, are rejected by the Wittgensteinian tradition. Mechanism ends where meaning begins (McDonough, 1989: 12).

Wittgenstein's pupil Norman Malcolm (1971) emphasizes that the possession of a concept (representation, knowledge) is not the same as possessing a mental image or idea in the mental theatre – rather, it is being able to *do* certain things. '[I]nner exhibition can contribute nothing to the understanding of a concept' (Malcolm, 1971: 56–7). According to Malcolm, the mind cannot be understood in isolation from the body and the community of human beings. The brain as such does not think; only a living person does (ibid.: 77).

The likeness to Ryle (see Chapter 2) will be clear: concepts are parts of a whole form of life, and it is the task of philosophy to explore and clarify concepts, not to explain them by inner mental causes. Philosophical conceptual analysis merges into theoretical sociology, which is elucidation of existing social conceptual practices (Winch, 1958). Linguistic analysis in a social context also touches hermeneutics. In contrast with the facts of natural science, concepts have a contextual structure, which is known by the members of a linguistic community, as it were from the inside, from the way they participate pre-reflexively in its transactions. This makes the hermeneutic conception of mental content clearly distinct from the naturalistic science of the mind, which is in the business of discovering empirical facts about mental processes.

Fodor rejects such a conceptual construal of mental discourse. He wants real explanations, and therefore causal mechanisms of mind. McDonough (1989) argues that Fodor needs to assume that meaning is a function of elementary meaning particles (cf. the elementary observation statements of logical positivism), and that language and the language of thought is thus analogous to a logical calculus. Contrary to the Fodorian school Wittgenstein holds that there is no underlying mechanism that explains meaning. The explanation of behaviour is not to be found in a semantic engine inside the skull, but the criteria for a semantic description of neuronal events can be traced to the semantical system outside them (McDonough, 1989: 19): a person's intentionality is to be understood, not from inside his or her brain, but from the outside, the cultural context. McDonough calls this a Copernican revolution: conceptual clarification goes in the opposite direction from what Fodor thinks.

For this reason Wittgenstein had great doubts about whether psychology and (neuro)physiology did match.

> No supposition seems to me more natural than that there is no process in the brain correlated with associating or with thinking; so that it would be impossible to read off thought-processes from brain-processes. . . . It is thus perfectly possible that certain psychological phenomena *cannot* be investigated physiologically, because physiologically nothing corresponds to them. (Wittgenstein, 1981: 106)

From this non-mechanist model of mind and language, later critics of cognitivism infer that there cannot be a universal mental syntactic or 'deep' structure, conceived of in Chomsky's theory of language and in the language of thought, which delivers meanings in a mechanical way. Our ability to understand sentences is not an ability to make 'lightning-quick calculations in which we derive the meaning of a sentence from the meanings of its constituents and their mode of combination,' write Baker and Hacker (1984: 354). They see this as a false idea, a remnant of the 'ancient myth of the "given" and of what the mind, contributing structure from its own resources, makes of it'; and they add that this myth 'is not rendered respectable by being dressed up in late twentieth century garb' (ibid.: 355).

To sum up, Wittgenstein and his followers can be seen as a kind of counterpoint to the dominant cognitivist paradigm, embodied by Fodor. The latter tries to explain mind by its computational mechanisms, the former consider cultural context, irreducible to physical mechanisms, as the essence of mind.

Putnam on representation and reality

Hilary Putnam's rejection of the computational theory of mind has some Wittgensteinian overtones. His famous article 'The meaning of "meaning"' (Putnam, 1975) shows, somewhat counterintuitively, that mental content, meaning and reference are not exclusively in the head. The thought experiment he proposed is known as 'Twin Earth'. Imagine that there is an exact copy of our earth somewhere, the only difference being that water over there is XYZ rather than H_2O. Twin Earth contains an exact copy of you and me; when we have a representation 'water' in our heads, this will be exactly the same as the thought 'water' in the heads of our identical twin. However, on earth this means H_2O, on Twin Earth it means XYZ: therefore, meaning is not in the head, but depends also on the environment.

There is no necessary relation between having mental states and understanding; what goes on in a person's head does not determine what he or she means or refers to. A mental state isolated from situations does not fix reference. Putnam tries to show this in another, much disputed thought experiment, 'Brain in a Vat' (Putnam, 1981: Ch. 1). When we imagine a brain that is disconnected from the world and gets its inputs from a computer that is connected to its nerve endings, then its experiences, representations and mental contents are in principle hallucinations – even if they are, *ex hypothesi*, exactly the same as in a healthy individual looking at the same environment through his or her own eyes. This proves in Putnam's analysis that having mental states is not a sufficient condition for seeing and understanding: what goes on in your head does not determine what you mean; a mental state isolated from its situation does not have the capacity to refer to the world (ibid.: Ch. 2). If mental content is not in the head, but in an organism–environment relation, then methodological solipsism must be a failure.

Putnam (1988) extends his theory of meaning into a critique of the representational theory of mind. Whereas Fodor and others treat meaning and representation as intrinisic properties of a computational system, Putnam thinks they are part of holistic interpretive practices, and therefore irreducible to internal (syntactic) processes in a formal mental language. Reference is partly determined by the physical environment, as shown by the Twin Earth example, and it is partly social, not intrinsic in mental processes, as is evident in what Putnam calls the 'division of linguistic labor': I use words like 'elm' and 'beech', of which I as an individual have no clear definition, and I rely on the foresters of my linguistic community to tell them apart. Meaning is not in an individual's head, but partly external to it. Mentalism of the Fodorian and Cartesian variety typically neglects the contribution of the environment and of the linguistic community to meaning and mental content. Therefore, Fodor's language of thought can be no theory of meaning. We cannot individuate beliefs without reference to the environment, and the states of the brain in isolation from their environment ('in a vat') are not representations. Meaning and beliefs are dependent on interpretive practices, and Putnam argues that these cannot be captured in an explicit procedure (a 'Master Algorithm'), since the latter presupposes such interpretational skills.

Here Putnam's view approaches the position of Wittgenstein: meaning is use, and reason goes beyond what reason can formalize. He seems effectively to abandon any pretence of reducing interpretation and meaning to something more basal; that is, an explanation, or a naturalistic account of meaning is out of the picture. The identification of beliefs takes place in an open-ended interpretive practice, not to be identified with computational states. You cannot reduce mental processes to computation, since the latter is insufficient for genuine intentionality.

Strictly speaking, Putnam's (1988) rejection of computation affects only Fodor's computational theory of mind, and similar broad metaphysical claims, much less the quest for computational models of certain domains of cognition and perception (Demopoulos, 1990). However, Putnam (1994) makes it clear that in his opinion AI has not achieved anything interesting in these domains either.

Vygotsky on the social origins of mind

The Russian psychologist Lev Vygotsky (1896–1934) has been considered one of the fathers of the idea that the social other plays a crucial role in the cognitive development of the individual. Two themes in his theoretical framework are of importance for his understanding of mind: the genetic or developmental approach, and the claim that (higher) mental processes in the individual have their origin in social processes (Wertsch, 1985). In the context of his research on the dynamics and prediction of children's intellectual development, for instance, he asserted that only in joint activity with others do children achieve what he calls *zones of proximal development*. These are levels of performance beyond their individual competence, higher cognitive skills than they could attain by acting on their own. It was shown that only under the guidance of or in cooperation with an adult could three- to five-year-old children perform some tasks, which five- to seven-year-old children were able to perform independently (Rogoff and Wertsch, 1984; see also Van der Veer and Valsiner, 1991: Ch. 13). Vygotsky proposed a more complex method for assessing and predicting children's intelligence than the 'Western' individualistic IQ test: he focused on the relation between teaching (socializing) and cognitive development, rather than on what the child can do herself.

Vygotsky saw the mental as an *internalization* of the social, a process in which social phenomena are transformed into psychological. Language is an important medium of internalization, it is a psychological tool for socializing children into the public domain, the means to communication and social contact, as well as the medium that shapes individuals' higher mental functions, such as thinking and memory. Language is by nature social, not organic or individual (Vygotsky, 1962; see also Wertsch, 1985: Ch. 4).

Contrary to Chomsky's theory that language is not taught but is an inborn mechanism, a 'language instinct' (Pinker, 1994), the social tradition considers language as a social product, the key factor in what Pinker disapprovingly calls the 'Standard Social Science Model', according to which the human psyche is moulded by the surrounding culture (Pinker, 1994: 23). The focus of the social psychologists is on language as social action, on language in pragmatic use rather than in a formal and abstract mental system, 'wired in' in a human being. Both sides of the controversy make a number of interesting observations (for an overview of – the social side of – this discussion and many related issues see Shanon, 1993: Ch. 9; Bickhard and Terveen, 1995: Ch. 11).

Many commentators have pointed to the similarity of some of Vygotsky's ideas to the thoughts of the American social philosopher George Herbert Mead (1863–1931) (Looren de Jong, 1991). Mead (1934) also claimed that mind is social by origin. His idea that the self is a product of social interactions (see also Chapter 3, p. 85 ff.) is pursued in social constructionists' studies on self and identity (Shotter and Gergen, 1989) and by those social psychologists who postulate that, because language is inherently social, thought is collective; that individuals take part in *social representations* created in the course of communication and interaction; and that reality is a matter of conventions (Farr and Moscovici, 1984).

The body in the mind

Let us end this section of various objections to the mechanist mind by refer-ring to a constant theme: embodiment. Orthodox cognitive psychology focused on 'higher' mental functions, rational thought and the production of language, and disregarded the body. Even behaviour was not a relevant topic, because it was seen as an unproblematic consequence of information-processing. There was no real cognitive difference between, say, problem-solving and playing piano; both activities involve knowledge, and all knowledge can be specified and represented in symbolic mental represent-ations. Being able to perform the activity is possessing the required knowledge.

Shanon (1993: 109) points out that two senses of the body are involved here: the identification with the neurophysiological system or the body in terms of motor activity; and the body in its phenomenological sense, that is, as experienced.

It is especially this second sense that plays a crucial role in cognitive activ-ity, according to many cognitive philosophers (e.g. Dreyfus, 1979; Johnson, 1987). What is meant is that our cognitive relation with the world (intention-ality) is mediated by our body. To perceive is to move our eyes, to grasp things, to walk around. For our daily habitation in the world we need a zillion skills, and these cannot be made explicit, spelled out in knowledge, that is, in *knowing-that*; what we use is *know-how*. Many philosophers have pointed out this distinction (e.g. Ryle, 1949). To know the rules is not the same as being able to play the piano; to think about them can even hamper the performance.

The body has a fundamental epistemological function in our *background knowledge*: this is pre-reflexive know-how, absolutely necessary knowledge we do not learn explicitly and just do not think about. To use one of John Searle's (1992; see also 1983) examples: we learn how to use a knife and fork, we hardly have to learn not to stick the food in our ears. Exploiting this con-cept of background (see also above, Chapter 2, p. 65 ff.), Dreyfus (1979) demonstrated 'what computers can't do'. Learning, he wrote, does not consist merely in mechanically acquiring more and more information about specific routine situations; rather it takes place against a 'background of shared prac-tices'. This background is also implicit know-how, and not formalizable in facts and beliefs; it is 'bodily skills for coping with the world' (ibid.: 47). AI researchers had difficulty in coping with the problem of representing everyday context, since they tried in vain to make the background of practices explicit as a set of beliefs (ibid.: 56).

Many of the inspiring thoughts about the phenomenological import of the body in our daily experience and conduct, especially perception, can be found in Merleau-Ponty's *Phénoménologie de la perception* (1945). His work has motivated studies about the cognitive role of the body, how the body shapes the categories of our world-understanding and world-activity. Mark Johnson's *The Body in the Mind* (1987) speaks of 'embodied schemata', cog-nitive structures 'that are constantly operating in our perception, bodily movement through space, and physical manipulation of objects' (1987: 23).

He takes as an example of embodied schemata those for *in–out* orientation in our experience, and in our use and understanding of language, as in: John went out of the room; let out your anger; hand out the information. He claims that our sense of *out* orientation in these daily examples is most intimately tied to the experience of our own body in its spatial orientation, since the body can take up the role of the 'thing contained' or the 'container'. We easily project this in–out orientation on to a tube of toothpaste and extend a schema metaphorically from the physical to the non-physical, as in: tell me your story again, but leave out the minor details; here the story event is used as container (1987: 32 ff.).

For all these authors, meaning is not solely wrapped up in the propositions of a language of thought; mind is not locked up in our head. On the contrary, it is situated and works in an environment, is embodied, develops in time, and is culturally formed.

Suggested reading

On the mind–body problem:
   Warner and Szubka (1994)
A reader on mind–brain identity:
   Borst (1970)

On the history of cognitive science:
   Gardner (1987)

A comprehensive reader on the philosophy of mind from Descartes to Dennett, and with short introductions:
   Rosenthal (1991)
Important readers on the philosophy of mind:
   Lycan (1990)
   Goldman (1993)
A collection with strong historical emphasis:
   Beakley and Ludlow (1992)
Brief reviews of philosophers from Plato to Searle on the mind:
   Priest (1991)
Good textbooks on the philosophy of mind:
   Bechtel (1988b)
   Churchland (1988)
   Kim (1996)
For a useful introduction to the philosophy of mind alphabetically arranged:
   Guttenplan (1994)

For criticism on 'cognitivism':
   Still and Costall (1991)
   Shanon (1993)
   Varela et al. (1991)

On the intellectual development towards a science of the mind:
 Flanagan (1991)

On consciousness:
 Dennett (1991)
 McGinn (1991)
 Searle (1992)
 Flanagan (1992)
 Chalmers (1996)
 Churchland (1995)

For a collection of readings on consciousness from many perspectives and with good introductions:
 Pickering and Skinner (1990)
 Metzinger (1995)

A collection of important papers on representations:
 Stich and Warfield (1994)

A philosophical introduction to AI:
 Copeland (1993)
A reader on the philosophy of AI:
 Boden (1990)

Approaches in artificial intelligence and their theoretical background:
 Franklin (1995)

Clear expositions of computational theories of mind:
 Crane (1995)
 Sterelny (1990)

Philosophically minded reviews of connectionist models and dynamic systems:
 Bechtel and Abrahamsen (1991)
 Port and Van Gelder (1995)
 Horgan and Tienson (1996)

Readings on folk psychology:
 Greenwood (1991a)
 Davies and Stone (1995a, 1995b)

A series of critical reactions to philosophers, with responses:
 Dahlbom (1993)
 LePore and Van Gulick (1991)
 Loewer and Rey (1991)
 McCauley (1996)

Theoretical issues in psychology:
   Valentine (1992)

Journals:
   British Journal for the Philosophy of Science
   Journal of Consciousness Studies
   Journal of Philosophy
   Mind
   Minds and Machines
   Philosophical Psychology
   Philosophical Review
   Philosophical Studies
   Philosophy of Science
   Synthese
   The Behavioural and Brain Sciences
   Theory and Psychology

Epilogue

In the preceding chapters, we have surveyed theoretical issues in psychology. Roughly, the first cluster concerned questions about the nature and practice of science in general, and the science of psychology in particular. The second cluster was about fundamental concepts in psychology, and about recent developments in cognitive and neuroscience that have consequences for the ways we think about mind, brain and consciousness.

In the first chapter, some ideas and concepts were introduced that concern scientific methods. The upshot was roughly that science is organized common sense, but the way of its organization is rather special and intricate. Perhaps the best way to describe scientific methodology is the empirical cycle: framing hypotheses, deriving predictions, testing them, and revising the hypothesis, deriving new predictions, and so on. In the standard view, science proceeds by formulating general laws (such as Newton's mechanics), and bringing many phenomena under them. Explanation is showing how (the description of) an event follows from a law; thus, it is logically the same as predicting. The preferred form of laws is mathematical.

Laws, let alone mathematical laws, are hardly a possibility in the social sciences. Nevertheless, the classical model inspired by the natural sciences, as briefly sketched above, is held in high esteem.

The opposition in the social sciences to the role model of (classical) physics is led by hermeneutics, which aims at understanding the inner motives of singular cases (a typical procedure in the humanities and social sciences), rather than at explaining through general laws, in terms of mechanical causation. It is dubious whether hermeneutics qualifies as a real method: it lacks the intersubjectivity and the cookbook-like precision of the classical methods of explanation.

Nevertheless, some additions and corrections must be made to the classical model. All-out reduction to a unified science (for all practical purposes, to physics) is not a feasible option; rather, reality can be seen as stratified, and sciences such as physics, biology, psychology and sociology as covering distinct levels of description. Hence, we see no reason to subsume every phenomenon under a physical description.

In this context, we should also take the description and explanation of behaviour in terms of reasons and motives seriously as an irreducible level of description, rather than trying to reduce it to physical causes, as the classical model preferred.

In the second chapter, a series of philosophical concerns about the nature and the foundations of science were discussed. As a central issue the notion of the demarcation criterion was identified: how to make out what is real science, and what pseudo-science. The history of the philosophy of science since the logical positivists shows that neither verification, nor falsification, nor research programmes, are a foolproof guarantee of rationality and scientific legitimacy.

Feyerabend and some followers of Kuhn concluded from this that the scientific community is as dogmatic as the Mafia or the Roman Catholic Church, and that whatever is considered true or warranted knowledge is determined by subjective and collective processes, not by adherence to canons of rationality and pure scientific method. Such relativism implies that the world is as it pleases us to see it, and that how we see it is a matter of sociology or social psychology, not necessarily a matter of rational reasons. We proposed that the failure of the search for hard and fast demarcation criteria does not mean that 'anything goes' in science. Success in research is a matter of pragmatic skills, the ability to make things happen. Such success is a matter of know-how, and not entirely to be captured in explicit methodological rules, let alone in a-priori philosophical constructs like a universal demarcation criterion.

This led us to a broadly pragmatist view of science. Only when the failure of a universal explicit philosophical criterion for rationality is equated with all-out relativism, do we have reason to despair about the rationality of science. The relativist threat to the standard view of science looks far less damaging when the scientific enterprise is seen as a human activity that has to cope with the world, and can do so more or less successfully.

In Chapter 3, the practice of science was considered as a human activity among others, to be studied by sociologists and psychologists. For sociologists, the communitiy of scientists needs an ethos, social norms by which to abide, to make publishing and criticizing results possible, in more or less the same way any group needs norms in order to function. The nettle of this approach to research, however, is that whenever a sociological explanation of the acceptance of a theory is offered, the theory's claim to truth seems compromised: it is apparently affirmed for sociological, not for rational reasons. This externalist approach contrasts with internalism, which holds that the development of science is to be explained as a result of internal scientific criteria (coherence, empirical adequacy, technological success, etc).

Sociological and psychological studies of scientific work are valuable in their own right, but in our opinion, externalism misfires when it becomes an ideology. All-out relativism must be missing something, since some theories obviously work, increase their empirical content, produce new technology, and so on, while others are rubbish. The difference must have something to do with internal factors, like empirical adequacy: Mother Nature talks back, so to speak.

The subject of Chapter 4, philosophy of mind, is that of the fundamental concepts of psychology. This field received a major impetus from the rise of Artificial Intelligence: for the true believers this was proof of the existence of 'mechanical rationality'. The early success of intelligent machines led to a focus on mechanical, in fact computational, models of the kind that consider the mind as a computer. Such ideas about mind have the advantage of being compatible with real science, with a materialistic view of the world. There is nothing mysterious about a computer performing intelligent tasks, so if the mind is a computer, then its mystery is in principle solved, after all these centuries of mysticism and obscurantism.

The second source of inspiration was analytic philosophy with its focus on questions of language, meaning, representation, logic and intentionality. Fodor brought these themes into a brilliant synthesis with his computational theory of mind, covering computation, mentality, and the language-like structure of mental processes. However, new technologies for computation (connectionism) have suggested new ways of thinking about the mind and its relation to the brain. The jury is still out on this issue.

An important problem in this field is how commonsense psychology may relate to the cognitive and neurosciences. Dennnett and Clark make a difference between an instrumentally useful way of describing and predicting our fellow beings' behaviour on the one hand, and the neuroscientific study of its underlying causes on the other. Fodor and Churchland suppose, each in his own way, a close correspondence between underlying mechanisms (symbolic computation or neural networks, respectively) and the way we talk about them in daily life. We face here a special case of reductionism; the conclusion seems to be that a relatively independent level of discourse about human motives and reasons is legitimate, and must not be sacrificed to (promises of) neuroscientific or computational reduction.

A somewhat fuzzy subject, around which much debate nevertheless centres, is so-called folk psychology. This refers not only to common sense, but serves also as a label for deep philosophical issues, like the reducibility of beliefs, desires, motives and reasons to computational and/or neurophysiological mechanisms.

One might think the philosophy of mind as sketched here somewhat 'technology driven'. In fact, its critics mostly belong to the school that rejects the mechanistic approach in its entirety as an implausible approach to humanity, and propose a radically different view of mind. Whereas the computational school is a branch of mentalism, going back to Descartes, and considers mind a kind of entity, the more or less Wittgensteinian view considers mental terms as part of a narrative about behaviour. Yet another branch of critics recognizes the value of science for the rest of nature, but feels that mind, or at least consciousness, will remain a mystery.

A final observation: you have probably recognized in the abstract and philosophical terminology of this book many commonsense concerns. Such as: what is so special about science in general, and about psychology as a science in particular? why do we think scientific knowledge is superior to prejudice and common sense? what is objectivity? what is thinking? are we our brains? are we no more than mechanical systems?

The technical language used in discussing such questions is not only sophistry, but also offers the opportunity to question and refine intuitions, and make assumptions and prejudices explicit (what is so terrible about being your brain? what does reduction mean? why do you want objectivity?). In this way, philosophy of mind and science might be, like science in general, a kind of organized common sense. Perhaps theoretical issues in psychology are not so purely theoretical after all.

Glossary[1]

ABDUCTION   Or *inference to the best explanation*. The art (or logic) governing the principles by which we arrive at hypotheses for subsequent testing. Unlike induction,* abduction goes beyond generalizing from empirical evidence; compare: all swans are white (induction), and: insufficient hygiene must be the cause of the epidemic (inference to the best explanation). Like induction, and unlike deduction* it is non-demonstrative. Thus, abduction is usually considered to belong to the context* of discovery, although some tried to develop a logic of prescriptive rules for hypothesis construction – with little success.

ACTION   What a human agent does. It should be distinguished from mere movement, and also from behaviour, in the technical sense of behaviourism (observable responses). Action involves intentionality* and rationality. However, not every action is done on purpose and it might be that a person cannot be held responsible for it. In this sense the problem of free will is related. To explain or to account for an action is asking/giving reasons* for it, rather than causes.*

ARTIFICIAL INTELLIGENCE   Making machines (computers, or better: computer programs) do things that would require intelligence, if done by men (in Minsky's definition), for example, playing chess, constructing mathematical proofs, answering insight questions about a story, etc. *Weak AI* aims at nothing more than a working program. *Strong AI* aims, in addition, at producing programs that do essentially the same as, and are 'equivalent' to, a human thinker. Strong AI thus entails the claim that mental activity is in essence computation,* be it symbol manipulation, or simulation of spreading activation in networks (see Connectionism).* There seem to be fewer believers in strong AI nowadays than there used to be; weak AI is a booming business.

BACKGROUND   A concept in the philosophy of mind meaning the general and implicit *know-how* and capacities that enable a person to function in, or to understand her environment. The background operates implicitly, implying that it need not, and even cannot, be explicitly formulated or reflected upon. Background know-how is opposed to *knowing-that* or declarative knowledge.

[1] Very useful dictionaries are: Blackburn, 1996 for philosophy; Reber, 1995 for psychology.

BELIEF   A mental state, a thought, by which a proposition is held to be true, and upon which one is prepared to act: which guides action,* as pragmatism* would add. Beliefs, together with desires, are taken as the paradigms of mental states – particularly of propositional attitudes* – in philosophy of mind. See also: Belief-desire psychology.

BELIEF-DESIRE PSYCHOLOGY   A theory in the philosophy of mind (main exponent: J. Fodor) that takes beliefs and desires, as used in folk psychology,* as the paradigms of mental states. According to Fodor, these mental categories from folk psychology do really exist as cognitive states and have causal efficacy, i.e. they cause behaviour and other mental states. The theory thus takes folk psychology seriously as the point of departure for scientific cognitive psychology.

CAUSE, CAUSALITY, CAUSATION   A relation between two events, such that the first can be said to bring about or to necessitate the second event, so that it *must* occur. It is a notorious philosophical problem how this can ever be empirically* established, and whether causes are not subjective constructions, rather than elements of reality. Hume held that we can say only that events occur with some regularity one *after* the other, not that one occurs *because* of the other. What is the difference between the going together of two events (the 'constant conjunction'), and the claim that one causes the other (e.g. smoking and cancer)? *Causal laws* describe an invariant relation between two events, where the cause is a necessary condition for the effect, i.e. the latter does not occur without the first. In this context, what counts as a cause is also dependent on explanatory* interests, since an event may have a number of causes, only some of which are relevant. Causal laws are contrasted with teleological* laws. See also: Reasons.

COHERENCE THEORY OF TRUTH   See: Truth.

COMMONSENSE PSYCHOLOGY   See: Folk psychology.

COMPUTATION   In the most general sense: manipulating symbols. The idea of a general-purpose computer was traditionally that it executes symbol manipulation according to formal mechanic procedures. One should distinguish between this classical symbolic view, as described, and the recent connectionist view on computation, as the spreading of numerical activation through a (neural) network. The computational theory of mind* holds that mental processes are essentially computation.

COMPUTATIONAL THEORY OF MIND   The theory that mental processes essentially consist in computation, i.e. symbol manipulation. CTM in its classical version, associated with Jerry Fodor, assumes that mental states are symbol states, strings in a formal language (imagine a computer language, or predicate calculus in logic) in the head, and mental processes are transformations of these symbol strings. Churchland's alternative, that mental processes are activation patterns in a multidimensional vector space, could also be called a computational view of mind, although a completely different kind of computation (numerical versus logical). See also: Language of thought; Connectionism.

CONFIRMATION Showing a statement to be supported by empirical* evidence (see also: Verification). Carnap thought he could develop a logic in which the degree of inductive* support could be assessed. Popper showed that a theory can only be corroborated, but can never be confirmed conclusively; it can however be proved wrong with absolute certainty (falsification).*

CONNECTIONISM An approach in cognitive psychology and Artificial Intelligence* that uses self-organizing networks (modelled on neural networks) of interconnected nodes, in which the changing of weights of the connections underlies the network's learning of a discriminating response. In this model of information-processing the network is supposed to tune itself to the environment, rather than following a programme of pre-set rules and commands. See also: Representation.

CONSCIOUSNESS The state of awareness, of being conscious. Also: the whole set of higher-order mental states and psychological functions that the subject can be aware of, such as thoughts, beliefs, desires, feelings, intentions. Consciousness is a much-debated topic in modern philosophy of mind. Some philosophers think that it is essentially private, first-person experience. Others try to demystify and to naturalize* consciousness, to make it available for third-person objective explanation (e.g. that it emerges from brain processes). Consciousness involves the problems of intentionality* and qualia.*

CONSENSUS THEORY OF TRUTH See: Truth.

CONSTRUCTIONISM, SOCIAL A position in (social) psychology and in the philosophy of science that considers all the products of knowledge and (social) science, such as categories, concepts, facts, data, measurements, etc. to be completely a matter of social artefacts, since all knowledge is conveyed only by language and communication. The role of language is not to refer to an extralinguistic world, but to contribute to mutual understanding and to sustain social relations. Truth* is defined by consensus, i.e. nothing more than what happens to be agreed upon. The position leans strongly towards relativism.*

CONTEXT OF DISCOVERY In this context the focus is on a reliable description of the historical, social and even psychological circumstances and influences that were relevant to the discovery of a scientific theory. It is the subject of a methodological programme for a contextual historiography of science, in opposition to the positivistic* programme of the context of justification* of theories.

CONTEXT OF JUSTIFICATION   In this context the focus is on the methodological requirements of a scientific theory, its logical argument, i.e. the degree to which the conclusions are supported by factual premises (induction),* or are inferred from general lawlike premises (deduction).* In this positivistic* programme it is maintained that it is not the business of science to pay attention to the social or psychological circumstances of the problem-solving situation.

CORRESPONDENCE THEORY OF TRUTH   See: Truth.

DEDUCTION   The reasoning process or argument in which a conclusion is logically drawn, or deduced from a set of premises. Induction* and abduction* are non-demonstrative, whereas deduction is demonstrative: its conclusions follow with logical certainty, on pain of contradiction. It is also seen as the argument that takes you from general statements (e.g. All birds are . . .) to particular conclusions (This bird is . . .).

DEDUCTIVE-NOMOLOGICAL MODEL OF EXPLANATION   The view that explaining is deriving a proposition describing the event to be explained (the *explanandum*) from a general law or set of laws (the *explanans*): for example, all plants containing chlorophyll are green, grass contains chlorophyll, therefore grass is green. Subsuming an event under a 'covering law', is considered tantamount to answering the question why it happened. The positivist* ideal of a theory as an axiomatic formal system accounts for the element of (logical, demonstrative) deduction; 'nomological' means lawful. See also: Explanation.

DEMARCATION   Since the logical positivists,* philosophers of science have tried to find an unfailing criterion separating rational scientific knowledge from metaphysical speculation, irrationality, superstition and pseudo-science. The logical positivists proposed as such verifiability,* Popper falsifiability.* Neither works.

DUALISM   A position in the mind–body problem, associated with the seventeenth-century French philosopher Descartes, and part of the whole tradition called 'Cartesianism'. Dualism divides human existence into having a mind and having a body. Mind and body are completely different substances, though they interact in a mysterious way. Mind is associated with a private inner mental world, to which the owner by a kind of inner eye has privileged access, whereas the body is part of the external observable world. See also: Consciousness.

DYNAMIC SYSTEMS THEORY   A general formalism for describing complex systems, using the notions of an abstract space of possible states of the system (state space), and of a trajectory through it, governed by laws that can be described mathematically. For psychological purposes, behaviour (like approach – avoidance, or walking) can be described, in a more or less geo-metrical way, as evolution (or 'flow') through state space. Important assets are its conceptualization of the agent-environment coupling and the evolution over time.

ELIMINATIVISM   The claim that folk psychological* categories like beliefs* and desires eventually can, and should, be eliminated and replaced by neuroscientific terms: we will talk about the firing of our neurons rather than about pain when hitting our thumb. In contrast, reductionism* allows us to keep our commonsense concepts (like 'water') even when they are identified with scientific concepts (water is 'really' H_2O).

EMPIRICISM   A doctrine in philosophy and, in particular, a position in epistemology* which says that all knowledge comes from the senses, and that only those expressions have a claim to knowledge and to truth* that can be translated, directly or indirectly, into sense impressions. These impressions, or *sense-data*, form the *given* content of our mental states of which we have direct awareness. This view was taken as the rock bottom of positivism.* See also: Theory-laden; Rationalism; Foundationalism.

EPISTEMOLOGY   The theory of knowledge, a main branch of philosophy. Its central problems are the origin and legitimacy of knowledge. This relates to questions about the credentials of the senses and of reason; about the nature of truth, of meaning, etc. The main historical positions in the field are rationalism* and empiricism.*

EXPLANATION   In normal discourse, to make something easier to under-stand, to elucidate, or to answer a why-question. In the theory of science, especially when logical positivism* held sway over the field, it was considered as a strictly logical relation between the *explanandum* (that which has to be explained) and the *explanans* (that which explains). This ideal was found in the *covering-law model of explanation*: an event is explained when it can be deduced from a natural law plus initial conditions. Accordingly, the model was also called *deductive-nomological** (D-N model; Greek *nomos* is law). This model has been challenged: the notion of law and the ideal of the logi-cal relation were disputed as requirements for explanation, in particular in the human/social sciences, where sometimes the *context* is seen as useful circum-stantial evidence for interpretation/explanation (see also: Reasons). The *inference to the best explanation* is the idea that one sometimes opts for the best among a set of possible explanations (see also: Abduction; Teleology).

FALSIFICATION   Showing a statement to be false. According to Popper, a theory is to be rejected when predictions derived from it turn out to be false. Thus, whereas a theory can never be verified,* it can conclusively be falsified.

FOLK PSYCHOLOGY   *Commonsense psychology*, the kind of explanation of everyday behaviour in terms of the goals, desires, beliefs, opinions and plans that supposedly drive one's fellow beings' behaviour. Fodor and others consider folk psychology as belief-desire psychology,* the kind of psychology that uses intentional* language, and requires representations* as explanatory concepts. Beliefs and desires, construed as propositional attitudes,* are, in this view, literally causes and lawful explanations, and can and should be preserved in a computational theory of mind.*

FOUNDATIONALISM   A (usually dismissive) label for those normative positions in epistemology or the philosophy of science, like positivism,* which demand that true knowledge and science should be demarcated* from irrationality or pseudo-science by building upon secure epistemological* foundations, such as empiricism,* rationalism* or other views which call upon universal, ahistoric principles or postulates of rationality.

FUNCTIONALISM   The thesis that mental states are functional states of a machine or a brain, implying that the actual physical make-up of the machine (the *implementation*) is irrelevant to the functional *role* it realizes. As a simple example of a functional description consider a carburettor: it can be made in infinitely many different materials and designs, all with the function of providing fuel to an engine. Analogously, mental states are functional roles: they have causal relations with input, with other mental states, and with behaviour, that can be described irrespective of the physical make-up of the system. An important consequence of functionalism in the philosophy of mind is that the same mental process (functional state) can be realized in brains as well as in computers (or in a contraption made of empty beer cans, for that matter); this is called *multiple realizability*. *Narrow (or machine) functionalism* considers a function solely in terms of the internal economy of the system. *Wide functionalism* is more like the biological notion of function: it includes the role a function has in the system's environment; for example a rattlesnake has a heat detector and a movement detector: this has the function of detecting mice only in an environment where the snake can feed on mice.

HERMENEUTICS   Originally (since the seventeenth century) the art or the method for the exegesis of classical, theological and juridical texts. At the end of the nineteenth century hermeneutics was made into a general methodology for understanding (*Verstehen*) and interpretation in the human sciences, in contrast with the objective method of explanation in the physical sciences. *Philosophical hermeneutics* was developed in the twentieth century; it became a philosophical theory of the fundamental historical and linguistic situation of human experiences. It is one of the main epistemological convictions in modern hermeneutics, that since in the human sciences *meaning* is the central concept, the knowing subject and the known object share a common background. Hence, to understand the sometimes subtle meanings in these sciences, subject and object confront each other, are partners in a discussion, so to say. To understand the meaning of social, historical or psychological concepts and actions, it is essential to understand the context; and to understand the context, it is essential to understand the parts; this is the *hermeneutic circle* (see also: Holism).

HOLISM The idea that the whole has priority over its parts. Holism is encountered in different domains. In contrast with the empiricist*/ associationist account of perception, Gestalt psychology contends that perception should not be analysed in atomistic sensations, since in normal perception a gestalt is predominant: perception is organized by certain configurations. *Epistemological holism* is the (Duhem–Quine) thesis that the meaning of a term or a sentence can only be understood in the context of a whole body of sentences, a theory, or even a worldview. This also means that observational data can only be appreciated within or in the context of a theory. See: Theory-laden.

HOMUNCULUS Literally: little man. Refers to the kinds of explanation where intelligent behaviour is explained by intelligent processes (the little man) inside the agent – which is a pseudo-explanation when the intelligent processes themselves remain unexplained. Dennett made a variety of the homunculus explanation respectable under the label of *intentional stance*: the prediction or description of intelligent behaviour (of, say, a chess computer) in terms of the goals and knowledge it has. This is legitimate as long as it yields adequate descriptions and successful predictions (it is perfectly OK if it helps you to win a game of chess), and if it can in the end be explained by specifying the *design* (e.g. the chess computer's program). This consists in decomposing the intelligent 'little man' inside, with its complex function, into an 'army of idiots', each with a much more simple function.

IDEALISM A philosophical doctrine holding that reality is essentially mental, consisting in something like the World Spirit (Hegel); this is called objective idealism. Idealism is usually considered as a subjective epistemology, implying that knowledge is first and foremost a product of the activity of the knowing subject, and that there is no way of finding out whether knowledge corresponds with, or refers to, something like an external reality. The idealist view of truth* is coherence, being consistent with the rest of knowledge. See also: Realism; Relativism.

IDENTITY THEORY A materialistic solution to the mind–body problem, which says that mental events are identical with physical events. The *mind–brain identity theory* identifies mental events with brain events. This is a strong conception of materialism,* type-materialism, saying that a type of mental state (e.g. being angry) is identical with a certain type of brain state (say, the firing of specific neurons x, y, z). Functionalism* (token-materialism) opposes it.

IDEOLOGY According to the Marxist interpretation, ideology is the production of ideas, the set of beliefs, conceptions, categories, moral standards, etc. of a social class, reflecting the material basis, the socioeconomic conditions of the group. Since in this view all groups, except the proletariat, have the wrong ideas or 'false consciousness', ideologies are deceptive. In later interpretations ideology has lost the connotation of 'false consciousness', though the ideas of a group are still supposed to be influenced by the socioeconomic circumstances and to guide the group's social and political action.

IDIOGRAPHIC   The method leading to the understanding of individual, unique events (Greek *idios* – unique, individual), as in the human sciences and history; it is opposed to the nomothetic* method.

INCOMMENSURABILITY   Literally: having no common yardstick. When two theories do not refer to a common set of facts, they are incommensurable. Since a paradigm* produces, according to Kuhn, its own evidence, and facts are theory laden, there is no neutral ground for comparing one paradigm with another and they make sense of the world in terms of completely different categories, concepts and meanings. This notion can be criticized for leading to relativism.*

INDIVIDUALISM   A thesis in the philosophy of mind holding that for purposes of psychological explanation, only the internal features of an organism are relevant, i.e. that 'psychology ends at the skin'. What someone believes can be described without reference to the things in his or her environment. Almost the same as internalism;* see also: Solipsism; Functionalism, narrow.

INDUCTION   The reasoning process or argument in which an empirical conclusion (a generalization) is inferred from empirical premises, that is observation statements. Unlike deduction,* induction is non-demonstrative: its conclusions are not logically certain. The conclusion of an inductive argument is *probable, supported by* the premises. It is also seen as the argument that takes you from particular statements to generalizations. See also: Abduction; Confirmation.

INFERENCE TO THE BEST EXPLANATION   See: Abduction; Explanation.

INSTRUMENTALISM   The view that scientific theories, concepts and entities are instruments or convenient tools that help us to understand the world and facilitate our thinking, but do not convey literal truths and do not have ontological* import.

INTENTIONALITY   The distinguishing property of mental states or psychological phenomena, implying that they have a content, are directed at, about, or involved with objects, whereas physical things lack this property. Words, or books, are directed at, are about objects, have meaning, but they take the intentionality from mental states, they have *derived intentionality*, not *intrinsic intentionality*. Intentionality in this technical sense has little to do with being intended or on purpose; to intend to do something is one among the many manifestations of intentionality. Materialist* theories aim at naturalizing* intentionality.

LANGUAGE GAME   A pattern of practices, a 'form of life', which explains the meaning of interconnected expressions and concepts. It is associated with the later Wittgenstein, who compared the use of language with a game and rules. The message that the meaning of a word or an expression can never be isolated from its practical context – *meaning is use* – can also be taken to imply the relativistic* notion that expressions or beliefs derive their meanings only from the social context of language games, and that language games are a matter of (arbitrary) consensus. (See: Truth.)

LANGUAGE OF THOUGHT   Fodor's hypothesis that mental activity has a structure like a formal, or logical, language. Mental representations* are strings of symbols that are characterized by their syntactical* structure (see also: Solipsism, methodological). Thinking is manipulating these symbols in more or less the same way as constructing logical proofs is. The LOT hypothesis explains the *systematicity* and *productivity* of thinking: you can think infinitely many thoughts by combining a finite number of mental elements, and these thoughts cohere with each other.

LAWS   A much-debated concept in philosophy of science. Historically it suggests a lawgiver, and during the seventeenth and eighteenth centuries it was the idea that the Creator had dictated that nature should progress according to His will, and that the scientist could discover its laws. Nowadays, laws are seen as rather lawlike, empirical generalizations. Some laws are causal (e.g. Frustration leads to aggression); others are not (e.g. All swans are white). Laws may contain *unobservables*: theoretical terms that cannot be directly seen, but from which testable predictions can be derived (e.g. the unconscious; genes). See also: Cause.

MATERIALISM   A metaphysical doctrine in philosophy that the world and all its entities and phenomena, including psychological phenomena, are manifestations of spatiotemporal matter. There are strong and more or less weak versions. The strong versions imply reductionism:* mental phenomena have to be seen as manifestations of body or brain processes and must, scientifically, be reduced to these processes. The identity theory,* physicalism* and eliminativism* are strong versions. Naturalism* might be seen as a weaker version of materialism, allowing for the non-reducibility of mental phenomena. Non-reductive materialism is also called *emergent materialism*: it holds that some objects or processes, while entirely dependent on matter, nevertheless have properties that transcend the vocabulary of physics (for example consciousness as a product of the brain). See also: Supervenience.

METAPHYSICS   A branch of philosophy that tries to answer questions about the general or abstract nature of reality, also about a reality that is supposed to lie behind the world and that is not accessible by scientific method. In psychology and the philosophy of mind, metaphysics includes questions about mind, consciousness,* intentionality,* qualia;* in philosophy of science it involves questions about causality,* matter, rationalism,* etc. Metaphysics is challenged, in a sense, by positivism,* materialism,* and naturalism,* though these positions themselves are supported by metaphysical presuppositions.

METHODOLOGICAL SOLIPSISM   See: Solipsism.

MODEL   A model is sometimes used as a synonym for a theory (as in: a model of the brain); it is mostly, however, a kind of mini-theory, usually in a more or less visual or metaphorical form.

MULTIPLE REALIZABILITY   See: Functionalism.

NATURALISM   claims that the methods of natural science can be applied to all phenomena, including mental processes. This can be construed as physicalism,* which holds that the concepts and methods of current physics can in the end explain everything. However, it can also mean that some phenomena, although beyond the realm of physics, can and should be investigated and explained in an objective, scientific way, i.e not necessarily in terms of physics, though at least not contradicting physics. In psychology this suggests a broadly biological approach, considering mind as a capacity for survival, developed from animal patterns of reactivity. By extension, naturalism may imply a rejection of solipsism:* minds are capacities for coping with the environment and mental functions should be considered in relation to the organism's world. *Naturalizing*, therefore, is the name of the programme that aims at demystifying, stripping a concept or a theory of its metaphysical* content, and using for its explanation objective, scientific methods, as in naturalizing epistemology,* or naturalizing intentionality.*

NATURAL KINDS   The ontological* view that natural kinds are the categories that divide things in natural classes, 'carve nature at the joints' (such as gold, water, animals). Some philosophers try to relate the notion of natural kinds to essences and necessary properties (like, 'Gold has necessarily the atomic number 79'). The issue of what natural kinds are is closely related to questions of *taxonomy*: what should the *classification* of science be? For example, consider the question of whether a whale should be classified as a fish or a mammal. Some opponents of the natural kind view hold that classifications are human-made and theory laden.*

NOMOTHETIC   The method for finding general laws (Greek *nomos* – law), as in the positivistic* notion of explanation.* It is the opposite of the idiographic* method.

OBJECTIVISM   The view in the philosophy of science that the scientific method should be objective, that is, based on observables, empirical matters of fact; and that science is a realistic enterprise. It is a dismissive label, affiliated to positivism* and opposed to subjectivism/relativism.*

ONTOLOGY   A main branch of philosophy, concerned with the question: what kinds of things, properties and events exist (fundamentally), as furniture of the world? A traditional and popular position is materialism:* only spatio-temporal matter exists. The Cartesian position, important in psychology, is dualism,* which presupposes two principal substances: mind and matter (body). See also: Natural kinds.

PARADIGM   A concept in the philosophy of science, introduced by Kuhn. It is a whole complex of methods, concepts and theories; techniques and laboratory apparatus; social processes and institutional structures, which determines what are legitimate problems and solutions in a field of scientific research. See also: Incommensurability.

PHYSICALISM   A reductive materialist* doctrine in the philosophy of science saying that all the sciences or scientific theories should be reduced to physics, and that only the language and methods of physics are scientifically respectable. See also: Reductionism.

POSITIVISM, LOGICAL   Positivism in general refers to philosophical positions that emphasize empirical data and scientific methods. Logical positivism (or neo-positivism) is mostly associated with the so-called Wiener Kreis (1920s–1930s), a group of philosophers, physicists and logicians who claimed that legitimate knowledge consists exclusively of observation sentences and logical connections between them. Statements that are not (empirically) verifiable* are meaningless nonsense or metaphysics.

PRAGMATIC THEORY OF TRUTH   See: Truth.

PRAGMATISM   The philosophical view that knowledge should primarily be considered as guiding our actions in coping with the world, rather than as a theoretical set of beliefs, or a picture corresponding in some way with the world. See also: Truth; Realism.

PROPOSITIONAL ATTITUDES   A mental state consisting of an attitude ('He believes', 'She expects') and a proposition ('that it is/will be raining'). Propositional attitudes make up folk psychology* (belief-desire psychology),* in the sense that mental states, such as beliefs and desires, figure as explanations of behaviour ('She buys an umbrella because she expects . . .'), and specify mental content in the form of propositions (which happen to fit nicely in a language of thought* theory). Hence, they are closely related to issues of intentionality* and mental representation.*

QUALIA (Singular: quale)   The *first-person* phenomenal qualities, experiences or feelings, such as feeling pain, seeing red wine, tasting a truffle, hearing 'God save the Queen'. Friends of qualia think that they exist, that humans/living beings do experience them, but that they are not accessible to objective, *third-person*, scientific means. Some materialists* deny the existence of qualia; others suggest they can be reduced to brain processes.

RATIONALISM   An answer to the epistemological* question about the origin of knowledge. Rationalists believe that knowledge is based on naturally given, *innate ideas*. The opposite position is empiricism* (or empirism).

REALISM   The view that our knowledge, or scientific theories correspond to reality. Specifying what 'correspondence' means is difficult. In the *naive* version it means something like 'mirroring' or 'copying'. *Scientific realism* holds that theories correspond to reality; that, for example, elementary particles cited in the laws of physics really exist. *Convergent realism* claims that the increased agreement between, and wider applicability of the scientific laws (e.g. elementary physics, or evolution) indicate that they somehow approach reality. Realism is less obvious than it seems: patently false theories can be useful, and may produce correct predictions. *Internal realism* (Putnam) rejects the naive copy-theory of truth and holds that knowledge is a human creation, without being subjective. In the *pragmatic* view it is claimed that the epistemological relation to the world should not be seen as exclusively linguistic or theoretical (intellectualistic), but that in the subsequent practice of intervention, manipulation and action the world makes a difference: replies, so to say. See also: Idealism; Relativism; Truth.

REASONS   The means by which we explain, or account for actions.* Reasons can be distinguished from causes,* because actions have meanings, to be interpreted in the light of (social) contexts, that cannot be traced in the physical/physiological events and processes that cause the movements of the action. Some philosophers maintain that reasons are causes.

REDUCTIONISM   See: Eliminativism; Materialism; Physicalism.

RELATIVISM   Holds that theories, concepts and categories are not absolutely true or valid, but are irredeemably dependent on subjective views, social contexts and historical processes: there is no such thing as objective knowledge, no knowable world independent from knowing subjects. Neither are there objective criteria to assess whether one of the many possible perspectives is more warranted than another. Informally speaking, truth* is in the eye of the beholder; it all depends on how you see things. Relativists challenge realism* and the correspondence theory of truth. Relativism is related to idealism.*

REPRESENTATION   Mental representation is a crucial but problematic concept in cognitive psychology. Mental states supposedly mean, refer to or stand for something else: they have mental content. The concept of mental representation is thus burdened with many of the problems of meaning and intentionality.* (See also: Semantics; Propositional attitudes.) One of the problems is that mental representation runs the risk of a homunculus* pseudo-explanation. Fodor assumes that mental representations have a symbolic format, as sentences in the language of thought.* Connectionists* consider them as activation patterns in neural networks. These theories one might call a *representational theory of mind*: thinking is essentially having and manipulating representations. This constitutes an attempt to exorcize the homunculus pseudo-explanation by naturalizing* representations. Some recent developments (such as dynamic systems theory*), question the usefulness of representation as an explanatory construct in cognitive psychology.

SEMANTICS   Concerning the *meaning* of linguistic representations* (utterances) and by extension of mental representations (thoughts). It is a deep philosophical question how words or thoughts can mean a thing in the external world; even more, how they can mean things that do not exist (e.g. how one can think of a unicorn). Some proposals suggest relations of causation or covariation between representation and referent. See also: Language game.

SENSE-DATA   Experiences that are, supposedly, directly *given* in the senses, such as colour or sound, and which are thus evident, indubitable, unadulterated by cognitive processing. Some empiricists* thought that sense-data could and should be the foundation* of knowledge. It is doubtful whether there is such a thing as pure sense-data, and even more dubitable whether they can carry the epistemological* burden that empiricism requires. See also: Theory-laden.

SOCIAL CONSTRUCTIONISM   See: Constructionism, social.

SOLIPSISM   The view that only oneself and one's experiences exist and that, accordingly, one can only know what is in one's own mind. *Methodological solipsism* is associated with Fodor's philosophy of mind, implying that only the syntactical (formal) structure of mental states is of psychological importance and that their semantics, such as the reference to the world, is not relevant for explaining mental states and how they affect behaviour and other mental states: Claire's *belief* can be about an extraterrestrial and cause her *desire* to meet him, her *visiting* a secret place in a cave, and her *waiting* for what is to come; though it might well be that the creature *does not exist*. So, we should approach mental states as if they were solipsistic states. See also: Language of thought.

SUPERVENIENCE   A relation between two epistemological domains. The notion of supervenience holds that no changes can occur at the mental level without some changes at the physiological level. This means that there is no such thing as a disembodied mind (mental processes without accompanying neurophysiological processes). Supervenience nicely fits with non-reductive materialism:* it only entails a rejection of metaphysical dualism,* but does not require lawful correspondences between mind and brain; it is therefore entirely compatible with functionalism.*

SYNTACTICAL   Refers to the *form* of statements, that is, the logical or formal linguistic relations between sentences or parts thereof. See also: Semantics.

TELEOLOGY   Goal-directedness. Teleological explanations invoke *functions*, *goals*, *purposes* or *end-states* as explanations* of behaviour (e.g. a thermostat has the goal of keeping the room temperature constant; the function of the heart is to pump blood; the purpose of their making so much noise was to scare off the animals). This poses a problem for classical physics, where only causes,* (events preceding the effect in time) are recognized: in teleological explanations, the effect follows the goal.

THEORY   A coherent (and non-contradictory) set of statements (concepts, ideas) that organizes, predicts and explains phenomena, events, behaviour, etc. Ideally, hypotheses (testable predictions) can be derived from a theory. Theoretical terms should be unambiguously defined. A formal-logical axiomatic structure is the ideal of clarity and coherence for theories; this can be seen in mathematical theories in physics, but is almost never realized in psychology.

THEORY-LADEN   An epistemological characteristic of observations, statements, etc., meaning that they only make sense in a system or context of other beliefs, a theory, or a worldview. The idea of theory-ladenness was mainly developed in contrast with the empiricist* doctrine of neutral, objective sense data;* this doctrine was criticized for implying the *Myth of the Given*. Since the idea of the 'given' proved to be untenable, the relation between the knowing subject and the known object became an issue in epistemology* and the philosophy of science, especially in the debate between relativism* on the one hand, and scientific realism* and pragmatism* on the other.

TRUTH   The term for the abstract concept *the* truth, as in 'The truth and nothing but the truth', as well as for the epistemological* quality of theories, beliefs, propositions, statements: 'What she says is true' or 'Which statement is true?' Realists* distinguish truth from *reality*: only conceptions, beliefs, statements, etc. *about* the reality or *about* the world can be true (or false). This realistic distinction, however, is in conflict with the relativistic* notion that thought and world are interconnected. A particular version of the abstract concept is the philosophical/epistemological problem of truth: 'What is truth, anyway?' There are different theories of truth. The *correspondence theory of truth*, which states that truth consists in the correspondence between thought and reality, is associated with realism. Critics of this theory contest the nature of the concept of correspondence, taken as a kind of *mirroring*, and they dispute the distinction between subject and object. Idealism* and relativism, therefore, adhere to the *coherence theory of truth*: the more beliefs in a system are coherent, the truer they are. Relativism also adheres to another theory, the *consensus theory of truth*: truth is what is agreed upon by common consent. Both theories of truth are criticized by realists, because the world does not play any role in the theories, and, as to the latter theory, realists do not like the idea that truth is dependent on group-think. The *pragmatic theory of truth* claims that the truth, or better the *reliability* (because truth is never absolute) of a belief cannot be conceived apart from its practical consequences, but is demonstrated in subsequent experiment, test or action. This theory is sometimes ridiculed in the phrase, 'True is what works.'

TURING MACHINE   The prototype of a symbol manipulator, a Turing machine can read a symbol from tape, perform an elementary operation on it, and write the result back. The English mathematician Turing proved that every task that can be written as a set of elementary operations (an algorithm) can be executed on a *universal* Turing machine. This is the basis for the claim of strong AI (see: Artificial Intelligence).

UNDERSTANDING/VERSTEHEN   See: Hermeneutics.

VERIFICATION   Assessing the fit between a theory (better, the prediction generated by the theory) and empirical facts. Logical positivists* proposed *verifiability* (specification of how to find empirical facts that make rejection or acceptance of the statement possible) as the criterion for a meaningful theory (see: demarcation).* However, it is impossible to verify general laws: they can only be confirmed or falsified.*

Bibliography

Allen, G. (1976) 'Genetics, eugenics and society. Internalists and externalists in contemporary history of science', *Social Studies of Science,* 6: 105–22.

Amabile, T. (1983) *The Social Psychology of Creativity.* New York: Springer Verlag.

Anderson, R.J., Hughes, J.A. and Sharrock, W.W. (1986) *Philosophy and the Human Sciences.* London: Routledge.

Apel, K.O. (1982) 'The Erklären–Verstehen controversy in the philosophy of the natural and human sciences', in G. Fløistad (ed.), *Contemporary Philosophy. Volume 2: Philosophy of Science.* Dordrecht, Holland: Martinus Nijhoff. pp. 19–49.

Ayer, A.J. (ed.) (1959) *Logical Positivism.* New York: The Free Press.

Baker, G.P. and Hacker, P.M.S. (1984) *Language, Sense and Nonsense. A Critical Investigation into Modern Theories of Language.* Oxford: Blackwell.

Baker, L. Rudder (1987) *Saving Belief. A Critique of Physicalism.* Princeton, NJ: Princeton University Press.

Baker, L. Rudder (1995) *Explaining Attitudes.* Cambridge: Cambridge University Press.

Baritz, L. (1960) *The Servants of Power. A History of the Use of Social Science in American Industry.* Middletown, CT: Wesleyan University Press.

Barnes, B. (1977) *Interest and the Growth of Knowledge.* London: Routledge & Kegan Paul.

Barnes, B. and Bloor, D. (1982) 'Relativism, rationalism and the sociology of knowledge', in M. Hollis and S. Lukes (eds), *Rationality and Relativism.* Oxford: Blackwell.

Barnes, B., Bloor, D. and Henry, J. (1996) *Scientific Knowledge: A Sociological Analysis.* London: Athlone.

Bates, A. and Elman, J.L. (1993) 'Connectionism and the study of change', in M.H. Johnson (ed.), *Brain Development and Cognition.* Oxford: Blackwell. pp. 625–42.

Beakley, B. and Ludlow, P. (eds) (1992) *The Philosophy of Mind.* Cambridge, MA: MIT Press.

Bechtel, W. (1985) 'Realism, instrumentalism and the intentional stance', *Cognitive Science,* 9: 473–97.

Bechtel, W. (1986) 'Teleological functional analysis and the hierarchical organisation of nature', in N. Rescher (ed.), *Current Issues in Teleology*. Lanham, MD: University Press of America. pp. 26–48.

Bechtel, W. (1988a) *Philosophy of Science. An Overview for Cognitive Science*. Hillsdale, NJ: Erlbaum.

Bechtel, W. (1988b) *Philosophy of Mind. An Overview for Cognitive Science*. Hillsdale, NJ: Erlbaum.

Bechtel, W. (1990) 'Connectionism and the philosophy of mind: an overview', in W.G. Lycan (ed.), *Mind and Cognition. A Reader*. Oxford: Blackwell.

Bechtel, W. (1993) 'Decomposing intentionality: perspectives on intentionality drawn from language research with two species of chimpanzees', *Biology and Philosophy*, 8: 1–32.

Bechtel, W. and Abrahamsen, A. (1991) *Connectionism and the Mind*. Oxford: Blackwell.

Bechtel, W. and Abrahamsen, A. (1993) 'Connectionism and folk psychology', in S.M. Christensen and D.R. Turner (eds), *Folk Psychology and the Philosophy of Mind*. Hillsdale, NJ: Erlbaum. pp. 341–67.

Bedau, M. (1990) 'Against mentalism in teleology', *American Philosophical Quarterly*, 27: 61–70.

Bem, S. (1989) 'Denken om te doen. Een studie over cognitie en werkelijkheid' (Thought for action. A study of cognition and reality). Dissertation, University of Leiden.

Bem, S. and Keijzer, F. (1996) 'Recent changes in the concept of cognition', *Theory & Psychology*, 6: 449–69.

Berger, P.L. and Luckmann, T. (1967) *The Social Construction of Reality*. Harmondsworth: Penguin Books.

Bernstein, R.J. (1983) *Beyond Objectivism and Relativism: Science, Hermeneutics, and Praxis*. Oxford: Blackwell.

Bickhard, M.H. and Terveen, L. (1995) *Foundational Issues in Artificial Intelligence and Cognitive Science. Impasse and Solution*. Amsterdam: Elsevier.

Bigelow, J. and Pargetter, R. (1987) 'Functions', *Journal of Philosophy*, 84: 181–96.

Billig, M. (1987) *Arguing and Thinking. A Rhetorical Approach to Social Psychology*. Cambridge: Cambridge University Press.

Billig, M. (1990) 'Rhetoric of social psychology', in J. Parker and J. Shotter (eds), *Deconstructing Social Psychology*. London: Routledge. pp. 47–60.

Blackburn, S. (1996) *Oxford Dictionary of Philosophy*. Oxford: Oxford University Press.

Bleicher, J. (1980) *Contemporary Hermeneutics. Hermeneutics as Method, Philosophy and Critique*. London: Routledge & Kegan Paul.

Block, N. (1978) 'Troubles with functionalism', in W. Savage (ed.), *Perception and Cognition: Minnesota Studies in the Philosophy of Science, Vol. 9*. Minneapolis: University of Minnesota Press. pp. 61–325. Excerpts reprinted in Lycan (1990) and Rosenthal (1991).

Bloor, D. (1976) *Knowledge and Social Imagery*. London: Routledge & Kegan Paul. (1991, 2nd edn). Chicago: University of Chicago Press.

Blumer, H. (1969) *Symbolic Interactionism: Perspective and Method.* Englewood Cliffs, NJ: Prentice-Hall.

Bochenski, I.M. (1973) *Die zeitgenössischen Denkmethoden.* 6th edn. Bern: Francke.

Boden, M. (1972) *Purposive Explanation in Psychology.* Cambridge, MA: Harvard University Press.

Boden, M. (ed.) (1990) *The Philosophy of Artificial Intelligence.* Oxford: Oxford University Press.

Bolton, N. (1991) 'Cognitivism: a phenomenological critique', in A. Still and A. Costall (eds), *Against Cognitivism. Alternative Foundations for Cognitive Psychology.* Hemel Hempstead: Harvester Wheatsheaf. pp. 103–21.

Boorse, C. (1984) 'Wright on functions', in E. Sober (ed.), *Conceptual Issues in Evolutionary Biology: an anthology.* Cambridge, MA: MIT Press. pp. 367–85.

Borst, C.V. (ed.) (1970) *The Mind–Brain Identity Theory.* London: Macmillan.

Boyd, R. (1984) 'On the current status of scientific realism', in J. Leplin (ed.), *Scientific Realism.* Berkeley: University of California Press. pp. 41–82. Also in Boyd et al. (1991) pp. 195–222.

Boyd, R., Gasper, P. and Trout, J.D. (eds) (1991) *The Philosophy of Science.* Cambridge, MA: MIT Press/Bradford Books.

Brannigan, A. (1981) *The Social Basis of Scientific Discoveries.* Cambridge: Cambridge University Press.

Brentano, F. (1924) *Psychologie vom empirischen Standpunkt,* ed. Oskar Kraus, 3 vols. Hamburg: Meiner. Originally published 1874.

Brooks, R.A. (1991a) 'Intelligence without representation', *Artificial Intelligence,* 47: 139–59.

Brooks, R.A. (1991b) 'Intelligence without reason', in *Proceedings of the Twelfth International Joint Conference on Artificial Intelligence.* San Mateo, CA: Kaufmann. pp. 569–95.

Brown, H.I. (1977) *Perception, Theory and Commitment. The New Philosophy of Science.* Chicago: University of Chicago Press.

Bruner, J. (1990) *Acts of Meaning.* Cambridge, MA: Harvard University Press.

Bunge, M. (1991–92) 'A critical examination of the new Sociology of Science, parts 1 and 2', *Philosophy of the Social Sciences,* 21: 524–60; 22: 46–76.

Burge, T. (1986) 'Individualism and psychology', *Philosophical Review,* 95: 3–46.

Callebaut, W. (1993) *Taking the Naturalistic Turn. How Real Philosophy of Science is Done.* Chicago: University of Chicago Press.

Cantor, G.N. (1975) 'Phrenology in early nineteenth century Edinburgh. An historiographical discussion', *Annals of Science,* 32: 195–208.

Chalmers, A. (1990) *Science and its Fabrication.* Milton Keynes: Open University Press.

Chalmers, D.J. (1996) *The Conscious Mind. In Search of a Fundamental Theory.* Oxford: Oxford University Press.

Churchland, P.M. (1979) *Scientific Realism and the Plasticity of Mind.* Cambridge: Cambridge University Press.

Churchland, P.M. (1981) 'Eliminative materialism and the propositional attitudes', *Journal of Philosophy,* 78: 67–90.

Churchland, P.M. (1985a) 'Reduction, qualia, and the direct introspection of brain states', *Journal of Philosophy*, 82: 8–28.

Churchland, P.M. (1985b) 'The ontological status of observables: in praise of the superempirical virtues', in P.M. Churchland and C.A. Hooker (eds), *Images of Science. Essays on Realism and Empiricism.* Chicago: University of Chicago Press. pp. 35–47. Also in Churchland (1989) pp. 139–51.

Churchland, P.M. (1988) *Matter and Consciousness.* 2nd edn. Cambridge, MA: MIT Press.

Churchland, P.M. (1989) *A Neurocomputational Perspective. The Nature of Mind and the Structure of Science.* Cambridge, MA: MIT Press.

Churchland, P.M. (1995). *The Engine of Reason, the Seat of the Soul.* Cambridge, MA: MIT Press.

Churchland, P.M. and Churchland, P.S. (1990) 'Stalking the wild epistemic engine', in W.G. Lycan (ed.), *Mind and Cognition. A Reader.* Oxford: Blackwell. pp. 300–11.

Churchland, P.S. and Sejnowski, T. J. (1990) 'Neural representation and neural computation', in W.G. Lycan (ed.), *Mind and Cognition. A Reader.* Oxford: Blackwell. pp. 224–52.

Clark, A. (1989) *Microcognition. Philosophy, Cognitive Science, and Parallel Distributed Processing.* Cambridge, MA: MIT Press.

Clark, A. (1993) *Associative Engines.* Cambridge, MA: MIT Press.

Clark, A. and Toribio, J. (1994) 'Doing without representing?' *Synthese,* 101: 401–31.

Copeland, J. (1993) *Artificial Intelligence. A Philosophical Introduction.* Oxford: Blackwell.

Copi, I.M. (1961) *Introduction to Logic.* 2nd edn. New York: Macmillan.

Costall, A. and Still, A. (1987) *Cognitive Psychology in Question.* New York: St Martin's Press.

Crane, T. (1995) *The Mechanical Mind.* Harmondsworth: Penguin Books.

Cummins, R. (1980) 'Functional analysis', in N. Block (ed.), *Readings in the Philosophy of Psychology.* Cambridge, MA: Harvard University Press. pp. 185–90.

Cummins, R. (1983) *The Nature of Psychological Explanation.* Cambridge, MA: MIT Press.

Cummins, R. (1989) *Meaning and Mental Representation.* Cambridge, MA: MIT Press.

Dahlbom, B. (ed.) (1993) *Dennett and his Critics.* Oxford: Blackwell.

Darnton, R. (1968) *Mesmerism and the end of Enlightenment in France.* Cambridge, MA: Harvard University Press.

Davidson, D. (1968) 'Action, reasons and causes', in A.R. White (ed.), *The Philosophy of Action.* Oxford: Oxford University Press. Reprinted in Davidson (1980a).

Davidson, D. (1980a) *Essays on Actions and Events.* Oxford: Clarendon Press.

Davidson, D. (1980b) 'Mental events', in *Essays on Actions and Events.* Oxford: Clarendon Press. pp. 207–27.

Davies, M. and Stone, T. (eds) (1995a) *Folk Psychology.* Oxford: Blackwell.

Davies, M. and Stone, T. (eds) (1995b) *Mental Simulation.* Oxford: Blackwell.

De Groot, A.D. (1969) *Methodology.* The Hague: Mouton.

De Mey, M. (1982) *The Cognitive Paradigm.* Dordrecht: Reidel.

Demopoulos, W. (1990) 'Critical notice: Hilary Putnam's *Representation and Reality*', *Philosophy of Science,* 57: 325–33.

Dennett, D.C. (1978) 'Intentional systems', in D.C. Dennett, *Brainstorms.* Brighton: Harvester Press. pp. 3–23.

Dennett, D.C. (1987) 'True believers', in D.C. Dennett, *The Intentional Stance.* Cambridge, MA: MIT Press. pp. 13–42.

Dennett, D.C. (1988) 'Quining qualia', in A. Marcel and E. Bisiach (eds), *Consciousness in Contemporary Science.* Oxford: Clarendon Press. pp. 44–62.

Dennett, D.C. (1990a) 'The myth of original intentionality', in K.A. Mohyeldin Said, W.H. Newton-Smith, R. Viale and K.V. Wilkes (eds), *Modelling the Mind.* Oxford: Clarendon Press. pp. 45–62.

Dennett, D.C. (1990b) 'Cognitive wheels', in M. Boden (ed.), *The Philosophy of Artificial Intelligence.* Oxford: Oxford University Press. pp. 147–70.

Dennett, D.C. (1991). *Consciousness Explained.* Harmondsworth: Penguin Books.

Dennett, D.C. (1994) 'Real consciousness', in A. Revonsuo and M. Kappinen (eds), *Consciousness in Philosophy and Cognitive Neuroscience.* Hillsdale, NJ: Erlbaum. pp. 55–63.

Dennett, D.C. (1995) *Darwin's Dangerous Idea: Evolution and the Meaning of Life.* London: Allen Lane.

Dennett D.C. and Kinsbourne, M. (1992) 'Time and the observer: the where and when of consciousness in the brain', *Behavioral and Brain Sciences,* 15: 183–247.

Derksen, A.A. (1985) *Wetenschap of Willekeur. Wat is Wetenschap?* (Science or Caprice. What is Science?). Muiderberg: Coutinho.

Devitt, M. and Sterelny, K. (1987) *Language and Reality.* Oxford: Blackwell.

Diggins, J.P. (1994) *The Promise of Pragmatism. Modernism and the Crisis of Knowledge and Authority.* Chicago: University of Chicago Press.

Dretske, F. (1988) *Explaining Behavior. Reasons in a World of Causes.* Cambridge, MA: MIT Press.

Dreyfus, H.L. (1979) *What Computers Can't Do.* 2nd edn. New York: Harper & Row.

Dreyfus, H.L. (1980) 'Holism and hermeneutics', *Review of Metaphysics,* 34: 3–23.

Elias, N., Martins, H. and Whitley, R. (eds) (1982) *Scientific Establishments and Hierarchies.* Dordrecht: Reidel.

Farr, R.M. and Moscovici, S. (eds) (1984) *Social Representations.* Cambridge: Cambridge University Press.

Faust, D. (1984) *The Limits of Scientific Reasoning.* Minneapolis: University of Minnesota Press.

Feigl, H. (1967) *The 'Mental' and the 'Physical'.* Minneapolis: University of Minnesota Press. Originally published 1958.

Feyerabend, P. (1975) *Against Method.* London: Verso.

Feyerabend, P. (1978) *Science in a Free Society.* London: NLB.

Feyerabend, P. (1980) *Erkenntnis für freie Menschen.* Frankfurt am Main: Suhrkamp.

Fisch, R. (1977) 'Psychology of science', in I. Spiegel-Rösing and D. de Solla Price (eds), *Science, Technology and Society. A Cross-disciplinary Perspective.* London: Sage.

Fiske, S.T. and Taylor, S.E. (1984) *Social Cognition.* New York: Random House.

Flanagan, O. (1991) *The Science of the Mind.* 2nd edn. Cambridge, MA: MIT Press.

Flanagan, O. (1992) *Consciousness Reconsidered.* Cambridge, MA: MIT Press.

Fleck, L. (1979) *Genesis and Development of a Scientific Fact.* Chicago: University of Chicago Press. Originally: *Entstehung und Entwicklung einer wissenschaftlichen Tatsache,* 1935; new edn. Frankfurt am Main: Suhrkamp, 1980.

Fodor, J.A. (1968) *Psychological Explanation. An Introduction to the Philosophy of Psychology.* New York: Random House.

Fodor, J. (1975) *The Language of Thought.* New York: Crowell.

Fodor, J. (1981) 'Introduction', in J. Fodor, *Representations.* Cambridge, MA: MIT Press. pp. 1–31.

Fodor, J. (1987) *Psychosemantics.* Cambridge, MA: MIT Press/Bradford Books.

Fodor, J. (1990) 'Why there still has to be a Language of Thought', in W.G. Lycan (ed.), *Mind and Cognition. A Reader.* Oxford: Blackwell. pp. 282–99.

Fodor, J. (1991) 'A modal argument for narrow content', *Journal of Philosophy,* 88: 2–26.

Fodor, J. (1994) *The Elm and the Expert.* Cambridge, MA: MIT Press.

Fodor, J. and McLaughlin, B.P. (1990) 'Connectionism and the problem of systematicity', *Cognition,* 35: 183–204.

Fodor, J. and Pylyshyn, Z. (1988) 'Connectionism and cognitive architecture: a critical analysis', *Cognition,* 28: 3–71. Reprinted in S. Pinker and J. Mehler (eds) (1988), *Connections and Symbols.* Cambridge, MA: MIT Press. pp. 3–71.

Franklin, S. (1995) *Artificial Minds.* Cambridge, MA: MIT Press.

Fuller, S. (1989) *Philosophy of Science and its Discontents.* Boulder, CO: Westview Press.

Fuller, S., De Mey, M., Shinn, T. and Woolgar, S. (eds) (1983). *The Cognitive Turn. Sociological and Psychological Perspectives on Science.* Dordrecht: Kluwer.

Gadamer, H.G. (1960) *Wahrheit und Methode*. Tübingen: Mohr. Trans. and ed. by G. Barden and J. Cumming as *Truth and Method* (1975). New York: Seabury.

Gardner, H. (1987) *The Mind's New Science. A History of the Cognitive Revolution*. New York: Basic Books.

Geertz, C. (1973) *The Interpretation of Cultures*. New York: Basic Books.

Gellner, E. (1974) *Legitimation of Belief*. Cambridge: Cambridge University Press.

Gellner, E. (1982) 'Relativism and universals', in M. Hollis and S. Lukes (eds), *Rationality and Relativism*. Oxford: Basil Blackwell. pp. 181–200.

Gergen, K. J. (1980) 'Towards intellectual audacity in social psychology', in R. Gilmour and S. Duck (eds), *The Development of Social Psychology*. London: Academic Press. pp. 239–70.

Gergen, K.J. (1985a) 'The social constructionist movement in modern psychology', *American Psychologist,* 40: 266–75.

Gergen, K.J. (1985b) 'Social constructionist inquiry: context and implications', in K.J. Gergen and K.E. Davis, *The Social Construction of the Person*. New York: Springer Verlag.

Gergen, K.J. (1989) 'Social psychology and the wrong revolution', *European Journal of Social Psychology,* 19: 463–84.

Geuter, U. (1992) *The Professionalization of Psychology in Nazi Germany*. Cambridge: Cambridge University Press. Originally, *Die Professionalisierung der deutschen Psychologie im Nationalsozialismus*. Frankfurt: Suhrkamp, 1984

Gholson, B., Shadish, W.R., Neimeyer, R.A. and Houts, A.C. (eds) (1989) *Psychology of Science. Contributions to Metascience*. Cambridge: Cambridge University Press.

Goldman, A.I. (ed.) (1993) *Readings in Philosophy and Cognitive Science*. Cambridge, MA: MIT Press.

Gould, S. and Lewontin, R. (1979) 'The spandrels of San Marco and the Panglossian paradigm: critique of the adaptationist programme', *Proceedings of the Royal Society of London,* B205: 581–98.

Gower, B. (1997) *Scientific Method*. London: Routledge.

Greenwood, J.D. (1991a) *The Future of Folk Psychology*. Cambridge: Cambridge University Press.

Greenwood, J.D. (1991b) *Relations and Representation: An Introduction to the Philosophy of Social Psychological Science*. London: Routledge.

Greenwood, J.D. (1994) *Realism, Identity and Emotion. Reclaiming Social Psychology*. London: Sage.

Gruber, H.E. (1974) *Darwin on Man: A Psychological Study of Scientific Creativity*. New York: Dutton.

Guttenplan, S. (ed.) (1994) *A Companion to the Philosophy of Mind*. Oxford: Blackwell.

Habermas, J. (1971) *Toward a Rational Society. Student Protest, Science, and Politics,* trans. J.J. Shapiro. London: Heinemann. (includes the essay 'Technik und Wissenschaft als "Ideologie"').

Habermas, J. (1984) *The Theory of Communicative Action*, 2 vols. Cambridge: Cambridge University Press. Originally *Theorie des kommunikativen Handelns*, 2 vols. Frankfurt am Main: Suhrkamp, 1981.

Hacking, I. (ed.) (1981) *Scientific Revolutions*. Oxford: Oxford University Press.

Hacking, I. (1983) *Representing and Intervening. Introductory Topics in the Philosophy of Natural Science.* Cambridge: Cambridge University Press.

Hahn, R. (1971) *The Anatomy of a Scientific Institution: the Paris Academy of Sciences, 1666–1803.* Berkeley and Los Angeles: University of California Press.

Hanson, N.R. (1958) *Patterns of Discovery. An Inquiry into the Conceptual Foundations of Science.* Cambridge: Cambridge University Press.

Harman, G. (1988) 'Wide functionalism', in S. Schiffer and S. Steele (eds), *Cognition and Representation.* Boulder, CO: Westview Press. pp. 11–20.

Harnish, R.M. (ed.) (1994) *Basic Topics in the Philosophy of Language.* New York: Harvester.

Haselager, W.F.G. (1995) 'The right frame of mind. Cognitive science, folk psychology and the frame problem.' Dissertation, Free University of Amsterdam.

Haugeland, J. (ed.) (1981) *Mind Design.* Montgomery, VT: Bradford Books.

Haugeland, J. (1991) 'Representational genera', in W. Ramsey, S.P. Stich and D.E. Rumelhart (eds), *Philosophy and Connectionist Theory.* Hillsdale, NJ: Erlbaum. pp. 61–89.

Hawking, S. (1988) *A Brief History of Time.* Toronto: Bantam.

Heil, J. (1992) *The Nature of True Minds.* Cambridge: Cambridge University Press.

Held, D. (1980) *Introduction to Critical Theory: Horkheimer to Habermas.* London: Hutchinson.

Hempel, Carl G. (1966) *Philosophy of Natural Science.* Englewood Cliffs, NJ: Prentice-Hall.

Hesse, M. (1980) *Revolutions and Reconstructions in the Philosophy of Science.* Brighton: Harvester Press.

Holland, J.H., Holyoak, K.J., Nisbet, R.E. and Thagard, P.R. (1986) *Induction.* Cambridge, MA: MIT Press.

Hollinger, R. (ed.) (1985) *Hermeneutics and Praxis.* Notre Dame, IN: University of Notre Dame Press.

Hollis, M. and Lukes, S. (1982) *Rationality and Relativism.* Oxford: Blackwell.

Horgan, T. and Tienson, J. (1996) *Connectionism and the Philosophy of Psychology.* Cambridge, MA: MIT Press.

Houts, A.C. (1989) 'Contributions of the psychology of science to metascience: a call for explorers', in B. Gholson, W.R. Shadish, R.A. Neimeyer and A.C. Houts (eds), *Psychology of Science. Contributions to Metascience.* Cambridge: Cambridge University Press. pp. 47–88.

Hughes, J. (1990) *The Philosophy of Social Research.* 2nd edn. London: Longman.

Hume, D. (1963) *Enquiry concerning the Human Understanding*, ed. L.A.

Selby-Bigge. London: Oxford University Press. Originally published 1748.

Hyland, M. (1981) *Introduction to Theoretical Psychology*. London: Macmillan.

Jackson, F. (1990) 'Epiphenominal qualia', in W.G. Lycan (ed.), *Mind and Cognition. A Reader*. Oxford: Blackwell. pp. 469–77.

Jacob, F. (1977) 'Evolution and tinkering', *Science*, 196: 1161–6.

Jarvie, I.C. (1993) 'Relativism yet again', *Philosophy of the Social Sciences,* 23: 537–47.

Jay, M. (1973) *The Dialectical Imagination. A History of the Frankfurt School and the Institute of Social Research, 1923–1950*. Boston: Little, Brown.

Johnson, M. (1987) *The Body in the Mind. The Bodily Basis of Meaning, Imagination, and Reason*. Chicago: University of Chicago Press.

Joravski, D. (1989) *Soviet Psychology*. Oxford: Blackwell.

Kantorovich, A. (1993) *Scientific Discovery. Logic and Tinkering.* Albany, NY: State University of New York Press.

Keijzer, F.A. and Bem, S. (1996) 'Behavioral systems interpreted as autonomous agents and as coupled dynamical systems: A criticism'. *Philosophical Psychology*, 9: 323–46.

Kettler, D., Meja, V. and Stehr, N. (1984) *Karl Mannheim*. Chichester: Ellis Horwood.

Kim, J. (1993) *Supervenience and Mind*. Cambridge: Cambridge University Press.

Kim, J. (1996) *Philosophy of Mind*. Boulder, CO: Westview.

Kirsh, D. (1991) 'Today the earwig, tomorrow man?' *Artificial Intelligence*, 47: 161–84.

Klahr, D. and Dunbar, K. (1988) 'Dual space search during scientific reasoning', *Cognitive Science*, 12: 1–48

Knorr, K.D., Krohn, R. and Whitley, R. (eds) (1980) *The Social Process of Scientific Investigation. Sociology of the Sciences Yearbook, Vol. IV.* Dordrecht and Boston: Kluwer.

Knorr-Cetina, K.D. (1981) *The Manufacture of Knowledge. An Essay on the Constructivist and Contextual Nature of Science*. Oxford: Pergamon Press.

Knorr-Cetina, K.D. (1983) 'The ethnographic study of scientific work: towards a constructivist interpretation of science', in K.D. Knorr-Cetina and M. Mulkay (eds), *Science Observed. Perspectives on the Social Study of Science.* London: Sage. pp. 115–40.

Knorr-Cetina, K.D. and Mulkay, M. (eds) (1983) *Science Observed. Perspectives on the Social Study of Science*. London: Sage.

Kornblith, H. (ed.) (1994) *Naturalizing Epistemology.* 2nd edn. Cambridge, MA: MIT Press/Bradford.

Kripke, S. (1980) *Naming and Necessity,* revised edn. Oxford: Blackwell. Originally published 1972.

Krohn, W., Layton, E.T. and Weingart, P. (eds) (1978) *The Dynamics of Science and Technology. Social Values, Technical Norms and Scientific*

Criteria in the Development of Knowledge. Sociology of the Sciences Yearbook, Vol II. Dordrecht: Reidel.

Kruglanski, A.W. (1991) 'Social science-based understandings of science. Reflections on Fuller', *Philosophy of the Social Sciences,* 21: 223–31.

Kuhn, T.S. (1962) *The Structure of Scientific Revolutions,* (1970) 2nd, enlarged, edn. Chicago: University of Chicago Press.

Kulkarni, D. and Simon, H.A. (1988) 'The process of scientific discovery: the strategy of experimentation', *Cognitive Science,* 12: 139–75.

Lakatos, I. (1970) 'Falsification and the methodology of scientific research programmes', in I. Lakatos and A. Musgrave (eds), *Criticism and the Growth of Knowledge.* Cambridge: Cambridge University Press. pp. 91–196.

Latour, B. (1987) *Science in Action: How to Follow Scientists and Engineers through Society.* Milton Keynes: Open University Press.

Latour, B. and Woolgar, S. (1979) *Laboratory Life. The Social Reconstruction of Scientific Facts.* London: Sage.

Laudan, L. (1981) 'The pseudo-science of science?', *Philosophy of the Social Sciences,* 11: 173–98.

Laudan, L. (1990) *Science and Relativism.* Chicago: University of Chicago Press.

Laudan, L. (1991) 'A confutation of convergent realism', in R. Boyd, P. Gasper and J.D. Trout (eds), *The Philosophy of Science.* Cambridge, MA: MIT/Bradford Books. pp. 223–45.

Laudan, L. (1996) *Beyond Positivism and Relativism.* Boulder, CO: Westview Press.

Leahey, T.H. (1992) *A History of Psychology.* Englewood Cliffs, NJ: Prentice-Hall.

Leplin, J. (ed.) (1984) *Scientific Realism.* Berkeley: University of California Press.

LePore, E. and Van Gulick, R. (eds) (1991) *John Searle and his Critics.* Oxford: Blackwell.

Lessnoff, M. (1974) *The Structure of Social Science.* London: Allen & Unwin.

Loewer, B. and Rey, G. (eds) (1991) *Meaning in Mind: Fodor and his Critics.* Oxford: Blackwell.

Looren de Jong, H. (1991) 'Intentionality and the ecological approach', *Journal for the Theory of Social Behavior,* 21: 91–110.

Looren de Jong, H. (1995) 'Ecological psychology and naturalism: Heider, Gibson and Marr', *Theory & Psychology,* 5: 251–69.

Losee, J. (1980) *A Historical Introduction to the Philosophy of Science.* 2nd edn. Oxford: Oxford University Press.

Lycan, W.G. (1987) *Consciousness.* Cambridge, MA: MIT Press.

Lycan, W.G. (ed.) (1990) *Mind and Cognition. A Reader.* Oxford: Blackwell.

McCauley, R.N. (ed.) (1996) *The Churchlands and their Critics.* Oxford: Blackwell.

McDonough, R. (1989) 'Towards a non-mechanistic theory of meaning', *Mind,* 98: 1–21.

McGinn, C. (1991) *The Problem of Consciousness.* Oxford: Blackwell.

Mahoney, M. (1976) *Scientist as Subject. The Psychological Imperative.* Cambridge, MA: Ballinger.

Malcolm, N. (1971) *Problems of Mind.* London: Allen & Unwin.

Mannheim, K. (1936) *Ideology and Utopia.* London: Routledge & Kegan Paul. Includes the essays: 'Ideology and utopia' (1929) and 'The sociology of knowledge' (1931).

Manuel, F. (1968) *A Portrait of Isaac Newton.* Cambridge, MA: Harvard University Press.

Marcuse, H. (1964) *One Dimensional Man. Studies in the Ideology of Advanced Industrial Society.* Boston, MA: Beacon Press.

Margolis, J. (1986) *Pragmatism without Foundations. Reconciling Realism and Relativism.* New York: Blackwell.

Marr, D. (1982) *Vision.* San Francisco: Freeman.

Masterman, M. (1970) 'The nature of a paradigm', in I. Lakatos and A. Musgrave (eds), *Criticism and the Growth of Knowledge.* Cambridge: Cambridge University Press. pp. 59–89.

Mayr, E. (1992) 'The idea of teleology', *Journal of the History of Ideas,* 55: 117–35.

Mead, G.H. (1934) *Mind, Self, and Society.* Chicago: University of Chicago Press.

Meja, V. and N. Stehr (eds) (1984) *The Sociology of Knowledge Dispute.* London: Routledge & Kegan Paul. Originally *Der Streit um die Wissenssoziologie.* Frankfurt: Suhrkamp, 1982.

Mendelsohn, E., Weingart, P. and Whitley, R. (eds) (1977) *The Social Production of Scientific Knowledge. Sociology of the Sciences Yearbook, Vol I.* Dordrecht: Reidel.

Merleau-Ponty, M. (1945) *Phénoménologie de la perception.* Paris: Gallimard. English trans. *The Phenomenology of Perception.* London: Routledge & Kegan Paul, 1962.

Merton, R.K. (1970) 'Science, technology and society in seventeenth century England', *Osiris,* 4(2), 1938. Reprinted with new preface, New York: Harper & Row.

Metzinger, T. (ed.) (1995) *Conscious Experience.* Paderborn: Schöningh.

Moya, C.J. (1990) *The Philosophy of Action.* Cambridge: Polity Press.

Mulkay, M., Potter, J. and Yearly, S. (1983) 'Why an analysis of scientific discourse is needed', in K.D. Knorr-Cetina and M. Mulkay (eds), *Science Observed. Perspectives on the Social Study of Science.* London: Sage. pp. 171–204.

Nagel, E. (1961) *The Structure of Science.* London: Routledge & Kegan Paul.

Nagel, T. (1980) 'What is it like to be a bat?' in N. Block (ed.), *Readings in the Philosophy of Psychology,* Vol.1. London: Methuen. pp. 159–68.

Napoli, D.S. (1981) *Architects of Adjustment. The History of the Psychological Profession in the United States.* Port Washington, NY: Kennikat Press.

Newell, A. (1980) 'Physical symbol systems', *Cognitive Science,* 4: 135-83.

Newton-Smith, W. (1982) 'Relativism and the possibility of interpretation', in M. Hollis and S. Lukes (eds), *Rationality and Relativism*. Oxford: Blackwell.

Nickles, T. (1980) 'Scientific discovery and the future of philosophy of science. Introductory essay', in *Scientific Discovery, Logic, and Rationality*. Dordrecht: Reidel. pp. 1–59.

Nisbett, R.E. and Wilson, D. (1977) 'Telling more than we can know. Verbal reports on mental processes', *Psychological Review*, 84: 231–59.

Noble, D. (1990) 'Biological explanation and intentional behaviour', in K.A. Mohyeldin Said, W.H. Newton-Smith, R. Viale and K.V. Wilkes (eds), *Modelling the Mind*. Oxford: Clarendon Press. pp. 97–112.

O'Hearn, A. (1989) *An Introduction to the Philosophy of Science*. Oxford: Clarendon Press.

Palmer, S.E. (1978) 'Fundamental aspects of cognitive representation', in E. Rosch and B.B. Lloyd (eds), *Cognition and Categorisation*. Hillsdale, NJ: Erlbaum. pp. 259–303.

Pickering, A. (ed.) (1992) *Science as Practice and Culture*. Chicago: University of Chicago Press.

Pickering, J. and Skinner, M. (eds) (1990) *From Sentience to Symbols. Readings on Consciousness*. Hemel Hempstead: Harvester Wheatsheaf.

Pinker, S. (1994) *The Language Instinct*. Harmondsworth: Penguin Books.

Popper, K. (1961) *The Poverty of Historicism*. London: Routledge.

Popper, K.R. (1966) *The Open Society and its Enemies*, 2 vols, 5th edn. London: Routledge & Kegan Paul.

Popper, K. (1974)*Conjectures and Refutations. The Growth of Scientific Knowledge*. 4th edn. London: Routledge.

Popper, K. (1976) *Unended Quest. An Intellectual Autobiography*. Glasgow: Collins.

Popper, K. (1979) *Objective Knowledge. An Evolutionary Approach*, rev. edn. Oxford: Oxford University Press.

Popper, K.R. and Eccles, J.C. (1977) *The Self and its Brain*. New York: Springer Verlag.

Port, R.F. and Van Gelder, T. (eds) (1995) *Mind as Motion. Exploration in the Dynamics of Cognition*. Cambridge, MA: MIT/Bradford Books.

Priest, S. (1991) *Theories of the Mind*. Harmondsworth: Penguin Books.

Putnam, H. (1961) 'Minds and machines', in S. Hook (ed.), *Dimensions of Mind*. New York: Collier. pp. 221–31.

Putnam, H. (1975) 'The meaning of meaning', in *Mind, Language and Reality. Philosophical Papers, Volume 2*. Cambridge: Cambridge University Press.

Putnam, H. (1980) 'Reductionism and the nature of psychology', in J. Haugeland (ed.), *Mind Design*. Cambridge, MA: MIT Press. pp. 205–19.

Putnam, H. (1981) *Reason, Truth and History*. Cambridge: Cambridge University Press.

Putnam, H. (1987) *The Many Faces of Realism*. La Salle, IL: Open Court.

Putnam, H. (1988) *Representation and Reality.* Cambridge, MA: MIT/ Bradford Books.

Putnam, H. (1990) *Realism with a Human Face.* Cambridge, MA: Harvard University Press.

Putnam, H. (1994) 'Artificial Intelligence: much ado about not very much', in *Words and Life.* Cambridge, MA: Harvard University Press. pp. 391–402.

Pylyshyn, Z. (1984) *Computation and Cognition. Toward a Foundation for Cognitive Science.* Cambridge, MA: MIT Press/Bradford Books.

Pylyshyn, Z. (1989) 'Computing in cognitive science', in M. Posner (ed.), *Foundations of Cognitive Science.* Cambridge, MA: MIT Press. pp. 49–91.

Quine, W.V.O. (1961) 'Two dogmas of empiricism', in *From a Logical Point of View.* New York: Harper & Row. pp. 20–46. Originally published in 1951.

Quine, W.V.O. (1969) 'Epistemology naturalized', in *Ontological Relativity and Other Essays.* New York: Columbia University Press. pp. 69–90.

Quine, W.V.O. (1992) 'Two dogmas in retrospect', *Canadian Journal of Philosophy,* 21: 265–74.

Ramsey, W., Stich, S.P. and Garon, J. (1991) 'Connectionism, eliminativism, and the future of folk psychology', in W. Ramsey, S.P. Stich and D.E. Rumelhart (eds), *Philosophy and Connectionist Theory.* Hillsdale, NJ: Erlbaum.

Reber, A.S. (1995) *The Penguin Dictionary of Psychology* London: Penguin.

Rescher, N. (1987) *Scientific Realism. A Critical Reappraisal.* Dordrecht: Reidel.

Rogoff, B. and Wertsch, J.V. (eds) (1984) *Children's Learning in the 'Zone of Proximal Development'.* San Francisco: Jossey-Bass.

Rorty, R. (1979) *Philosophy and the Mirror of Nature.* Princeton, NJ: Princeton University Press.

Rorty, R. (1980) 'A reply to Dreyfus and Taylor', *Review of Metaphysics,* 34: 39–46.

Rorty, R. (1982) 'Contemporary philosophy of mind', *Synthese,* 55: 323–48.

Rorty, R. (1993) 'Consciousness, intentionality and pragmatism', in S.M. Christensen and D.R. Turner (eds), *Folk Psychology and the Philosophy of Mind.* Hillsdale, NJ: Erlbaum. pp. 389–404.

Rosenberg, A. (1985) *The Structure of Biological Science.* Cambridge: Cambridge University Press.

Rosenthal, D.M. (ed.) (1991) *The Nature of Mind.* Oxford: Oxford University Press.

Rouse, J. (1987) *Knowledge and Power. Toward a Political Philosophy of Science.* Ithaca, NY: Cornell University Press.

Russell, B. (1988) 'Knowledge by acquaintance and knowledge by description', in N. Salmon and S. Soames (eds), *Propositions and Attitudes.* Oxford: Oxford University Press. pp. 16–32.

Ryan, A. (1970) *The Philosophy of the Social Sciences.* London: Macmillan.

Ryle, G. (1949) *The Concept of Mind.* London: Hutchinson.

Ryle, G. (1971) *Collected Papers,* 2 vols. London: Hutchinson.

Salmon, W.C. (1990) *Four Decades of Scientific Explanation.* Minneapolis: University of Minnesota Press.

Sanders, C., Van Eisenga, L.K.A. and van Rappard, J.F.H. (1976) *Inleiding in de grondslagen van de psychologie* (Introduction to the Theoretical Foundations of Psychology). Deventer, Holland: Van Loghum Slaterus.

Schafer, W. (ed.) (1983) *Finalisation in Science.* Dordrecht: Reidel.

Schwartz, J. (1991) 'Reduction, elimination and the mental', *Philosophy of Science,* 58: 203–20.

Searle, J. (1983) *Intentionality.* Cambridge: Cambridge University Press.

Searle, J. (1990a) 'Consciousness, explanatory inversion, and cognitive science', *Behavioral and Brain Sciences,* 13: 585–642.

Searle, J. (1990b) 'Minds, brains and programs', in M. Boden (ed.), *The Philosophy of Artificial Intelligence.* Oxford: Oxford University Press. pp. 67–88.

Searle, J. (1992) *The Rediscovery of Mind.* Cambridge, MA: MIT Press.

Secord, P.F. (ed.) (1982) *Explaining Human Behavior. Consciousness, Human Action and Social Structure.* Beverly Hills, CA: Sage.

Seebass, G. and Tuomela, R. (eds) (1985) *Social Action.* Dordrecht: Reidel.

Sellars, W. (1963) *Science, Perception and Reality.* London: Routledge & Kegan Paul.

Shanon, B. (1993) *The Representational and the Presentational. An Essay on Cognition and the Study of Mind.* Hemel Hempstead: Harvester Wheatsheaf.

Shapin, S. (1975) 'Phrenological knowledge and the social structure of early nineteenth century Edinburgh', *Annals of Science,* 32: 219–43.

Shepherd, G.M. (1990) 'The significance of real neuron architecture for real network simulations', in E.L. Schwartz (ed.), *Computational Neuroscience.* Cambridge, MA: MIT Press. pp. 82–96.

Shotter, J. (1975) *Images of Man in Psychological Research.* London: Methuen.

Shotter, J. (1991) 'The rhetorical-responsive nature of mind. A social constructionist account', in A. Still and A. Costall, *Against Cognitivism. Alternative Foundations for Cognitive Psychology.* Hemel Hempstead: Harvester Wheatsheaf.

Shotter, J. and Gergen, K.J. (eds) (1989) *Texts of Identity.* London: Sage.

Shrager, J. and Langley, P. (eds) (1989) *Computational Models of Discovery and Theory Formation.* San Francisco: Morgan Kaufmann.

Silvers, S. (ed.) (1989) *Rerepresentation. Readings in the Philosophy of Mental Representation.* Dordrecht: Kluwer.

Simonton, D.K. (1988) *Scientific Genius. A Psychology of Science.* Cambridge: Cambridge University Press.

Slezak, P. (1994) 'A second look at David Bloor's *Knowledge and Social Imagery*', *Philosophy of the Social Sciences,* 24: 336–61.

Smolensky, P. (1988) 'On the proper treatment of connectionism', *Behavioral and Brain Sciences,* 11: 1–74.

Smolensky, P. (1991) 'Connectionism, constituency and the Language of

Thought', in B. Loewer and G. Rey (eds), *Meaning in Mind: Fodor and his Critics*. Oxford: Blackwell. pp. 201–27.

Sober, E. (1985) 'Panglossian functionalism and the philosophy of mind', *Synthese*, 64: 165–93.

Sosa, E. and Tooley, M. (eds) (1993) *Causation*. Oxford: Oxford University Press.

Sterelny, K. (1990) *The Representational Theory of Mind*. Oxford: Blackwell.

Stich, S. (1983) *From Folk Psychology to Cognitive Science. The Case Against Belief*. Cambridge, MA: MIT/Bradford Books.

Stich, S. (1990) *The Fragmentation of Reason*. Cambridge, MA: MIT Press.

Stich, S. (1992) 'What is a theory of mental representation?', *Mind*, 101: 243–61.

Stich, S. and Warfield, T.A. (eds) (1994) *Mental Representation*. Oxford: Blackwell.

Still, A. (1991) 'Mechanism and romanticism', in A. Still and A. Costall (eds), *Against Cognitivism. Alternative Foundations for Cognitive Psychology*. Hemel Hempstead: Harvester Wheatsheaf. pp. 7–26.

Still, A. and Costall, A. (eds) (1991), *Against Cognitivism. Alternative Foundations for Cognitive Psychology*. Hemel Hempstead: Harvester Wheatsheaf.

Suppe, F. (1977) 'The search for philosophical understanding of scientific theories', in F. Suppe (ed.), *The Structure of Scientific Revolutions*. 2nd edn. Urbana: University of Illinois Press.

Taylor, C. (1971) 'Interpretation and the sciences of man', *Review of Metaphysics*, 25: 3–51.

Taylor, C. (1980) 'Understanding in human science', *Review of Metaphysics*, 34: 25–38.

Terwee, S. (1990) *Hermeneutics in Psychology and Psychoanalysis*. New York and Heidelberg: Springer Verlag.

Thagard, P. (1992) *Conceptual Revolutions*. Princeton, NJ: Princeton University Press.

Thompson, J.B. and Held, D. (eds) (1982) *Habermas. Critical Debates*. London: Macmillan.

Toulmin, S. (1990) *Cosmopolis. The Hidden Agenda of Modernity*. New York: Free Press.

Trigg, R. (1973) *Reason and Commitment*. Cambridge: Cambridge University Press.

Trigg, R. (1985) *Understanding Social Science*. Oxford: Blackwell.

Trigg, R. (1993) *Rationality and Science. Can Science Explain Everything?* Oxford: Blackwell.

Tweney, R.D. (1985) 'Faraday's discovery of induction: a cognitive approach', in D. Gooding and F.A.J.L. James (eds), *Faraday Rediscovered*. New York: Stockton. pp. 182–209.

Tweney, R.D. (1989) 'Fields of enterprise: on Michael Faraday's thought', in D.B. Wallace and H.E. Gruber (eds), *Creative People at Work*. Oxford: Oxford University Press.

Tweney, R., Doherty, M.E., and Mynatt C.R. (eds) (1981) *On Scientific Thinking.* New York: Columbia University Press.

Valentine, E.R. (1992) *Conceptual Issues in Psychology.* 2nd edn. London: Routledge.

Van der Veer, R. and Valsiner, J. (1991) *Understanding Vygotsky: A Quest for Synthesis.* Oxford: Blackwell.

Van Fraassen, B.C. (1980) *The Scientific Image.* Oxford: Clarendon Press.

Van Gelder, T. (1990) 'Compositionality: a connectionist variation on a classical theme', *Cognitive Science*, 14: 355–84.

Van Gelder, T. (1995) 'What might cognition be, if not computation?' *Journal of Philosophy,* 91: 345–81.

Van Gulick, R. (1989) 'Metaphysical arguments for internalism and why they don't work', in S. Silvers (ed.), *Rerepresentation.* Dordrecht: Kluwer. pp. 151–9.

Van Rappard, H. (1979) *Psychology as Self-knowledge. The Development of the Concept of the Mind in German Rationalistic Psychology and its Relevance Today.* Assen, Holland: Van Gorcum.

Varela, F.J., Thomson, E. and Rosch, E. (1991) *The Embodied Mind. Cognitive Science and Human Experience.* Cambridge, MA: MIT Press.

Von Wright, G.H. (1963) *Norm and Action.* London: Routledge & Kegan Paul.

Von Wright, G.H. (1971) *Explanation and Understanding.* Ithaca, NY: Cornell University Press.

Von Wright, G.H. (1993) 'On the logic and epistemology of the causal relation', in E. Sosa and M. Tooley (eds), *Causation.* Oxford: Oxford University Press.

Vygotsky, L. (1962) *Thought and Language.* Cambridge, MA: MIT Press.

Warner, R. and Szubka, T. (eds) (1994) *The mind–body problem.* Oxford: Blackwell.

Weinberg, S. (1992) *Dreams of a Final Theory.* New York: Pantheon.

Weizenbaum, J. (1976) *Computer Power and Human Reason. From Judgment to Calculation.* San Francisco: Freeman.

Wertsch, J.V. (1985) *Vygotsky and the Social Formation of Mind.* Cambridge, MA: Harvard University Press.

Wilkes, K.V. (1978) *Physicalism.* London: Routledge & Kegan Paul.

Wilkes, K.V. (1980) 'Brain states', *British Journal for the Philosophy of Science,* 31: 111–29.

Winch, P. (1958) *The Idea of a Social Science and its Relation to Philosophy.* London: Routledge & Kegan Paul.

Wittgenstein, L. (1953) *Philosophical Investigations,* trans. G.E.M. Anscombe. Oxford: Blackwell.

Wittgenstein, L. (1961) *Tractatus Logico-Philosophicus*, trans. D.F. Pears and B.F. McGuiness. London: Routledge & Kegan Paul. Originally published 1922.

Wittgenstein, L. (1981) *Zettel,* ed. G.E.M. Anscombe and G.H. von Wright. 2nd edn. Oxford: Blackwell.

Woolgar, S. (1988) *Science. The Very Idea.* Chichester: Ellis Horwood.

Wright, L. (1973) 'Functions', *Philosophical Review,* 82: 139–68.

Wright, L. (1976) *Teleological Explanations.* Berkeley: University of California Press.

Wyer, R.S. and Srull, T.K. (eds) (1984) *Handbook of Social Cognition,* 2 vols. Hillsdale, NJ: Erlbaum.

Yates, F. (1964) *Giordano Bruno and the Hermetic Tradition.* London: Routledge & Kegan Paul.

Yates, F. (1972) *The Rosicrucian Enlightenment.* London: Routledge & Kegan Paul.

Name Index

Subject Index

DATE DUE

OCT 2 3 2001			
GAYLORD			PRINTED IN U.S.A.